A HISTORY OF THE ATHENAEUM OF OHIO 1829-1960

A History of the Athenaeum of Ohio 1829-1960

A dissertation submitted to the graduate school of the
University of Cincinnati in partial fulfillment of the requirements
for the degree of Doctor of Education
1964

by
Francis Joseph Miller

A.B. Athenaeum of Ohio, 1947

BS Athenaeum of Ohio, 1957

S.T.L. Pontifical University of St. Thomas Aquinas, 1951

M. Ed. Xavier University, 1960

DEDICATION

This book is dedicated to my sisters and brother:
Mildred Gilland, Lorraine Miller, William Miller and Ethel Zwick

ACKNOWLEDGMENTS

The writer wishes to express his appreciation for the guidance given by Dr. R. L. Pounds, Dr. Frank E. Liguori, and Dr. Leonard Chaffee.

The writer also wishes to extend his appreciation to the Most Reverend Karl J. Alter, Archbishop of Cincinnati, the Most Reverend Paul F. Leibold, Auxiliary Bishop of Cincinnati, for their encouragement in making this study possible, and to the Right Reverend Joseph J. Schneider, for his cooperation. Appreciation is also expressed to Mrs. Mildred Gallant for the critical reading of the text and to all those whose assistance made this dissertation possible.

TABLE OF CONTENTS

FOREWORD

It has been forty years since the first publication of this history of the Athenaeum (in photocopy form) by the University of Michigan. During those intervening years, being procurator and teacher at the major seminary, principal in a regional high school, pastor of two parishes, and many years in Catholic social work, I just deferred, sad to say, the formal publication of this history of the Cincinnati seminaries.

But it always flickered on the back burner of my mind, and retirement from the pastoral ministry finally allowed me the time and the incentive to get back to undertaking its publication. With the patient and able assistance of my editor, Kathleen Carroll, I finally found the professional help necessary to publish that original manuscript.

Had I had the opportunity I might have, somewhere along the line, thought of bringing the present history (which ends in 1964) up to date. But the Spirit works in many ways, and I now think bringing this history of the seminaries up to the present would call for the settled scholarship of one or two generations hence. In the meantime, it is hoped that this history will inspire any future historian to fill in those forty years, while going back and expanding on so many fascinating personalities and absorbing ideas that were given just passing notice.

However I must say that one of the first things that surprisingly happened while preparing for this publication was a pleasant revival of my old admiration and regard for the contribution of so many dedicated individuals to the seminaries of the Archdiocese of Cincinnati. The Archbishops, the Bishops, the rectors, the professors, and the students in its sweeping history could never have realized how much their indomitable spirit and brilliant ideas wove a colorful tapestry of a remarkable era.

After those forty years, I still regard with the highest of admiration the contribution of Archbishop Purcell. It was indeed very sad that such an illustrious life was tarnished by the financial failure of the 1870's. But that failure should never have obliterated the enormous stature of the man. I often wonder what the condition of the Church in America would be today if his ideas on the seminaries had been allowed to become the paradigm of seminary life in America.

His great design was that located next to the theological seminary would be a college. The college was to be "mixed," that is, the college would accept all male students in the community for a classical education in Latin and Greek, and be solidly grounded in the English classics as well as the science of the day. The students in the major seminary, in turn, would teach the majority of those subject to the students in the college. The system provided for the seminarians a remarkably successful experience in pedagogy while providing an excellent opportunity for the assessment of future clerical qualities necessary in the priesthood. The number and quality of the vocations to the priesthood during its time proved it wisdom.

In the last chapter of this book, I stated forty years ago that the prime purpose of this history was to document the history and development of the Athenaeum from its founding in 1829 to 1964. Since there had been no comprehensive and complete history of this institution and since the educational needs of the times made it imperative that much more be known about the development of the individual Catholic seminaries in these United States, this story was presented as a detailed historical study of one particular individual diocesan seminary institution. The one essential purpose, therefore, of this chronological record has been to be of help to those who in the future must proceed with the work of evaluating and assessing Roman Catholic seminary education in the United States. Closely allied with this purpose were several others. One was to give due recognition to the many excellent rectors and dedicated professors of the Athenaeum lest their names be forgotten and their work go unheralded.

In finishing, just a personal note in this Foreword: I am now eighty-one years of age. I entered the seminary back in 1942. In preparing for this publication, another thing I noticed in the rereading the text was again to be put back in touch with the names of so many old pastors, priests and classmates of my seminary days. It then occurred to me that so many of them then were as old as I am now. Looking back on all the old stories that were told about them, I realized that I was looking back on a substantial amount of diocesan history peopled by so many colorful clerics and long-gone friends.

Rev. Francis J. Miller
March 5, 2005
Cincinnati, Ohio

CHAPTER ONE

Founding and Early History of the Seminary and College

INTRODUCTION

This chapter will treat of the first plans put forth for a seminary and college in the early history of the diocese of Cincinnati (1822-1851). Bishop Fenwick made one unsuccessful attempt (1826) to start a college and a seminary before seeing the actual beginning of Francis Xavier Seminary (1829) and the Catholic College of the Athenaeum (1831). It will be one of the important endeavors of this chapter to show that in Bishop Fenwick's time, these two institutions, as finally formed, were separate and distinct, but that nonetheless they were "joined" in a common purpose. Understood in light of the practices of the day, this educational arrangement was a type of institution known as a "seminary-college." Another important consideration of this chapter shows that in the very earliest days of its existence, the college section, the Athenaeum, was "mixed"; that is, it was both a preparatory seminary and a lay college. Mainly because of the uncertainties of obtaining qualified men for the administration of the college and for teaching in the college section, Bishop Purcell, successor of Bishop Fenwick, gave the college over to the Jesuit Fathers in 1840. But the diocesan seminary of St. Francis Xavier continued its precarious existence for a little more than eleven years before its name was changed (1851) to Mount St. Mary's Seminary of the West. Its future was then assured.

THE APPOINTMENT OF FENWICK AS BISHOP OF CINCINNATI (1822)

On March 30, 1822, the Liberty Hall and Cincinnati Gazette announced the arrival in Cincinnati of the "Right Reverend consecrated Catholic Bishop of Cincinnati and State of Ohio." Edward Dominic Fenwick, O.P., the person referred to in this early news item, was born on August 19, 1768, in St. Mary's county, on the Patient River, in Maryland. His father was Ignatius Fenwick of Wallington, a descendant of Cuthbert Fenwick of the Fenwicks of Fenwick Tower, Northumberland, England. Ignatius Fenwick was a large landowner in Maryland.

Edward's early education was probably received privately in the Fenwick Manor, but on December 24, 1784, he enrolled at Holy Cross College, Bornheim, Belgium—a school conducted by refugee Dominicans of England. He entered the order of St. Dominic on September 4, 1788, adding to his baptismal name of Edward, that of Dominic. He was ordained a priest on February 23, 1793.

In 1804, having returned to America, he was urged by Bishop Carroll of Baltimore, the first bishop of the United States, to visit the western state of Kentucky and investigate the possibilities of establishing the Dominicans in that area. In October of 1806, he bought five hundred acres of land situated about two miles from the town of Springfield, Washington county, Kentucky, and upon them he began the construction of a convent known as St. Rose. At the same time he founded a college called St. Thomas Aquinas, which was attached to St. Rose.

In 1807, upon his own petition, he was released from the office of Superior of the Order in Kentucky to embark on his famous missionary journeys into Kentucky and Ohio. The journeys into Ohio were to win for him the title of "Apostle of Ohio." It was his work in Ohio that finally gained for him the recognition of the bishops of the young country and the appointment by Rome to the See of Cincinnati on June 19, 1821.[1]

The following October of 1821, the Bull of Appointment arrived in Kentucky; and at St. Rose on the 13th of January, 1922, Fenwick was consecrated the Bishop of Cincinnati by the most Reverend B. J. Flaget of Bardstown, Kentucky, assisted by the Fathers Hill and Wilson. Bishop David of Bardstown preached the sermon.[2]

EARLY CINCINNATI AND THE CATHOLIC CHURCH (1822)

As a member of the Dominican Order, Father Edward Fenwick had visited Ohio as early as 1814. Coming twice each year to the state he soon discovered the existence of seven Catholic families. One of the most prominent of these sturdy Catholic pioneer families was that of Mr. Michael Scott, who had come to Cincinnati from Baltimore in 1805. The first Catholic service in this city was held in the house of Mr. Scott on Walnut Street near Fourth, the present site of the Dixie Terminal and the Old South Restaurant. The names of the early congregation of Catholics were Michael Scott, James Gorman, J.M. Mahon, J. Whiet, P. Walsh, F. Geoghegan, Edward Lynce, and Robert Ward. In subsequent visits to Cincinnati, he encouraged the Catholics to build a church.

On September 8, 1817, a meeting was held to discuss and plan the building of a church. No definite action was taken, however. On May 15, 1818, Bishop Flaget of Bardstown, Kentucky, visited Cincinnati and encouraged the building of a church. In 1918, the corporation limits of the city had been extended as far as Liberty Street. A piece of plotted ground consisting of lots one and two located on the northwestern corner of Vine and Liberty streets, was purchased from Mr. James Finley. The first Catholic Church in Cincinnati was erected on that spot. The Church of St. Francis Seraph stands there today.

When Fenwick came to Cincinnati, he thought that this first church north of Liberty Street was too far from town. On July 26, 1822, he purchased the lot of twenty-five feet on Sycamore Street, and moved the church from Liberty Street to this location. The new church was called St. Peter's and the site next to it was to be the place where the future seminary of St. Francis Xavier would be located.[3]

Fenwick was a bishop in a large state and one that boasted over one-half million inhabitants. Between 1810 and 1820 the population in Ohio had more than doubled. It had increased from 230,760 in 1810 to 581,295 in 1820. Partly because of its water facilities and partly because of its immense agricultural backcountry, Cincinnati and the southwestern part of the state had become its most flourishing portion.[4]

FIRST PLANS FOR A COLLEGE (1822)

Bishop Fenwick made it a condition of accepting the bishopric that Father Wilson, the

Provincial of the Dominicans, would come to Cincinnati in the capacity of his vicar-general. On March 23, 1822, the bishop, with Fathers Wilson, Hill, Hynes and De Raymaecker arrived in Cincinnati.[5] The fact that Father Wilson, at this early date, accompanied Bishop Fenwick to his diocese in Ohio in highly significant. For it is now known that father Wilson, on arriving in Cincinnati, called three members of his order from Kentucky to come to Cincinnati for the purpose of helping him in the establishment of a new college in the city. It had already been decided by Wilson and Fenwick that the college of St. Thomas attached to St. Rose in Kentucky would be closed and that the college would be brought to Cincinnati. The three Dominicans called by Wilson to staff the contemplated college were Stephen H. Montgomery (later to be the first rector of the Seminary of St. Francis Xavier), Thos. H. Martin, and John H. Grady. The plan never materialized because Bishop Flaget of Bardstown disapproved of it and appealed to Cardinal Consalvi in Rome. Through the Cardinal the proposal was dropped and the plan for a college at Cincinnati at this early date came to an end.[6]

The fact that Bishop Fenwick had intended to begin a school at this early date and that he intended to use the members of his community to staff it, must have been widely known in early Cincinnati. In the March 30, 1822, issue of *Liberty Hall and Cincinnati Gazette* the following news item appeared:

> We congratulate the Roman Catholiks [sic] of this city and environs on the arrival of the Rt. Rev. Dr. Fenwick, lately consecrated Bishop of Cincinnati and the Sate of Ohio. This circumstance interests not only the Catholiks [sic] but all the friends of literature and useful knowledge, as we understand that his intention is ultimately to open a school, aided by the members of his order long distinguished for their piety and learning.[7]

THE CONCEPT OF THE SEMINARY-COLLEGE

Even though the plan for the college came to naught due to the influence of Bishop Flaget, it is inspiring to note the importance Fenwick at this early date attached to higher education. Actually, this emphasis on higher education seems to have been a common characteristic of all the early Catholic bishops and missionaries of the country. There were many reasons for the emphasis. But, above all others, it is quite certain that Fenwick and all the others realized that if the church were to succeed in America, it needed a place to produce a native clergy while it went about the tasks of educating the laity.

Yet in the development of higher Catholic education here in the United States, it was true then, as it is true now, that finances constituted the real stumbling block and problem. In the development of the matter, the early bishops found that the most efficient, economical, and expedient way of proceeding was to begin with an educational arrangement known as a seminary-college.

The early American bishops with only one exception (Kenrick's seminary at Philadelphia) resorted to this combination. Generally, the bishops had been in favor of diocesan seminaries of the type prescribed by the Council of Trent.[8] Yet precisely because of these financial conditions most bishops in the first half of the nineteenth century found themselves forced into the seminary-college modification of the strictly Tridentine plan. As has been pointed out, at the time Fenwick served as bishop, all the seminaries with one exception were compelled by reason of finances to resort to the educational arrangement known as the seminary-college.[9]

In the seminary-college educational arrangement, the men in the seminary taught in the attached college. In this way, only one or two competent theologians were needed for the seminary, and perhaps one or two classical scholars were needed for the college. Beyond this, the students in the seminary carried the burden of teaching and maintaining discipline in the college. The ecclesiastical students would have a class or two each day in the Sacred Sciences, allowing them a great deal of time to teach and supervise the younger men. Under this arrangement of classes, the seminary became a mere annex for providing an inexpensive teaching staff for the college.[10] On the other hand it was the tuition of the men of the college, especially the non-clerical students, which provided for the support of the work in the seminary. McDonald writes, "Poverty made it impossible to maintain a seminary alone. The seminarians taught in the college and the revenue in the college maintained the seminary."[11]

In this thesis, it will be seen that this concept of the seminary-college was the idea that Fenwick had in mind in the establishment of St. Francis Xavier Seminary and the College of the Athenaeum on sycamore Street. In a letter written to the Association for the Propagation of the Faith[12] in 1829, this notion in the mind of Fenwick was very clearly outlined.

> The erection of the seminary is of the greatest necessity if we do not wish to lose the results of all our labor. I might, indeed, without a seminary obtain some priests from Europe from time to time; but they would always be too few in number to answer all the needs of the missions. Besides, I should be obliged to support them for two or three years in order to allow them time to learn English, etc. With a seminary, I do not lose those who come from Europe while a the same time I form a native clergy, bred to the customs of the country, accustomed to the hardships and well acquainted with the language, etc. Furthermore, I can start a college, and through it obtain in some means to better our lot and to set on foot other necessary or useful institutions. Likewise, I shall acquire an interest in the education and instruction of the youth of this state, which will be great advantage, to religion. In a word, sir, with a seminary, I have a most consoling future. I am therefore full determined to direct all my efforts to this object, and to make no further delay. I will commence by shortly purchasing the lot of which I have spoken, using for this purpose the money I have left and part of that which your have had to goodness to assign to me. Then I will give my attention to building the necessary structures. I can obtain a few young Europeans and Americans who have made their humanities, so that by the time the edifice is completed, or even before I shall have seven or eight seminarians. These I will employ, at first, in teaching the elements of Latin to some boys fourteen or fifteen years of age. I have every reason to hope that, in this way, the project will succeed, but I shudder when I think of the expense. The balance of the sum will not suffice for the construction of the building, and yet I shall, at the same time, be obliged to furnish board and lodging to the seminarians and perhaps most of the young boys; all this will probably put obstacles in the way of building the college. Nevertheless, with the example of the Bishop of Bardstown before me, I am going to commence.[13]

When Purcell[14] came to Cincinnati, he had been president of the college section of the same type of institution at Mount St. Mary's in Maryland. Throughout his life he had a great predilection for this type of arrangement, and even when forced to give up the College of the Athenaeum to the Jesuit Fathers in 1840, he resisted the idea of establishing a separate seminary. In 1856 he established Mount St. Mary's College in Price Hill. It, too, was attached to the major seminary. Actually, it was not until after Purcell's death that the idea of a separate minor seminary for clerical students only was accepted in the diocese of Cincinnati.

In this concept of the seminary-college still another important idea should be kept in mind. These early colleges attached to the seminary are known as "mixed." They were both preparatory seminaries and secular colleges at one and the same time. Their aim was to function as a seminary and also offer a preparatory college curriculum for strictly non-clerical students. Students who wanted to prepare for the priesthood entered the "mixed" college where they studied with the lay students. After receiving their classical training, they entered the seminary section, which was equivalent to what is known today as the major seminary. Edward Power estimates that of the forty thousand men who were graduated from these colleges throughout the country before 1855, ten thousand became clergymen.[15]

In the light of subsequent history, it also developed that these "mixed" colleges became very fine recruiting grounds for the secular college. It is interesting to consider what might have been the effect on recruiting vocations to the diocesan priesthood had this early plan of the "mixed" colleges continued to the present day. It is evident that Purcell recruited a very ample supply of priests for his diocese through the seminary-college arrangement.[16]

FENWICK SEEKS HELP FOR THE SEMINARY-COLLEGE (1823)

In tracing the events of his life, when the college project failed, Bishop Fenwick went to Europe in 1823 to seek financial help for his diocese. Foremost in his mind were the educational needs for the diocese.[17] On his arrival at Bordeaux in France, he wrote a letter (August 6, 1823) to the Reverend M. Badin who was then in Paris. In it he mentioned that "the object of my journey is also to procure means for securing, in the vicinity of my Episcopal town, the domain of a small tract of land, and a large convenient house, well calculated for a seminary . . . for you will conceive how great is the want of missionaries in my extensive diocese, when you learn that I possess only seven priests, and have neither seminary, professors, nor schools."[18]

The "domain of a small tract of land, and a large convenient hose, well calculated for a seminary" about which Fenwick spoke was a five-acre piece of property with a large house, 150 by 100 feet, containing twenty-three fireplaces, property upon which he had taken a lease in April. Ultimately he found the price of $26,000 far out of his reach.[19]

The Bishop was still convinced that a seminary and college in or near Cincinnati was essential for the good of religion in his diocese. While abroad he left nothing undone to obtain the means for their construction and to secure priests to conduct them. He believed, furthermore, that the wisest plan would be to place these institutions under the management of the Order to which he belonged. The Dominicans were already established in Ohio, and he felt that this territory could long depend upon them for its supply of missionaries and for teachers in his college. Accordingly, in addition to soliciting the wherewithal to build a seminary and college, he sought to interest his European brethren not only in the cause of his missions, but in that of his educational projects. To further materialize these plans, as well as to secure a worthy and able successor to the See of Cincinnati, while in Rome he urged the appointment of Father Thomas Hyacinth Cipoletti as his coadjutor. Father Cipoletti was Italian and a learned Dominican who spoke English.[20]

Several Friar Preachers, at least three of them were Italian, an Irishman, and a Frenchman, all living in Italy, offered themselves for service to the American mission. Unfortunately, although Bishop Fenwick did not appear to realize it at the time, circumstances abroad and the positions held by these fathers were to prevent them from giving their services to the Church in Cincinnati. The fact that these friars were all learned men, and of high standing in their order, attests to the caliber of men the prelate sought for his diocese.[21]

THE FIRST PLANS FOR THE SEMINARY (1825)

Early in the year 1825, Bishop Fenwick returned to his Episcopal city. On February 15, 1825, he purchased from Elmore Williams and wife the remaining fifty feet of the lot No. 73 fronting 49 feet on Sycamore Street, and immediately adjoining the property previously bought for the sum of $1,200. He then set about to prepare for the erection of a Cathedral.[22]

On March 29, 1825, Bishop Fenwick wrote the following letter to Mr. P. Pallivaiscini in Turin, Italy.

> …Here I am, with a cathedral without a pastor, and a seminary…for one was begun in my absence…without a professor. The ecclesiastic who took upon himself the burden of the latter work leaves me next week to go to New Orleans. He had only accepted the charge until my return from Europe, and having made previous arrangements with Msgr. Debourg he considers himself bound to fulfill his promise.[23]

It is known that in August of 1825 the bishop had asked Badin in London to make overtures in Europe for a priest to conduct his seminary. A young man by the name of de Gaussancourt of the Seminary of St. Nicholas du Chardonnet, Paris, had been obtained in 1825. But in 1826, he disappointed both Father Badin and Bishop Fenwick by taking up other work in Italy.[24]

In the fall of 1826, Drake and Mansfield, speaking of the Catholics of Cincinnati, said:

> The Cathedral belonging to this congregation is a neat specimen of Gothic architecture . . . the edifice for the literary college is to correspond in its exterior with the cathedral and be connected with it in the rear by the frame church originally occupied by the Society; and the whole will then form three sides of a square and when properly ornamented with a steeple, will present a magnificent appearance.[25]

Before the dedication of the cathedral on December 17, 1826, the old frame church that had served as the cathedral was moved to the rear of the property. Work was begun in remodeling it for use as the Episcopal residence as well as seminary until a better structure could be erected.[26]

Fenwick in December of 1826 had everything ready for his seminary except competent men to staff it. The many letters written by him during the years of 1827 and 1828 clearly indicate his continuing search for men to run his seminary. During these two years he met with no success at all, even though he had appealed through Badin to both the Jesuits and Benedictines.[27]

This move seems to have been especially for the purpose of placing him in charge of the seminary as well as the three seminarians that had accompanied Father De Raymeicker to America the previous spring. These seminarians were John Martin Henni[28] (destined to become Milwaukee's first bishop and archbishop), Martin Condign, and John Baptist Clicteur. All of these seminarians were nearly ready for ordination. Clicteur had come to America with the expressed purposed of joining the Dominicans, and the other two men seemed to be thinking of it.[29] It is not known why they did not become Dominicans.

Fenwick, because of lack of personnel, still could not open the seminary. As a result, the three candidates were sent to the seminary at Bardstown until they were prepared for the priesthood. Here they received form Flaget all the orders except priesthood. This only stirred the bishop to redouble his efforts for opening of the seminary.[30]

In January of 1829, Bishop Fenwick wrote to the officials of the Association for the Propagation of the Faith. In his letter he mentioned the fact that he had already purchased the land for the seminary, work on which was scheduled to begin in May. He was now thinking about purchasing the land upon which he would build his seminary-college in 1831.

> In Cincinnati, I purchased ground for the contemplated seminary. A good opportunity was presented and I thought it well to take advantage of it, as I would later on be compelled to pay $20 per front foot for the lot. Outside of this, I am now free of debt. Strictly speaking, I have some money on hand, which I propose to use in the following manner. I shall first of all endeavor to secure two zealous priests of good oratorical ability, who will be charged solely with visiting congregations as yet without resident priests. Secondly, I shall within a short time purchase in the immediate neighborhood of the cathedral another lot for the seminary, although to do so will entail an expenditure of about $4,000.[31]

On February 2, 1829, Bishop Fenwick ordained the Reverends John M. Henni, Martin Kundig, and John B. Clicteur to the priesthood. Father Clicteur became the Bishop's secretary two weeks after ordination. For a number of months they all assisted at the cathedral.

THE OPENING OF THE SEMINARY OF ST. FRANCIS XAVIER (1829)

On May 11, 1829, Bishop Fenwick opened his seminary in the old frame church that stood behind the new cathedral. On June 28, Father Clicteur wrote of this event:

I have the pleasure to announce to you that at last we have a seminary in Cincinnati. It was to have been opened on the 15th of March, but owing to unforeseen circumstances, the opening took place on the 11th of May. After the Veni Creator and Mass, Monseigneur read the regulations and made an address to the new seminarians. The Seminary has been dedicated to St. Francis Xavier, whose name it will bear. There are four seminarians, all clerics studying theology, who are regularly given one lesson a day, and six young men who are taught Latin; we hope their number increases by the arrival of some young men we expect from Europe. To judge from the start it has made, the institution promises excellent results. The discipline, patterned after the best European model and modified only to the degree called for by the customs of the country, is already I full force, and some missionaries from abroad, in passing through here recently, expressed their astonishment at the progress made in so short time. Besides the prayer recited for all the benefactors of the Mission, they recite here every day and in common a special prayer for the members of the Propagation of the Faith, to whom almost exclusively the seminary owes its existence. [32]

Presumably, the four theological students were the Reverends Reid, Denis A. DeLoughery, Emanuel Thienpont and James H. Clarkson.[33] In the first issue of the *Catholic Telegraph*, October 22, 1832, there is a news item recording the conferring of deacon Clarkson, a Dominican student, received the four minor orders.

MONTGOMERY, RECTOR (1829-1830)

The Reverend Stephen Montgomery, a talented Dominican, was appointed the seminary's first rector. Father Stephen Hyacinth Montgomery was born in Charles County, Maryland, about 1789 or 1790. With his father, Basil Montgomery, and his mother, who appears to have been an Elder and a relative of the future Archbishop Elder, he went to Washington county, Kentucky, as a young boy. Here he was ordained a Dominican, along with Father Miles, S.S. Montgomery and Willett, on September 21, 1816. He taught in the college of St. Thomas Aquinas until 1822 at which time he was sent to Ohio. After work in Zanesville, Ohio, he came to Cincinnati in 1828 and was appointed rector of the seminary in 1829. In the spring of 1830 he left for Kentucky and was prior of the Dominicans at St. Rose. In 1833 he attained the status of Covington. In 1845 he went to Natchez, Mississippi, where he labored for some years. In the early 1850s he seems to have retired to New Orleans where he died in 1855. Father Montgomery was possessed of great ability and was highly educated. It is interesting to note that a street near the cathedral in Covington is named after him. [34]

Father Montgomery's first faculty consisted of the Reverends J.B. Clicteur and Martin Kundig. Also, Brother James Vincent Bullock (an excellent classical scholar and linguist), Charles Dominic Bowling, and James Hyacinth Clarkson were brought from St. Rose Kentucky, although Clarkson had not yet completed his course in theology.[35] Bullock and Bowling were both Dominican novices and their course of study in theology was complete. "Clarkson was brought just after his profession from the same place...apparently that he might both study in the seminary and teach in college."[36]

As for curriculum in these early days, the four major seminarians were given a class or so a day in theology. The rest of the time they taught the younger students, and acted as prefects of discipline. Except for Latin, there is not evidence as to precisely what the younger students were taught.

It appears that in these early seminaries, intellectual training was very deficient.[37] Nonetheless, it does seem that they did produce some excellent missionary priests. What was the reason? One might suggest that the character stimulus gained from daily association with the self-sacrificing pioneer bishops and priests in the Episcopal residence and seminary more than made up for the inadequate intellectual training afforded the students.

As will be seen, the recurring perplexity of getting and keeping a stable faculty caused most of the difficulties for the seminary (and the future college of the Athenaeum.)[38] The desire to maintain a stable faculty for his seminary and college prompted Fenwick, just before he died, to ask for a coadjutor. He requested the services of Father Kenney, the Jesuit Provincial. Because of Father Kenney's age and the unwillingness of the Jesuit Superior in Rome, the request was denied. Purcell, in his turn, was actually forced by this very reason—the lack of competent men to staff his seminary and college—to relinquish the college to the Jesuit Fathers in 1840.

On August 1, 1829, Henry Gregory sold to the bishop Lot No. 74 in Spencer's Subdivision for the sum of $3,000.[39] This property, which was adjacent to the cathedral, and extended one hundred feet from the cathedral grounds, was the site upon which the completed buildings of the college and seminary finally rested.[40] It was the property to which he had referred in his letter of January 1829.

From a letter dated September 3, 1829, it was learned that the bishop had brought with him to his seminary two Indian youths from Mackinac. The intention was that when they became sufficiently advanced, he would send them to the College of the Propaganda[41] to finish their ecclesiastical education in the Capitol of Christendom, after which they would return to America and labor among their own people. As far as can be ascertained, this seems to be the first attempt on the part of the American hierarchy to recruit Indians as clergy. It illustrates well the missionary zeal of the first bishop of Cincinnati.[42]

In October of 1829 Bishop Fenwick attended the First Provincial Council of Baltimore summoned by Archbishop Whitfield. The subject of a common and metropolitan seminary for the entire province was suggested and discussed. Most likely because of the great distances involved at a time when travel was very difficult, any thought of a common seminary seemed impossible. At any rate, nothing was done about a metropolitan seminary at this time.[43]

After the adjournment of the Council, Fenwick visited the religious and education institutions of Baltimore, as well as his friends and relatives. It was while on this trip that he wrote from Georgetown College in Maryland to the Reverend Martin Kundig, a member of the faulty of the first seminary. Apparently Kundig and a student named Bullock had written to him complaining that the order in the seminary was not too good while he was away. The Bishop reminded him the "order is heaven's first law. If unruly students will not obey, they are to be dismissed. I will prefer to have no priests nor seminarians if I cannot have such as are pious, regular and obedient."[44]

About the middle of December 1829, Reverend Rese,[45] the Vicar-General, returned from his European trip accompanied by four clergy for the diocese. In stating this fact in a letter to the "annals" he says: "As you are aware, we have opened here a seminary, but, it is not very unlike to a stable. We must have suitable buildings in order to house the students properly, but whence should the means come from? We now have fifteen students, amongst them two young Indians from Michilimakinsk, who give great promise."[46]

In April of 1830, S. Montgomery, the rector, was sent back to St. Rose to teach the students there. The novices Bullock and Bowling, who were teaching in the seminary in Cincinnati, were also sent back to Kentucky. It seemed certain that up until this time Fenwick had cherished the idea of having the Dominican Fathers for his seminary-college. Many things certainly indicate this. But with the removal of Montgomery, this plan also came to naught. For the next ten years Fenwick and Purcell struggled to staff the college and seminary with diocesan priests. It is interesting to note that it was the Dominican Fathers who had the first opportunity of staffing the institutions of Catholic higher learning and education in Cincinnati.[47]

FENWICK, RECTOR (1830-1832)

With the departure of Montgomery, Fenwick himself became the superior of the seminary. Father Rese, the vicar-general, was vice-rector. It would seem that Fenwick had all the requisite knowledge and ability to successfully hold the office of rector. However, ten years later, Fenwick was to conclude that the visiting of the missions and work of the bishop interfered too much with the office of superior of a seminary.[48]

In the year of 1827, Father Rese had been sent to Europe by his bishop to make an appeal to its charitable missionary spirit in behalf of the vast diocese of Cincinnati. While on his errand the missionary conceived the idea of extending the work for the Lyons Society into Bavaria and Austria. He first went to Lyons, thence to Rome, where he spent a year, devoting most of the time to considering the question of a religious vocation with the Dominican Order.

Father Rese next proceeded to Bavaria. Here he explained to some of the bishops the needs of the American Missions. He was successful in establishing a society known as the Ludwig-Missionsverein. During the first decade of its existence nearly all the funds collected were sent to Cincinnati, about 36,000 marks. This society functioned independently of the Lyons Society after 1838. From that year to the year 1863 it contributed to the missions of the United States nearly 3,339,343 marks.

Elated over his success, Father Rese journeyed to Vienna. Upon his arrival in the Austrian capitol in the fall of 1828, he presented his plan to the Archbishop Leopold Maxmilian von Firmian, who was so well disposed toward it that he determined to take up the matter with the emperor. The greatness of the cause gained the favor of Francis I.

The society was to be formed and called "Leopoldenische Stiftung" (Leopoldine Society) in memory of Leopodina, late Empress of Brazil, and favorite daughter of the Emperor. The central Bureau was to be located in the Dominican Monastery in Vienna.

Membership in the Society was to include not only the rich and the dignitaries of the land, but also the lower classes of people. All from the highest to the lowest, could join this crusade of charity. The members were not to be burdened with many or difficult obligations.

In a letter to the Leopoldine Varien of Vienna on January 31, 1831, the Reverend Frederick Baraga gives a fine description of life in the little seminary of St. Francis Xavier, which was part of the residence for the cathedral clergy.

Frederick Baraga was born at Dobernic, Illyrin, June 29, 1797, and was ordained September 21, 1823. He made his way to America and stayed for a time at the seminary on Sycamore Street. From his correspondence, it is quite evident that he enjoyed his stay here. Later he went to Upper Michigan, where he soon became famous for his success among the Indians. He published catechisms of Christian doctrine, dictionaries in various Indian dialects. He became Vicar-Apostolic of Upper Michigan in 1853 and Bishop of Sault Sainte Marie, January 1857. He died at Marquette, January 19, 1868.[49]

It should be noted that in this letter Fenwick is indicated as the superior of the seminary. Some former lists of the rectors at Mount St. Mary's Seminary mention Rese as the second rector. It seems that this was not the case; Rese was vice-rector and in charge of a great deal of administration, but there is no indication that he was ever given complete charge of the seminary. It would also seem from this same letter that the students who were taking the Latin courses did not reside at the seminary at this time.

It is also interesting to not Baraga's description of the new building and its cost:

> We are living here in a small not very safe building known as the Seminary. The rules of the house are as in a convent, and are to my taste. The bishop is our superior. At five in the morning we rise. There are now in the house five priests and four students. Among the latter is an Indian about 18 years of age. It is with sorrow one perceives the many fissures in the walls of our present domicile, which threatens to tumble. On the other hand it is with feelings of pride and thanks, one sees the new college building arise, which will be used for education purposes. It is a well-planned building. The walls are finished and the roof has also been completed. It will, when thoroughly done, be of a lasting and inestimable value to this country, at present so largely devoid of educational facilities. The building is composed of three stories, and each of the floors will contain two large classrooms and eight smaller ones. The upper floor will be used as the dormitory. I am told, that thus far, the building has coat $7,600; the completion and furnishing for the interior require $4,000 or more.[50]

THE FOUNDING OF THE COLLEGE OF THE ATHENAEUM (1831)

In the early part of 1830 it had become readily apparent that the old frame church that housed the Episcopal residence and seminary was far too small to meet the growing educational needs of the diocese. At about this time Bishop Fenwick determined to begin work on a set of buildings that, together, were destined to become an architectural monument in early Cincinnati. The Cathedral of St. Peter was located on the south end of his property. The erection of the college building known as the Athenaeum was completed in 1831. The bishop then had the old frame structure razed and joined the cathedral and Athenaeum by having an Episcopal residence and seminary built across the rear of the property. This was completed in 1832.[51]

In February 1830 Bishop Fenwick wrote that they were at that very time beginning to procure materials for the construction of the college, which was to be one hundred and thirty feet long by fifty feet wide. He seemed to rejoice very much over the fact that, at last, there was a beginning.[52]

On May 14, 1830, the cornerstone[53] the future Athenaeum was laid. Although this was a very significant event in the history of the Church in Ohio, Bishop Fenwick could not be present since he was occupied with other pastoral duties in another part of the state. Accordingly, the Reverend J. J. Mullon, doubtless as a token of regard for his faithful services, was awarded the honor of presiding at this function.[54]

It is interesting to note that on November of 1830, J. J. Mullon wrote from Cincinnati that he was not quite sure if the proposed college would succeed.[55]

It was probably on his return from the northwest that bishop Fenwick received a letter from his cousin, Doctor Fenwick of Boston, dated April 6, 1831. His cousin congratulates him on the

> Starting of your college for the education of priests . . . from the fullness of my heart do I wish you success in this well-considered and richly blessed enterprise; for such an institution to the best of my judgment must be of incalculable benefit for firmly planting our Holy Faith in the valley of the Mississippi. I cannot better tell you my joy in this matter than by telling you that I believe such an institution . . . by which one can obtain priests educated in the native tongue, under one's own direction and imbued with one's own spirit . . . to be the most desirable and useful of all undertakings. And on that account I sincerely admire your wise measure in seeking the aid of pious Europeans; for if one has a good supply of such workers in the vineyard of the Lord, then parishes and churches must follow. Nor can the churches already establish last for any time without resident pastors. Would to God that I might soon start on a similar foundation! What immeasurable good it would do here in Boston . . ."[56]

In October 1831, a party of Jesuits traveling from the east of St. Louis reached the city of Cincinnati. The party consisted of Father Peter Kenney, visitor of the Jesuit houses in North America, Father McSherry, his assistant, and Mr. James Oliver Van de Velde who was joining the teaching staff of St. Louis College. Eager to reach their destination shortly, they spent but a single day in Cincinnati where they were entertained by Bishop Fenwick. The latter was most anxious to engage the services of Van de Velde as president to the Athenaeum and petitioned Kenney to this effect. Under the circumstances, it was an impossible request for Van de Velde had been committed to St. Louis College.[57]

Van de Velde was impressed by the recently erected building of the Athenaeum and this is mentioned by him in letters addressed to a friend in the East.

> *Cincinnati, October 14, 1831.* The good Bishop came to our hotel this morning to invite us to dine with him. It happens well, for this is a day of abstinence. We went there accordingly at about one o'clock p.m. After dinner we visited the church and the college. The college called Athenaeum is a building somewhat similar to the church, but of modern style. It has, like the church, a small turret of steeple, which looks very pretty. The Bishop's house, which is rather small, joins the two other buildings. The whole, take together, presents an imposing sight. The college is ample enough to receive a large number of students. The rooms are large, but the dormitory, though spacious, does not admit enough fresh air. The boys will suffer in the summer. There is a printing establishment attached to the College. Next week will be published the first religious newspaper under the name of the *Catholic Telegraph*.[58]

> *Cincinnati, October 15, 1831.* I must state that the college is 130 feet long and fifty feet wide and that the church has about the same dimensions. Only ten years ago there was neither church nor any resident priest. At present there are priests in several parts of the State of Ohio and the Bishop has fifteen or sixteen young men who are preparing for the priesthood in his seminary. Of that number, three are Belgians. As they were not introduced to me, although I wished to see them air did not become acquainted with any of them. Perhaps they suspected that I might want to make Jesuits out of them. If such was the case, the suspicions were not well founded.[59]

The Athenaeum was opened on Monday, October 17, 1831.[60] Doubtless this was one of the happiest days in Bishop Fenwick's life for it marked the consummation of a work devoutly prayed for. The building was described as "elegant and commodious," or "spacious and beautiful." Two stories and a half high, with an ample and well-lighted basement, it was one hundred and twenty or thirty feet long by fifty in width. It ran parallel with the cathedral to which it was later joined across the rear of the property by new structures housing the seminary and Episcopal residence. Above each of the structures, when they were ultimately completed, rose a commanding tower. The spires of the cathedral and the seminary-residence were crowned with splendid gilded crosses. Alpheus White, a convert and one of Cincinnati's most noted early architects, drew the plans and superintended the construction of the college and seminary-residence. When completed the group was regarded as one of the architectural attractions of a city which has always taken an honest pride in its public buildings. That the college and seminary residence, like the cathedral, were solidly and substantially built is shown by the fact that a part of it remained in use for educational purposes until 1891, or for sixty years.[61]

The college was opened under the name of the Athenaeum, or under the full title of "Cincinnati Athenaeum Religioni and Artibus Sacrum."[62]

The word *Athenaeum* is a name originally applied in ancient Greece to buildings dedicated to Athena, the goddess of wisdom, called sometimes Minerva by the Romans. The name was used later as the designation of a temple is Athens where poets and men of learning were accustomed to meet and read their literary productions. The academy for the promotion of learning which the emperor Hadrian built about 135 A.D. at Rome near the Forum was also called the Athenaeum. Poets and orators still met and discussed their productions there, but a new element injected into the idea of the Athenaeum was that at Hadrian's Athenaeum the regular courses of instruction were given by a staff of professors in rhetoric, jurisprudence, grammar, and philosophy. The institution, later called the Schola Romana, continued in high repute till the fifth century. Similar academies were founded in the provinces and at Constantinople by the emperor Theodosius II.[63]

After the Middle Ages, as a result of the love of things Greek, as reflected in the spirit of the Renaissance, the Latin word "universitas," or university, was replaced with the Greek, "Athenaeon." The Athenaeum was truly the universitas scientiarum, the universitas studiorum. In this sense, the various universities of Rome, like the Gregorian and the Angelicum, are still referred to as the Athenaeum.

Most likely Fenwick, in picking out this word "Athenaeum" to designate his college, did not want to use the word "university." It seemed entirely too pretentious in respect to his college. Perhaps he used the word "Athenaeum" because it would appear a little more reserved and not quite so ambitious. The words used at the time in this country designated the type of liberal arts college that Fenwick had in mind. In 1807, the monthly *Anthology* stated, "the trustees with their associates are made a body corporate by the oath of the Proprietors of Boston Athenaeum." In 1810, the Massachusetts Commonwealth laws describe, "An act to incorporate certain persons by the name of the Salem Athenaeum." In 1837, Peck's New Guide mentions, "The Athenaeum (of Cincinnati) is an institution under the management of Catholic priests."[64]

From the very beginning it was both a boarding school and a day school. The following somewhat pretentious advertisement appeared in the *Catholic Telegraph* announcing its opening:

> It (the Athenaeum) is now opened for the reception of pupils. The scholastic exercises commenced on Monday, the 17th inst. From the number and proficiency of the professors connected with the Athenaeum, it will be enabled to sustain a respectable standing among the literary institutions of the west. Like every similar institution, which must depend for success on the patronage of the public, its chief dependence is placed in the consciousness of possessing the means, and the assurance, which is hereby given, to make every exertion to merit the patronage of a liberal and enlightened public. All communications relative to the admission of students must be made to the Rev. Rese, Vice-President of the Athenaeum.[65]

The educational philosophy of the institution was outlined in these words: [66]

> The many and important advantages arising from a virtuous and liberal education, are too well felt, and acknowledged to need discussion or development. A good education is esteemed by the enlightened people of this country as the principal source of social and individual happiness. If it be true, as it has been so well remarked, "that a nation is on the decline when its youth are corrupted," it must be equally true, that when the youths are well educated, the

social body must then be blessed with comparative heath and vigor: so intimately is education connected with the better interests of society. To establish institutions; to devote, to the instruction of youth, our time, and the talents, which Divine Providence may have bestowed on us; is then, to deserve well of society, whose future supports and ornaments we prepare, in the pupils confided to our solicitude.

No labours are more useful than those of the directors of youth: to no functions is attached a higher responsibility, than to the moral magistracy with which they are invested: — no mark of public confidence more honorable that that by which they become the substitute parents of the children entrusted to their care; —no joy more pure that what they experience in witnessing, under their directions, the progress of their pupils in science and in virtue.

No duties, however, are more painful and laborious, or which require more patience and self-denial.

All theses motives, together with the conscious purity of our own views; the disinterested zeal for the public good, which animates us; and a certain degree of successful experience, to which we may be permitted to look back with honest pride; induce us to hope for a reasonable share of public patronage.

Convicted of the truth of our holy religion, we are adverse to all religious bigotry. And the student who differs with us in creed, will not be less cherished, than his companion, who believes and kneels with us at the same altar. Full of respect for the religious feelings, and religious freedom of others, never in our own establishment, shall we manifest a spirit of sectarian proselytism.

As our religion, however, is now better known than in less enlightened days; as it is now universally acknowledged, that our worship is as pure as our model is sound and scriptural; we do not deem it an infringement on liberty, to require for the good order of the community, (as it is practiced in similar institutions) that all our pupils should assist together at the religious exercises. We shall also consider as a paramount obligation, to inspire them with the love of those Christian maxims, which alone, can successfully inculcate our various duties towards God, ourselves and our fellowmen. The most particular attention shall likewise be made to maintain and perfect within them, the sentiments of filial piety, of self-esteem, and of respect for others: to infuse into their minds the love of truth and mutual benevolence; to teach them habits of order, of industry, of cleanliness; in a world, to bring them up in the practice of those virtues which makes good men and good citizens.

Of the health of our pupils, we shall take the most paternal care. The diet shall be nutritious, wholesome, abundant, and to the hours of class, shall regularly succeed the exercises of a moderate recreation. One day in each week, as the season and weather will permit, the collegians will go to the country house, situated on a beautiful eminence near the city, and shall there be exercised in common, according to their standing and progress, in recitation and public speaking.

Such are the advantages which the Athenaeum offers to the public, and if we consider its elevated and healthy position; the happy distribution of its spacious halls, chambers and dormitory; and above all, the city in which it stands, and which already gives such fair promise of importance and grandeur, may we not reasonably expect much encouragement from the stranger, as well as from our fellow-citizens? We shall endeavor to meet their esteem and answer the expectations of its venerable founder, the Rt. Rev. Dr. Fenwick.

The *Catholic Telegraph* of April 10, 1832, revealed that the curriculum set up in the early Athenaeum was indeed excellent. The *Telegraph* gave it as follows:

First Year—*Latin*—Gould's Grammar and Epitome. *French*—Levizac's Grammar and Directeur des enfrans. *English*—Murray's Grammar and introduction; writing under dictation, and arithmetic.

Second Year—*Latin*—Viri Romae, Caesar's Commentaries, Exercises, and Mythology. *French*—Grammar Continued, Receuil Choisi La Fontaine—*Spanish*—Josse's Grammar Exercises and Colmena Espanola. *English*—Grammar continued, Exercises, Scott's Lessons, Writing under dictation, Geography, Rational Arithmetic.

Third Year—*Latin*—Sallust, Phoedrus, Ovid, Exercises continued, Prosody and Roman Antiquities, *Greek*—Valpy's Grammar and Testament. *French*—Telemachus, Odes of J.G. Rosseau. *Spanish*—Extratos Exercises continued. *English*—Composition, Writing Essays and Letters, Geography continued, Algebra.

Fourth Year—*Latin*—Cicero de Senectutue, de Amicitia, de Officities Livy, Virgil's Pastorals, Aenied and Geogics, exercises continued. *Greek*—Graeca Minora, Prose and Poetry Exercises. *French*—L'Abeille Francaise and Boileau. *Spanish*—Extratos, Exercises and Dialogues. *English*—Composition Elocution, First Class Book. Mathematics—Geometry, Plain Trigonometry, Mensuration of heights and distances, Geography continued, History.

In the sixth year there will be a course of Rhetoric, Moral and Natural Philosophy and Chemistry.

The classical curriculum as listed here remained fundamentally unchanged until the beginning of Mount St. Mary's College. At this time it seems that the study of English and English literature rose to take an honored place in the curriculum along with the previous singularly honored subjects of Latin and Greek. After the financial failure in 1891, when the students entered the new minor seminary of St. Gregory's, there was a marked increase of time and study given to the science courses. This, too, made a great difference in the amount of time devoted to the study of Latin and Greek. In the modern era, it can be readily seen that over and above the study of the classics of antiquity the study of English and English literature, the natural sciences, and a fourth element, the study of the social sciences, had claimed their rightful place in the scheme of things.

THE EARLY PERIOD OF STRUGGLE FOR THE SEMINARY-COLLEGE (1821–1832)

In this period the Athenaeum and the seminary had an early era of prosperity, only to falter and almost fail in the last years of the 1830s. During Fenwick's time, it seems that the seminary and the Athenaeum were in a flourishing state. When he died, there was trouble on the faculty in the sense that there was a great deal of bickering. This difficulty does not seem however, to have affected the development of the seminary or the college to any marked degree. After Purcell came, both institutions seemed to grow and expand. But by the mid-1830s, the call upon his priests for the work of the missions, combined with an inability to obtain enough learned men to run an educational institution, caused a period of rapid decline. In this section, it will be seen how this came about.

About September 25, 1831, it is known that the Bishop had asked that the reverends Michael F. Wheeler and Charles C. Pise, both of the diocese of Baltimore, come to Cincinnati and teach in his seminary and college. Americans, all else being equal, he felt, were better suited for the instruction of the native youth. For this reason, the Bishop looked largely to the older East for English–speaking additions to his clerical force and seminary faculty.[67]

On October 16, 1831, the Bishop ordained James Reid as Deacon and Dennis DeLoughery as Subdeacon, gave the four minor orders to Emanuel Thienpont, and admitted Brother James H. Clarkson, O.P., to Tonsure. On the eighteenth, the day after the dedication of the Athenaeum, he administered Deaconship to DeLoughery, Subdeaconship to Thienpont, and the minor order to Mr. James H. Clarkson. [68]

That same day, Fenwick set out for Washington and Baltimore.[69] During this trip he tried again to secure teachers and students for his seminary-college.

At Mount St. Mary's Seminary, Emmitsburg, Maryland, several students volunteered for the missions in Ohio. Two of these, name Meline and Weiz, were young lay students in the college section from Cincinnati. Reverend Joseph V. Wiseman, who was teaching at Mount St. Mary's, tendered his services for the purpose of teaching at the Athenaeum institution in Cincinnati. At first, this offer of Wiseman was declined, but was afterward accepted on the recommendations of Reverend John B. Purcell, president of the college. Edward T. Collins,[70] destined to occupy and outstanding place in this history of the church in Cincinnati, was another student who volunteered.

Arriving in late November, Fenwick wrote in December 1831, to Reverend Peter P. Potier, O.P., Weybridge, Surrey, England, to thank him for some copies of the *Catholic Tract*. In the course of the letter he mentioned: "If some of the fathers would come to Ohio, they could find a congenial field for their zeal. The Order in the United States promises well. The church prospers in both Ohio and Michigan. Fourteen years before there was not a Catholic Church in the former state. Now he has twenty-four priests and twenty-two churches under his jurisdiction, not to count several congregations that have no house of prayer. A college is in full swing at Cincinnati and gives good promise, while the seminary united to the college and cathedral has thirteen students."[71]

From his home country in Maryland late in January of 1832, Fenwick wrote that on his arrival at Mount St. Mary's in Emmitsburg he would probably ordain Mr. Collins subdeacon; but he would leave that seminarian, as well as the other two students, at the college until the end of the year if their services were needed. He said that he now felt disposed "if you (Father Purcell) yet recommend it," to accept Father Wiseman and to take him along to Cincinnati. [72]

On his return in March of 1832, Bishop Fenwick had good reason to rejoice over the continued progress of religion in his diocese. Among other things, the Athenaeum already gave promise, perhaps beyond his most sanguine hopes.[73]

MULLON, PRESIDENT; WISEMAN, RECTOR (1832)

Due, no doubt, to his frequent and long absences from his episcopal residence, the Bishop on April 21, 1832, appointed Mullon as president of the Athenaeum. The Reverend Joseph J. Mullon was born in Ireland in 1793. Coming to this country as a child, he became a midshipman under Admiral Porter in the War of 1828. After the war he became a schoolteacher in a small village in Frederick County, Maryland. In 1815, he was invited by Father Dubois to teach at Mount St. Mary's College, Emmitsburg. While there he completed his seminary course and was ordained a priest by Purcell. In Cincinnati he preached so well that, "an entire pew was rented by non-Catholics, attracted by his lectures." In 1832, he became president of the Athenaeum and later, for a short time, rector of the seminary. On October 22, 1832, the *Catholic Telegraph* appeared for the first time with Mullon as its editor. In 1834 he went to New Orleans and became pastor of St. Patrick's parish there. During the Civil War he was strongly for the cause of the south. When General Butler, the Union general, captured New Orleans, he complained to Mullon about the matter of burying soldiers. Mullon, it is reported, stated that he was "only too happy to bury the Union soldiers." He was a man known for his piety, learning, and zeal. He died on September 11, 1866, at the age of 73. [74]

About the same time, Fenwick appointed Father Wiseman superior of the seminary. In a letter, dated May 25, 1832, to the Reverend Francis Jamison, Vice-President of Mount St. Mary's, Emmitsburg, he describes conditions at the college while referring to his appointment of Wiseman.

> Rev. and Dear Sir:
>
> Your favor of the 17th is before me . . . I had a severe spell of chills and fever which reduced me much. I am now, I hope, better, having missed both these last three days. I shall probably be absent in Michigan about the time Fr. Collins might be here. If health will permit me after Pentecost, I shall visit my Indian Missions. His services are really much wanted here for the college and congregation, and in my absence he will be as cordially received by my Vicar-General, Mr. Rese, and my Messrs. Mullon, Wiseman and DeLoughery as by myself. Rev. Mr. Wiseman does well, gives great satisfaction, edifies all by his regularity and piety. I have constituted him Superior of the Seminarians; he conducts them well, teaches a Latin class and Spanish, and bookkeeping, preaches alternately and hears confessions. [75]

With Mullon in charge of his college and Wiseman in charge of his seminary, he began in the late spring of 1832 to build his new seminary building at the rear of the Athenaeum and cathedral.

On May 5, 1832, there appeared this notice in the *Catholic Telegraph*:

"During the alterations, etc., included to the building of the Seminary, access may be had to our office, most readily, through the alley at the left hand of the Church."[76]

In a letter to Father Peter Potier on June 12, 1832, he writes:

> "My college is increasing daily and I have very little doubt, will in a short time secure a considerable share of public patronage. I am now building a seminary for my diocese, which will unite the College and Cathedral, and present to the view a range of buildings calculated to adorn our rising city." [77]

In a letter to a friend, written from Mackinac on August 12, 1832, he wrote that,

> "My college is in operation. The Seminary, now in the course of construction, is in brick with a stone foundation. It will be surmounted by a splendid tower, which will correspond with that of the Cathedral on one side and the College on the other . . ."[78]

It would seem that the seminary building and Episcopal residence that connected the cathedral with the Athenaeum at the rear of the property were completed by the opening of the school year in September of 1832. The theological students then moved out of the college building and into the new building. Also in the summer of 1832, James and Florent Meline, graduates of Mount St. Mary's, Emmitsburg, accepted positions as teachers in the Athenaeum. [79]

On September 26, 1832, just as school was opening, Bishop Fenwick died while visiting the northern limits of his far-flung congregation. He contracted cholera and died in Wooster, Ohio. The *Telegraph* wrote: "Few persons have been more esteemed and beloved than Bishop Fenwick; for, he was a man of the greatest simplicity, sincerity and piety and his death received the tribute of many tears and heart-felt sighs."[80]

THE INTERIM PERIOD (1832–1833)

Between the time of Fenwick's death and Bishop Purcell's coming to Cincinnati, the Diocese of Cincinnati was administered by Rese, who was the vicar-general. During the year of his administration, he erected a German and an English School which were under the direction of the seminarians.[81] Bishop Rosati of St. Louis had the ordinations in January of 1833. D. DeLoughery, E. Thienpont, and G. Bohem were ordained for the diocese.[82] On Monday, February 11, 1833, the seminarians assisted at the requiem of Fenwick immediately preceding the commitment of his body to the vault under the Cathedral of St. Peter's.

It is worthy to note that in December of 1832 a large proportion of students attending the Athenaeum were non-Catholic.[83]

Very few of the sixty registered students were of the Catholic faith. Further insight into how the college was regarded by these non-Catholic people may be gathered from and estimate of it that appeared in a survey of education in Cincinnati:

> The institution which is now the College of St. Francis Xavier was then established—at first under the title of the "Atenaeum," with the inscription on its front, "Religioni et Artibus

Sacrum," and a good school was organized, with a sufficient number of teachers to attend closely to all pupils, both in the hours of study and recreation.

This feature, in which most of our prominent seminaries are defective, gave the school a reputation that induced a number of Protestants to prefer it to any of our other schools for the education of their sons. It had then become (as it has since continued in the west) an established rule that teachers should not be allowed to punish pupils for any fault. The consequence was that such a degree of lawlessness prevailed in our schools as to deprive them of much of their usefulness. The arrangement of subordinate teachers in numbers sufficient to keep every pupil constantly in view, served as a substitute for the old-fashioned system of discipline by the rod and rule, and caused the Athenaeum to become a popular and flourishing state, and although the denomination increased so rapidly that it now possesses thirteen very large churches, with a splendid Cathedral, one of the best specimens of Grecian architecture in the city, all of which are crowded with worshippers on Sundays, yet the College did not seem to partake of their progress, and it was a few years since transferred to the order of the Jesuits.

During this interim period it is revealed that, "Father Edward Collins was teaching about two and one-half hours a day in the Athenaeum while taking care of the parochial duties at the cathedral."[84] He was a great collector of books. Upon his death, his collection was willed to the seminary library.

On July 28, 1833, Mullon wrote to Bishop-elect Purcell that things were in dreadful shape at the Athenaeum. It seems that Mullon was very much at odds with Rese. The priests at the seminary and college had divided into factions, and it was now that Mullon was very pessimistic about the future of the college. He wrote to Purcell:

When you accept, which I humbly beg you will, notify me, that I may make the necessary arrangements for continuing the College, which never could be reopened with respect, with the present members. Its prospects are fair and even flattering; but Rt. Rev. Sir, I entreat you, for its support to use your efforts to send some four or five efficient, and exemplary young men to assist us in the duties of it—the present with the exception of three are anything but what you would expect to see in Seminarians.[85]

THE APPOINTMENT OF PURCELL AS NEW BISHOP (1833)
Of the four candidates proposed as successor to Bishop Fenwick, the one finally chosen by Pope Gregory was John Baptist Purcell. [86]

On May 11, 1833, the *Telegraph* announced the coming of the "talented, amiable, learned and pious President of Mount St. Mary's College, Emmitsburg to See of Cincinnati."[111] On the occasion of Purcell's leaving the "Mountain" previous to his consecration, he remarked. "It indeed shall be among the greatest pleasures and holiest occupation of my present station to exert renewed energies that the students frequenting the College of Cincinnati, the Athenaeum, my rival, I dare not say, surpass you in talents, in love of science, morality and virtue."[87]

At the end of the school year, prizes were given to David Wade, Aug. Eberle, Francis Miller, Patrick McGroarty, Pierson Richardson, Francis O'Rielly, Jonathan Broadwill, Nicholas Lawlir, Sidney Sindder, Charles Williams, Joseph Allgaier, Julius Talant, Christ Julinsons, William Harris, William Paxton, Thompson Strurman, Alex Adams, Grourville Williams, John Teer and W. Oliver.[87] These are listed because the names of many prominent Cincinnati families of today are included among them.

CAVANAUGH, RECTOR (1833)

In September of 1833, Father Bernard O. Cavanaugh was superior of the seminary. Why he succeeded Wiseman we do not know. We assume it had something to do with the bad conditions existing because of dissension among the faculty stationed at the cathedral.

On October 13, 1833, John Baptist Purcell was consecrated Bishop of Cincinnati. On November 14 he arrived in his Episcopal see. No doubt because of the many letters he had received intimating distracted conditions in Cincinnati, immediately upon his arrival the bishop complained of many things that were wrong with the seminary-college. It would seem that the faction associated with Rese (now appointed Bishop of Detroit) found little favor in the eyes of Purcell. Undoubtedly he did have some reasons for complaining. But evidence seems to support O'Daniel and Deye[88] who contended that Purcell more or less magnified the problem. It was not quite as bad as he pictured it in his journal:

> Thousands upon thousands of dollars had been expended on buildings which are ill-constructed and inconvenient, of wretched materials, half finished, leaking mildewed roofs and walls; floors loose and badly, hydrants left insecure against external injury . . . property not enclosed and people stealing our wood and coal. House full of filth . . . meals ill-cooked and most ungainly and uncleanly servants.[89]

When Bishop Purcell arrived at the cathedral in Cincinnati, the following men resided there: James I. Mullon, Joseph V. Wiseman, Edward T. Collins, E. Thienpont, Bernard O'Cavanaugh, Denis DeLoughery and Jerome Vogeler. These priests cared for both the English-speaking and German congregations, both of which worshiped in the cathedral but at different hours. Their names are listed here because they were part of the first faculty who administered the college and seminary.

In the same journal in which the bishop criticized the physical aspects of the building, Joseph Wiseman and Bernard O'Cavanaugh, the third and fourth rectors of the seminary, also came in for a lion's share of the criticism. Both departed the seminary in the latter part of the year.[90]

MULLON, PRESIDENT AND RECTOR (1834)

Soon after Purcell's arrival, Mullon was made superior of the seminary, in addition to his duties as president of the Athenaeum.

In January 1834, Mullon left for New Orleans to see if he could recruit more students from that area to the Athenaeum. He also went to seek more subscribers for the *Catholic Telegraph* and supplies for the orphans. Purcell assumed Mullon's classes in theology and philosophy during his absence.[91]

At the same time Mullon left for New Orleans, S.H. Montgomery arrived in Cincinnati from that same city. He had experienced some difficulties with his own Dominican Order, and now wanted to join the diocese of Cincinnati as a secular priest. It seems that Montgomery had gained favor in Purcell's eyes. Young, the Provincial of the Dominicans, later attributed Purcell's seeming dislike of Dominicans to the influence of Montgomery.[92]

Mullon now returned from New Orleans. He asked Purcell's permission to leave the diocese of Cincinnati in order that he might work in New Orleans. But Purcell noted in his diary that one of the reasons Mullon left Cincinnati for good was his dislike for Montgomery.[93] Mullon departed fro New Orleans at the end of June, 1934,[94] and gained quite a reputation in his new home.

On July 3, 1834, James Conlon, a seminarian, wrote to Bishop Purcell concerning the seminary. From it a little knowledge is gained about the curriculum of the day.

> Rt. Reverend Father, Your communication to the young men of the seminary was kindly made known by Dr. Hermanger . . .your advice given the night previous to your departure has been punctually observed. We have regularly attended our Catholic instructions, but I'm sorry to add that the youth of Cincinnati does [sic] not warrant any economium for their attendance...you will be surprised, My Lord, to hear of the rapid strides Mr. Mullon and I have made in our Theological Science. We have brought to light all that was mysterious in the tracts of Trinitate, Incarnatione, Ecclesia, Sacramentis in Genere and Confirmationi. You are already aware of the departure of our excellent superior. We daily assault heaven for his return to Cincinnati.[95]

PURCELL, PRESIDENT AND RECTOR (1834)

On Montgomery's advice, Purcell made himself president of the college and rector of the seminary in the summer of 1934. The two posts previously had been held by Mullon. Purcell, both in ability and learning, was eminently suited for these offices. He had been president of the college of Mount St. Mary's in Maryland. There was one difficulty! He was now also bishop of a large diocese. In only a year's time he was to find that he could not be both bishop and professor.[96] Fenwick had had the same experience.

School began on August 18, 1834. Purcell was assisted in the administration of the seminary and college by S.H. Montgomery and J. M. Henni. It is interesting to note that the *Telegraph* contained a notice of the appointment of Doctor Hermanger as a member of the faculty. More than likely he had arrived early the previous spring. He taught the classics and mathematics. When he left the Athenaeum is not known.[97]

Writing to Brute in January of 1835, Badin told of the many duties of Purcell:

> He is overpowered by being obliged to attend all sorts of offices and functions, which would

keep several men very busy. . . . He must perform all the duties of a Professor of Divinity in the Seminary and of humanities in the College. . . . He must trouble himself with a variety of temporal affairs and domestic economy and government, besides the discipline of the college and Seminary. . . . He is destitute of a secretary, of a theologian and there is no class of Divinity during the protracted visits of his diocese. Conformable to his request, I relieve him now of the theological lectures.[98]

At this time, Purcell was conscious of the fact that he was trying to do too much. Writing to the Prefect of the Congregation Propaganda Fide on January 28, 1835, Purcell itemized his report as "Reasons for Joy" and "Reasons for Sorrow." Under the latter, in addition to his financial complaints, he mentioned the lack of priests, and especially the lack of a "pious and learned professor of theology and a president of the seminary." As for himself, he was so distracted with a variety of duties and cares that he was unable to do any one of them properly.[99]

In October, the *Telegraph* mentioned that Purcell had fourteen students studying for the diocese in the "Seminary of St. Francis Xavier" attached to the cathedral. He had one studying in Baltimore, too.[100]

On October 9, 1834, Purcell wrote to Bishop England, then in Rome:

> The church I have named (Holy Trinity) was dedicated last Sunday. It is allowed to be the finest public building in Cincinnati. . . . Bishop Flaget kindly assisted at the ceremony of dedication. Mr. Abell preached. Thus, two bishops, ten priests, sixteen seminarians, formed and processioned out there. I am much in debt for the church. . . . Could you not possibly induct the Propaganda, through Fr. O'Finan, to grant Reverend J.H. Montgomery an indult to secularization? Bishops Rosati, Flaget, David and myself agreed this would be much better for religion in Ohio and Kentucky and for the Dominican Order. I ask for this most special favor that you try and have him attached to this city as a Dominican, if you cannot effect his secularization, which I much prefer. I wrote to Cardinal Pedicine after my consecration but have not received an answer.[101]

Parents, guardians and the public were invited to the recitations held at the College of the Athenaeum on Monday and Tuesday, the 22 and 23 of December, 1834.[102] In June 1835, an exhibition was held in the Athenaeum.[103] In an editorial concerning the sending of students abroad for an education, an article was written in *Western Man,* published in Cincinnati, pursuing the fact that in the Athenaeum a nucleus was being formed "around which is collecting the fire of western energy."[104] It was really a manifestation of the fact that early citizens of Cincinnati were anxious for the growth of their educational institutions.

MONTGOMERY, PRESIDENT; JAMISON, RECTOR (1835)

In September of 1835, Francis B. Jamison[105] was named rector of the seminary and S.H. Montgomery, the former first rector, became president of the Athenaeum. Francis Jamison came from Fredericks, Maryland, and was of Anglo-American stock. He was related by blood to Leonard Calvert and many other famous colonists. He was described as "tall, very handsome, with a long black beard, gentle, polished, of beautiful manners, humorous, chess player, a linguist, and a good teacher." On August 20, 1833, he had succeeded Purcell as the fifth president of Mount St. Mary's Seminary, Emmitsburg. He resigned five months later, February 7, 1834, in a disagreement with the faculty. Coming to Cincinnati, he was rector for two years—1835-36 and 1836-37. At that time he left for St. Louis. He died at Cape Gerardian on October 15, 1858.

On January 21, 1836, Jamison organized the Seminary Fund Association.[106] Its purpose was to help the financial difficulties of the seminary but it lasted only a few years.

Making a correction in the *Catholic Almanac* for the year, the *Catholic Telegraph* stated:

> Reverend Francis B. Jamison should, also, have been numbered with the clergy of the cathedral. This gentleman is likewise Superior of the Ecclesiastical Seminary of St. Francis Xavier. Finally, Right Reverend J.B. Purcell, read Reverend S.H. Montgomery, President of the Athenaeum.[107]

The annual commencement and distribution of premiums was again held in the Athenaeum on Thursday, June 30, 1836. (The lists of the students receiving prizes in reading, arithmetic, algebra, geography, Latin, Greek, French and bookkeeping were given.) Some of the names of the Athenaeum students from Cincinnati receiving the prizes this year were: Henry Morris, William McLean, Joseph Darr, John Duffy, Alexander Pune, Richard McGuire, Rudolph Lawler, William Hughes, John Manning, William Hall, John Phillips, William Lytle, and Hiram Goodrich. General Harrison, major General Lytle, Major Neville, and Judge Hall were among the distinguished guests to attend this graduation, and a dinner was served later in the "College Refectory."[108] Other students receiving the prizes indicated that they came from Kentucky, Maryland, Mississippi, Pennsylvania, and Washington, D.C.[109]

The respected place the Athenaeum held in the community could be seen by the list of references for the school among the prominent citizens of the day: General W.H. Harrison, T. D. Carneal, Doctor David Drake, Nicholas Longworth, Esq., Honored B. Storer, General R. Lytle, and Elan P. Langdon.[110]

On a visit to Cincinnati in July of 1836, Badin found idleness at the Athenaeum "without rule or ruler," as S.H. Montgomery was on a trip to New York at the time.[111] The school had begun to flounder again.

On September 19, 1836, the Most Reverend Doctor Eccleston, Archbishop of Baltimore, arrived in Cincinnati and visited the Athenaeum. "He was greeted by one of the students with a poetical address, (which we will publish next week") to which the Bishop replied in his usual happy and eloquent style."[112]

On January 11, 1837, the college of the Athenaeum witnessed the meeting in which the terms for the famous debate between Campbell and Purcell were arranged.[113]

Purcell, quick and violent in his temper, at least according to Montgomery's description, dismissed the latter in the summer of 1837 after returning from the third Provincial Council of Baltimore. In the spring of 1837, Jamison moved to St. Louis and thus, after two years,

Purcell was again without a rector for the seminary or a president for his college.

In the spring of 1837, after Jamison had moved, Purcell tried to induce "Deacon" John McCaffrey of Mount St. Mary's Emmitsburg to take charge of the seminary.[114] He did not succeed and McCaffrey went on to become president of the Emmitsburg school.

STOKES, RECTOR AND PURCELL, PRINCIPAL (1837)

In September of 1837 the Reverend Stokes, with only seven students in the seminary, became rector. Stokes was born in Ireland, studied at Carlow, and was ordained there for the diocese of Charleston on December 21, 1822. He then spent a year in the Archdiocese of Dublin, probably at Maynooth, preparing to teach in Bishop England's seminary and college. The *U.S. Catholic Miscellaney* of June 15, 1825 says: "Columbia (South Carolina) the Reverend Joseph Stokes has been appointed to take charge of this and the neighboring congregations until some further arrangements can be made, and he has arrived to take charge of his flock" This is the first mention of him in the United States.

He remained in South Carolina until about 1829, when he was transferred to Savannah, Georgia, where he was pastor until 1835. All of these ten years he was one of the most active missionaries of the Charleston Diocese. From Savannah he went to Portsmouth, Virginia. After about a year, he came to Cincinnati where he became rector of the seminary. After two years he then went to Nashville. In all of these places he was regarded as a fine scholar and eloquent preacher. He was vicar-general of the Nashville diocese until about 1842. He the entered the Society of Jesus. He left St. Mary's College in Kentucky, and then labored for a while (1844-1845) at St. Joseph Church, New York City. From 1845 to 1851 he was at Utica, New York. In 1851 he became pastor of New London, Connecticut. In 1852 the Bishop of Hartford, who then lived in Providence, Rhode Island, took him to that city and made him his vicar-general. He died on July 16, 1854, at Saratoga, where he seems to have gone for his health. O'Daniel says of him: "He was a splendid priest, but seems to have somewhat of a roving disposition, perhaps brought about by his long missionary life."[115]

In the same issue of the *Catholic Directory* of 1838 it is noted that Edward Purcell[116] is listed as the Principal of the Athenaeum and that J.M. Young[117] as the prefect of studies. Edward Purcell, the brother of the bishop, was the youngest in the Purcell family of four. He was born in 1818 in Ireland. Coming to this country, he took up the study of law. Then, suddenly in the summer of 1836, he decided to give up law to study for the priesthood in the diocese of Cincinnati. The precise date of this decision is not known.

In February of 1835, Father Hughes, writing from Philadelphia, still described Edward as "a hot politician." But during the summer of 1836, he was studying for the priesthood in Cincinnati. Bishop Purcell took his brother into his confidence immediately. Already in January of 1837, while still a seminarian, Edward was answering some of the Bishop's mail while the latter was out of town. Edward received minor orders on May 30, 1837, and in the following March, he was ordained. Thus he was made the principal of the day school now conducted at the Athenaeum. No two brothers were closer than the Bishop and his brother Edward for the next forty years.

It would seem that due to the financial panic of this year, the Athenaeum was reduced from a boarding school to a day school for the years 1837-1839. This would explain why there was enough room in the buildings to erect a private chapel for the seminarians.

In October of 1838, a spiritual retreat was preached for the clergy in the Seminary of St. Francis Xavier. The retreat, lasting from October 13-20, was followed by a synod in the seminary building. The synod began on Sunday morning and the Reverend M. Stokes, Superior of the Seminary of St. Francis Xavier preached the sermon. It held five sessions.[118]

On December 19, 1838, in a letter Stokes wrote to Purcell about his desire to join the Jesuits, he stated that he was having trouble with Collins (in the course of the letter, he mentions the five students attending his theology class). They were studying the tracts of Penance, the Eucharist, the Trinity, the Incarnation, the Sacraments in general. The also had a class in Scripture and church history.[119]

The other young men who were members of the seminary are James Kerney, Francis Rodriques, John Mervin, John McCary, Timothy White, Edward Norman, James Hickey and Norm Gormell. The last five had just arrived and were beginning their classical studies and were being " useful" in the college. Again in September 1839, Stokes wrote to Purcell from Nashville. He complained about his treatment by others at the seminary. He had continued in the seminary until July of 1839. He and Collins apparently had disagreed over the fitness of one student, McLaughlin. He closed by recommending two students to orders.[120] The letters show that the seminaries of these early days tried to go over the fields of dogma, morals, Scripture, canon law, and church history. The student lists also show that the college of the Athenaeum was still a "mixed" college.

On September 17, 1839, after sixteen months absence, Purcell arrived in Cincinnati with eight new missionaries.[121] Things had not improved in his absence.

J.J. O'MEALY, RECTOR (1839)

In September, J.J. O'Mealy was appointed rector, while Edward Purcell served as principal. O'Mealy was born in Limerick, Ireland, in 1809. His family later migrated to America. His studies were made at Mount St. Mary's, Emmitsburg, and at the Propaganda in Rome. Not long after his ordination, he was placed in charge of the seminary. After resigning in 1842, he went to Portsmouth, Ohio, and returned to the Cathedral (1845) in Cincinnati. Then he went to Pittsburgh, where he was editor of the *Pittsburgh Catholic* from 1846-1849. He was an author of some repute, having written two books, Later, he was pastor in Dayton, and he organized the parish of St. Augustine in Cincinnati. He died in Springfield, Ohio, on October 20, 1856.[122]

The feast of the patron saint of the seminary was celebrated with "more than usual fervor" by the students on December 3, 1839. "A beautiful chapel had been prepared in one of the ample rooms of the college, in which divine service was held in the morning, and in the evening an admirable panegyric of the Saint was delivered by one of the students."[123]

In late December, Father Machebeuf, one of the French missionaries who had returned with Purcell (and later became a bishop), wrote of life at the seminary:

> Well, to prove to you that the Bishop sought only our greater good in every respect in sending us out immediately, I have only to tell you that it would have been impossible for me to become accustomed to America if I had remained much longer at the Seminary. I was there but three weeks, sick nearly fifteen days of that time. There was no one to teach classes, and with the exercise of the ministry, a few moments after dinner were all that could be given to us.[124]

The bishop himself was overwhelmed with business and visitors all day long, and it often happened that his room was filled with visitors while he was taking his meals.

Apparently when Purcell started the work on his Cathedral on Plum Street, the seminarians and professors living at Sycamore Street lent a helping hand. "In doing this, I was only imitating our Bishop, who, at the head of his seminarians, used the shovel for half a day digging for the foundation of his Cathedral, while Fathers Gacon, Cheymol and others filled the wheelbarrows. You see that we are obliged to turn ourselves to everything."[125]

On Sunday, March 21, 1840, "Our Sanctuary never presented a more edifying spectacle than on the last Sunday. All the clergy who made the ten day retreat assisted in surplice and stole at the Solemn High Mass celebrated by the Bishop. They worked with the members of the Seminary, thirty-eight in number."[126]

On June 29, premiums were awarded to the students. The *Catholic Telegraph* of July 4 carried the announcement that "at the annual examination of the students of this College, the following young gentlemen distinguished themselves for progress and proficiency in their respective classes."[127] The article lists the subjects and the students receiving premiums.

THE JESUITS TAKE OVER THE ATHENAEUM (1840)

As early as March 23, 1838, in a letter to Eccleston, Purcell stated that he was very desirous of obtaining a group of Jesuits for a college in Brown County.[128] Again in August of that year, Purcell was considering the property in Brown County as a site for such a college.[129] On September 24, 1839, Purcell asked his friend, the Reverend John McElroy, S.J. to intercede for him in obtaining the Jesuits.[130] On May 17, 1840, the minister general, Father John Roothaan, S.J., after weighing Purcell's request against a similar one from Rese in Detroit and against the fact that the French Jesuits already had a college at St. Mary's in Kentucky, decided in Purcell's favor and recommended to Father Peter Verhaegen, S.J., head of the Vice-Province of St. Louis, to take over Purcell's Athenaeum.[131]

When Purcell received this news in Verhaegen's letter of August 10, 1840, he replied immediately and with even more than his usual enthusiasm. He offered the Jesuits in perpetuity the college, seminary, the episcopal residence, the cathedral, and if they desired, also the property in Brown County or elsewhere. Lest they hesitate due to lack of teachers, Purcell promised them the aid of his seminarians and a couple of priests he was expecting from France.[132]

In a letter to Verhaegen on August 17, 1840, Purcell wrote:

I propose then Reverend and Dear Friend, to give up to your forever on the condition that they should ever be held scared for church and school, the College, Seminary and Church with the real estate on these buildings which I now occupy, are located…that you may have there a College and Parish Church to be served by you society in perpetuity. This property is about two hundred feet square…the College is in good repair, at present, having been newly shingled (on time, for its former covering) since I have been here. In it, is a new cabinet of Natural Philosophy, which I have imported from France, for two thousand dollars, and which should be yours.

If you think it fit to employ them I can employ under your direction, as teachers in the College, in Cincinnati, twelve seminarians…even one or two French priests…in addition to, or instead of the foregoing, just as you please, I would give you 500 acres of land in Brown County, forty miles from Cincinnati, with a first-rate McAdamized road, 22 miles of which are completed, passing by the door of the small brick collet, already built thereon. I should think a College in the country indispensable…or instead of this in Brown County, you can have six-teen hundred acres or 2000 as you prefer in Gallia County, 12 miles from the Ohio River, and 18 miles from Gallipolis, which property has been deeded to me for a College by a wealthy and enlightened Irish Catholic.[133]

The *Catholic Telegraph* of September 5, 1840, announced that the Athenaeum, now renamed Francis Xavier College, would open under Jesuit auspices.[134] In a letter written shortly after his return from St. Louis in September 1840, Verhaegen acquainted the Father General with the step he had taken:

I have visited the Right Reverend Bishop of Cincinnati who received me and Father Elet, my companion, with every token of love and benevolence. All arrangements regarding his college have been made. He has deeded to the Society in perpetuity all the buildings, which were erected for a boarding school and diocesan seminary, and has given along with them a rather large and handsome church. The College will be opened at the beginning of November under the title of St. Francis Xavier . . . since, however, there is not a sufficient number of professors, the Bishop will lend a helping hand by allowing certain of the seminarians to assist ours in teaching as long as will be necessary.[135]

The Reverend Thomas Butler,[136] the predecessor of McCaffrey at Mount St. Mary's, in September 1840, superintended the extensive preparations that were going on for the open-ing of the college.[137]

St. Francis Xavier College opened on November 3, 1840, and by the middle of December there were seventy-six students in attendance.[138]

Five or six of Purcell's seminarians continued to reside at the college in order to assist in teaching as Purcell had promised.[139] Thus, it was in 1840 that the College of the Athenaeum, founded by Fenwick and at times heroically maintained by Purcell, passed to the control of the Jesuit Fathers to continue its existence and to flourish in after years as Xavier High School and Xavier University.

It is important to note that the Athenaeum, now under the Jesuit Fathers, ceased being, in any way at all, a preparatory college for the seminary. It was no longer the "mixed" college that was mentioned.

Why did Purcell give up the Athenaeum? It would seem, as was mentioned before, that the main reason was the lack of a competent and stable faculty. Both he and Fenwick had found it almost impossible to find men among the secular clergy suitably educated to take over the responsibilities of the Athenaeum. When the two bishops did find such men, as in the case of Montgomery, Mullon, Jamison, and Stokes, they found it impossible to keep them. It seems that it was hard for a missionary in those days, no matter how well educated he might be, to confine himself to the limited area of a seminary and college and to the quiet life of a scholar and teacher.

THE MOVING OF THE SEMINARY TO BROWN COUNTY (1840)

In 1823 General William Lytle conveyed to Bishop Fenwick a tract of land comprising three hundred acres to be used for educational purposes. General Lytle was an accomplished soldier and at the time, Governor Surveyor of the Virginia Military District. He had taken a prominent part in the campaign of Boone in Kentucky, and had been a soldier with Kenton and Washbourn in Ohio. The land which he presented to the bishop was situated in the section of Brown county now occupied by the Convent of the Brown County Ursulines. In 1830 Reverend Martin Kundig was sent by Bishop Fenwick to minister to the spiritual needs of a few Catholic families then residing in the neighborhood, and dedicated to his patron, St. Martin. Reverend James Reed built a house on the property and organized a school in November 1832, and completed it in October of 1833. It was into this school building built by Reed that the Seminary of St. Francis Xavier moved in 1840. It was brick and two stories high.[140]

In the first year at Brown County, O'Mealy was the rector and he was assisted by three priests: Lamy, Gacon,[141] and Cheymol.[142] These men had charge of the meager band of ten seminarians that made up the student body. Very little is known of their activities except that the faculty and students at this time attended the solemn blessing of the cornerstone of St. Peter's Cathedral in downtown Cincinnati on May 20, 1841.[143] The following year they walked over to Fayetteville, Ohio, to attend the ceremonies connected with the dedication of St. Patrick's Church.[144]

During this first year, O'Mealy did a great deal to enlarge and improve the buildings. The chapel, the school building, and the residence for the priests were all improved. O'Mealy also did a great deal in landscaping and improving the grounds.[145]

At the beginning of the second year in Brown County, September 1841, O'Mealy was still the rector. Cheymol and Gacon stayed on, but Lamy went off to his famous future on the missions of the southwest. Two more seminarians came and the enrollment stood at twelve.

During all of this time, however, Purcell had some seminarians (at least two or three) helping the Jesuits by teaching in the college on Sycamore Street. During the time the seminary was in Brown County, the seminarians also taught[146] students who continued to attend the free day school set up there by Reed.

On Ascension Day, May 5, 1842, Purcell journeyed to Brown County for the ordination of Cornelius Daly, held in the little chapel.[147]

THE VINCENTIANS TAKE OVER THE SEMINARY (1842)

In July and August of 1840, when Purcell was engaged in turning over the Athenaeum to the Jesuits, he was thinking again of turning over the training of his diocesan seminary students to a religious order, in this case the Eudist Fathers,[148] whose special mission was the management of ecclesiastical seminaries. The request had to be refused by Abby Lewis of Rennes, France, because he did not have priests available. However, in 1842, Purcell succeeded in getting the Lazarist Fathers[149] of Missouri to come and take over.

The *Catholic Telegraph* of July 16, 1842, announced that Joseph O'Mealy resigned as rector and was appointed pastor of Portsmouth and that the priests of the Congregation of the Missions founded by St. Vincent de Paul would take over the direction of the seminary.[150]

BURLANDO, RECTOR (1842)

In September 1842, the *Catholic Almanac* carried this text:

> The diocesan Seminary of St. Francis Xavier, at present situated on a large farm in Brown County is under the care of Rev. F. Burlando and Rev. Charles Boglioli, priests of the same congregation of the Missions. There are two lay brothers of the same congregation attached to the Seminary. The students are twelve in number; besides whom there are four or five seminarians who teach in St. Francis Xavier College, Cincinnati, under the direction of F. De Theux, of the Society of Jesus. There are also alumni of the diocese in Propaganda at Rome, St. Sulpice at Paris, and at St. Mary's at Emmitsburg.[151]

James Francis Burlando was born on May 6, 1814, in Genoa Italy. He was ordained in Turin on July 9, 1838, and immediately set out for the missions in New Orleans. Later he was sent to St. Mary's Seminary of the Barrens in Missouri. Here he made his vows as a Vincentian on December 25, 1839. In 1842, he was asked to take charge of the seminary in Brown County. He died on February 16, 1873, at Emmitsburg, Maryland, in the Central House of the Sisters of Charity.[152]

Purcell at this time began to have a little trouble with the newly arrived German immigrants. They complained that the priests who came from the seminary did not know enough German. In 1842, while O'Mealy was rectory of the seminary, Purcell had introduced a course in German to take care of this problem. For many reasons the attempt failed, and after two years the study of German was dropped. There were more complaints. In February of 1844, Purcell, somewhat exasperated, took some of the Germans in his flock to task in that they had made these complaints yet they had never contributed in any way to his seminary. He stated that he had brought to the diocese "nine priests and ten students of theology, all Germans, for their benefit." And yet he had not received a single cent from them. This, of course, was a mild confrontation. There were to follow many similar mild conflicts. It must be said, however, that by and large, Irish-born Purcell got along extremely well with his rapidly increasing flock.[153]

The school years of 1843 and 1844 passed by uneventfully. Burlando and Boglioli ran the seminary and were assisted still by Gacon and Cheymol. However, it soon was apparent that Burlando and Purcell were not able to get along with each other. Burlando constantly complained to his superior, Father Timon, about the interference of Purcell. Timon's letters were written over the three years that he was there. Purcell, too, wrote letter after letter defending himself to Timon. Timon tried to recover the situation but found that it was hopeless. According to Burlando, Purcell failed to give adequate financial support to his seminary. There seems to be a measure of truth in this charge, as Purcell then was busy with the work of constructing his cathedral. However, it seems that the one who was really parsimonious with the seminary was not the bishop but his brother Edward. In Purcell's, defense, it must be said that Burlando really wanted the Vincentians to have the seminary as their own. This Purcell would not permit.[154]

When Purcell finally decided to move the seminary back to the city with the idea of temporarily housing the students in the third floor of the Episcopal residence, Burlando's patience was exhausted. Even though Purcell assured Timon that this was only to be a temporary arrangement until the new seminary could be built, Timon withdrew his congregation before the end of the school year in 1845.[155]

When this happened Purcell placed Father Thomas Butler, the former rector of Mount St. Mary's, Emmitsburg, in charge. Father Peter Senez, a priest who had written to Purcell and asked if he could stay at the seminary and do some work on translating, assisted Butler. Gacon and Cheymol were there also.[156]

There were again many reasons why Purcell abandoned the seminary at Brown County. After one hundred years and more, it seems that in its section, this was an ideal site and a marvelous place for an ecclesiastical seminary. But it must be kept in mind that the seminary at Brown County in those days was practically inaccessible; the roads were terrible and there were no direct railroad lines to the area. Probably Purcell very quickly realized how impractical it was since he directed the moving of the seminary back to Sycamore Street.[157]

On Thursday, July 21, 1845, the Ursuline Sisters from France arrived in Cincinnati. Purcell told them they could have their choice of any one of several sites for their proposed new convent. Included among the list was the site at Brown County.[158] After investigation of all the possible locations, the sisters chose the Brown County site. In the late summer of that year, the sisters were received on the seminary grounds by Fathers Gacon and Cheymol and all the seminarians. With their coming, the seminary once again pulled up stakes and returned to the old location in Cincinnati.

The Moving of the Seminary Back to Sycamore Street (1845)

At the beginning of the school year in 1845, the diocesan seminarians were back in their old quarters on Sycamore Street. The old Athenaeum building was now the college, and the old seminary and residence was now the scholasticate. It seems that during most of the time that the seminary was located at Brown County, there were two or three seminarians of the diocese living at the scholasticate and teaching tat the college. The only difference now was that all the seminarians moved in. It seems that during the next couple of years they, too, besides studying theology, taught several of the classes in the college.[159]

While they stayed at Sycamore Street, the seminarians were placed under the direction of a Jesuit priest, Leonard Nota, who was born November 25, 1807, and was a native of Italy. He entered the Jesuit Novitiate of the Province of Naples on September 27, 1824. After his ordination, he and three others were sent to the American missions by Father Roothan, the General of the Society. In America he taught theology and philosophy in the Missouri Province. He was then sent to St. Louis in 1841, where he taught the classics. There he remained until 18434. In 1845 he was sent to Cincinnati and taught philosophy and theology. In 1848 he was transferred to the Maryland Province of the Society.[160]

During the years that the seminary was located on Sycamore Street under the direction of Nota, the entire student enrollment for the seminary, as such, was about ten. Purcell, about this time, had begun the practice of sending some of his seminarians to different seminaries around the country and also to Europe. This accounts for the whereabouts of some of the ten seminarians when even this arrangement with the Jesuit Fathers did not prove satisfactory.[161]

The Seminary at the Episcopal Residence (1847)

In September 1847, there were still some seminarians living with the Jesuits on Sycamore Street. However, it seems that Purcell always wanted a direct and immediate hand in the supervision work of the diocese. For that reason, he made over the attic of the Episcopal residence behind the new cathedral into a dormitory and study hall for his seminarians. Gradually the number of students was increased until there were about twelve studying there.

A young student named F.J. Goetz arrived in Cincinnati at this time and was the first to occupy the seminary at Eighth and Central. Others students who arrived during the year were: Borgess, Rosecrans, Quinlan, Kreckel, Gavienzel, Groeadier, and Goetz who years later, wrote of these days in a series of articles for the *Telegraph*:

> For some time, I was the only student in the Bishop's house. There were several in Bardstown, Kentucky, in Rome, Paris, St. Xavier's, Cincinnati, and at other places. The first one associated to me was Mr. John Quinlan, afterwards Bishop of Mobile; then Mr. Sylvester Rosecrans, afterwards Bishop of Columbus—both already gone to their eternal reward. At one time, we formed a considerable little flock. There was Mr. Groeadier, Mr. Kreckel, Mr. C.H. Borgess, now Bishop of Detroit, and Mr. Gavienzel a new convert to the Church. WE were all fed at Bishop Purcell's frugal table. And we were all, I believe, educated at his expense. But as to the latter point, I have to answer only for myself.

He [Purcell] sent me to Fr. Nota, one of the Jesuit Fathers on Sycamore Street who was to examine me, and see whether I was fit for the course of philosophy. The wise father decided that I should first learn English. Bishop Purcell gave me some English lessons himself, and at the same time, placed me under the care of a seminarian whose kindness, cleverness and gentlemanliness I shall ever fondly remember. The same afterwards, commenced with me and John Quinlan, the late Bishop of Mobile, a course in Philosophy. The bright, talented and kind-hearted seminarian and teacher was C.H. Borgess, now Bishop of Detroit.[162]

The Bishop at this time placed Father David Whalen in charge of the students studying in the seminary. He was born in 1807. It seems that he was ordained rather late in life, being about forty-two years of age at the time. He did, however, spend most of his life as a priest in the work at the cathedral. He taught for a few years when the seminary was built on Price Hill. He died on December 18, 1867.[163]

While the students were studying in the attic-seminary, the generous offer of the Slevins and the Considines started the work on the new seminary. On July 19, 1848, Purcell laid the cornerstone for the new building and on October 2, 1851, Mount St. Mary's Seminary of the West began its existence. It was the end of a long and frustrating era, and the beginning of a great and glorious one.

SUMMARY

This chapter is devoted to a general chronological history of the seminary of St. Francis Xavier and the College of the Athenaeum from the time of the coming of Bishop Fenwick to the See of Cincinnati in 1821 until the founding of Mount St. Mary's Seminary in Price Hill in 1851.

In this chapter it has been observed that Bishop Fenwick, in 1822, already had the idea of founding a college. The plan, however, never materialized. In 1825, a seminary was started in Cincinnati, and in 1826, Fenwick had seminary all ready but no professors. The seminary, with faculty, itself started in 1829.

In 1831 the Catholic College of the Athenaeum was founded. It was a mixed college, that is, a college for both clerical and lay students. During 1831-32 both seminary and college enjoyed a period of eminent success. On the death of Fenwick and before the appointment of Purcell to Cincinnati, there was a slight period of confusion in the college-seminary. This was mainly due to internal bickering among the faculty.

When Purcell came in 1833, he found a somewhat unsettled condition among the faculty. Yet in spite of these things, the seminary and the college enjoyed a period of relative prosperity until the middle thirties. Due mainly to financial reasons and to the pressure of missionary work that precluded a stable faculty, in the late thirties this seminary-college hit upon a period of rapid decline.

In 1840, the Athenaeum was turned over to the Jesuit Fathers and the seminary moved to Brown County. During this time the seminary had a very precarious existence. Here in 1842, the seminary was turned over to the Lazarist Fathers.

Mainly because of the inaccessibility of the Brown County location, the seminary was moved back to Cincinnati in 1845, and the seminarians resided at the scholasticate of the Jesuit Fathers on Sycamore Street.

In 1847 Purcell had some seminarians living at his house at the cathedral. This nomadic life of the seminary came to an end when Mount St. Mary's Seminary was built on Price Hill in 1851.

The dominant figures of the history of the seminary during this period were Purcell, Fenwick, Montgomery, Mullon, Jamison, Stokes, Edward Purcell, O'Mealy, and Burlando.

For the administration of the seminary-college, both Fenwick and Purcell borrowed their ideas from Mount St. Mary's at Emmitsburg. In this arrangement there was a superior for the seminary and a president for the college. Each enjoyed complete jurisdiction in his own sphere. As was pointed out in this chapter, the seminarians taught in the college and acted as the disciplinarians for the lay students.

In this period, there is very little material available on the curriculum of the theological seminary. It seems to have lasted, at most, for about two years. The theological students were ordained priests when it was felt that they had derived enough education from their nearness to the Episcopal work.

It can be seen from the data available that the core of the theological curriculum, dogma, morals, Sacred Scripture, church history, and canon law were taught at this time. However, at the very most, the theologians had one or two classes a day. A great deal of their time was spent teaching in the college. There is no evidence, at this time, of the textbooks that were used.

The curriculum of the Athenaeum, however, from the very beginning was very well organized and thorough in its coverage. It was a solid classical course, both for the day students and for boarders, lasting over a period of six years.

The first years in the history of the seminary were concerned with two problems: one—financial support, and two—obtaining competent men to teach. During this period these two problems were never completely solved. It seems no consistent basis was ever devised for the support of the seminary. The main problem, however, was the lack of competent teachers. The men who taught were men of find individual and academic background. The main trouble was that these capable men had sort of a wandering spirit. The work of the missions attracted them much more than the academic halls on Sycamore Street.

Fenwick was plagued with these problems and so was Purcell. The fact that neither of these problems was satisfactorily solved at this time is why the struggles and labors of this period seem so frustrating and difficult.

It is impossible not to admire the sound educational dreams and ideals of both Fenwick and Purcell, together with the toil that they invested in this institution.

NOTES

[1] V. F. O Daniel, the *Rt. Rev. Edward Dominic Fenwick, O.P.* New York: Frederick Pustet, 1920, pp. xiv-473.

[2] *Ibid.*, p. 239.

[3] Lamott, *op. cit.*, p. 34.

[4] *Ibid.*, p. 38.

[5] *Ibid.*, p. 251.

[6] *Ibid.*, p. 252.

[7] *Liberty Hall and Cincinnati Gazette*, March 30, 1822.

[8] The Council of Trent, on July 15, 1556, in the Twenty-third Session, in essence laid down the fundamental law of the Church in the education of priests. Seminaries were to be established in which the elements of a liberal education were to be taught together with the professional knowledge necessary for the ministry. The education of priests, according to the Tridentine ideal, was to be accomplished in institutions for clerical students alone. They were not to be "mixed."

[9] Lloyd Paul McDonald, *The Seminary Movement in the United States: Projects, Foundations and Early Development* (1784-1833), p. 54. Washington: The Catholic University of America Press, 1927.

[10] McDonald, *op. cit.*, p. 62.

[11] *Ibid.*, p. 62.

[12] The Society for the Propagation of the Faith was founded in Lyons, France in 1822 by a French laywoman named Pauline Jericot. The Society was not established to send out missionary personnel, but to raise funds for the missions. On May 3, 1922, the centennial date of its founding, the headquarters of the Society were transferred from Lyons to Rome.

[13] *The Catholic Telegraph*. This newspaper has an unbroken history form its founding in 1831 to the present. For a short period in the 1850s it added "Advocate" to the above title, the *Louisville Advocate* having merged with it for that period, and since 1937, it has added "Register" after becoming part of the Denver newspaper chain. In this work the title *Catholic Telegraph* will be used throughout. The complete history of the *Catholic Telegraph* is in the Centenary Edition issued October 22, 1931. This excerpt is taken from the editions of October 5, 1911, p. 1, and November 19, 1891, p. 1.

[14] Cf. p. 42.

[15] Edward J. Power, *A History of Catholic Higher Education in the United States*, pp. 35-36. Milwaukee: The Bruce Company, 1958.

[16] Cf. chapter three, p. 156.

[17] Lloyd Paul McDonald, *op. cit.*, p. 51.

[18] Quoted in *Catholic Telegraph*, August 16, 1891, p. 1.

[19] Letter, Fenwick to Badin, Cincinnati, April 16, 1825, UNDA.

[20] O'Daniel, *op. cit.*, p. 261.

[21] *Ibid.*, p. 262.

[22] *Catholic Telegraph*, April 2, 1891, p. 1.

[23] *Ibid.*, April 2, 1891, p. 1.

[24] Lamott, *op. cit.*, p. 61.

[25] O'Daniel, *op. cit.*, p. 306.

[26] O'Daniel, *op. cit.*, pp. 311-312.

[27] *Catholic Telegraph,* July 18, 1929, p. 8.

[28] There is no satisfactory biography of Fr. Henni, who later became bishop and archbishop of Milwaukee. See Martin Mary, O.S.B. Dr Johann Martin Henni: *Erster Bishopf und Erzbishopf,* etc. Deye, p. 93. It is interesting to note that while a priest in Cincinnati he had tried to found a German seminary in Covington. He gave up the plan when made a bishop in 1843.

[29] O'Daniel, *op. cit.*, pp. 347-348.

[30] Victor Francis O'Daniel, p. 69. *The Dominican Province of St. Joseph,* New York: Holy Name Society, 1942.

[31] *Annals of the Propagation of the Faith,* IV, 502, 504, 05. *Catholic Telegraph,* November 19, 1891, p. 1.

[32] Letter, J. B. Clicteur, Cincinnati, Jun 28, 1829; to Lyons, France (Annales 1830, IV, 516-517) UNDA. The prayer which the Bishop's seminarians recited daily for their benefactors in Europe was as follows: Let us pray for those associated in Europe for the Propagation of the Faith. O Lord, Thou, who, where two or three are altered together in Thy name, art in the midst of them, be also, we beseech Thee, with all of those in Europe constitute the Association for the Propagation of Thy Faith; grant that their efforts may bear abundant fruit and that Faith in Thee may increase everywhere; bestow on these so associated, in reward for their generosity and zeal, happiness, temporal as well as eternal. St. Francis Xavier, pray for them.

[33] In later years, the fields of labor for Clarkson were Kentucky, Ohio and Tennessee, in all of which he left an imperishable name. His parents were Henry and Elisabeth (Worland) Clarkson, and he was born in Washing County Kentucky, about 1811. He died a valiant missionary in Memphis on August 25, 1849, esteemed, revered, and venerated. He was the first priest in that city. In the beginning, he was buried in the yard that lay at the side and towards the rear of St. Peter's Church. Some twelve or fifteen years later, when he was taken up that he might be placed beneath the sanctuary of a new church, the body was found to be intact The servant of God appeared to be asleep rather than dead, very little decomposition having taken place. Quite naturally this amazed the people and convinced many that he was a saint. The phenomenon is still not infrequently spoken of in and around Memphis. O'Daniel, *op. cit.*, p. 76.

[34] O'Daniel, *op. cit.*, p. 100.

[35] O'Daniel, *op. cit.*, p. 356.

[36] *Ibid.*

[37] "Seminary," *Catholic Encyclopedia.* New York: Encyclopedia Press Inc., 1913, Volume 13, p. 698.

[38] *Catholic Magazine,* 1846.

[39] Deed, Henry Gregory to Edward Fenwick, recorded December 17, 1829, Hamilton County

Recorder's Office, Book No. 33, pp. 408-409.

[40] Letter, Fenwick, Cincinnati, 1829; to Lyons, France (Annales, IV, 505) UNDA.

[41] Propaganda Congregation was canonically erected 336 years ago by Pope Gregory IV in accordance with the *Bull Inscrutabili* previous created by Gregory XIII (1572-1585) for the purpose of trying to effect a reconciliation of the Easter Churches with the Roman Catholic Church. In 1622 this commission was transformed into a permanent Congregation whose aim was to spread the Roman Catholic Faith in missionary territories. A second factor leading to its establishment was the need to coordinate the missionary activities of the numerous religious communities entering between the Vatican on the one hand the Kings of Spain and Portugal on the other, with respect o Episcopal patronage, i.e., the power to nominate and appoint bishops.

Because of the importance of the Congregation de Propaganda Fide, its Cardinal Prefect is sometimes referred to as the "Red Pope" in the same manner that the Superior General of the Society of Jesus is sometimes appointed Gregory Peter Cardinal Agagianian (Patriarch of Cilicia of the Armenian Rites of the Roman Catholic Church) serve in the capacity of Proprefect of the Propaganda.

The Propaganda has authority over the major and minor seminaries within its territorial jurisdiction. It also has authority over those seminaries, wherever located, which have been founded exclusively for service abroad. The Congregation for the Eastern Church supervises the seminaries within its areas; and the seminaries which are located in the areas under the administrative jurisdiction of the consistorial and the Extraordinary Ecclesiastical Affairs Congregations are supervised by the Seminaries Congregation.

[42] The two Indian youths were named William (Blackbird) Maccatebinessi and Augustine (Kanapima) Hamelin. Maccatebinessi was a full-blooded Indian and son of the chief of the Ottawas at Arbre Croche, probably the chief named Blackbird. Hamelin was a half-breed born of a French Canadian father and an Indian wife.

About the time of his return from the east, Bishop Fenwick received a letter from the prefect of the Propaganda, in answer to Kenrick's letter, agreeing to admit his two Indian youths, William (Blackbird) Maccatebinessi and Augustine (Kanapima) Hamelin, into the Propaganda College. On April 10, therefore the prelate dispatched Father Rese with these youths to New York that he might place them on a boat for Marseilles, whence they would continue their way to Rome. They had spent two years in the Cincinnati seminary. (A letter from Gregory XVI dated April 14, 1932, accepting the two youths, was received in July and published in the *Catholic Telegraph*.)

Cardinal Pedicini, Prefect of Propaganda informed Fenwick in a letter dated July 28, 1832, that the two Indian youths had arrived safely in Rome.

William Maccatabinessi dies in Rome, June 9, 1833. Hamelin returned (1834) and led an edifying life at Pointe St. Ignace.

Sources: O'Daniel, *op. cit.*, p. 408; *Ibid.*, *op. cit.*, p. 408; *Catholic Telegraph*, April 21, 1832, p. 4; *Ibid.*, July 7, 1832; *Ibid.*, April 21, 1832, p. 215; *Ibid.*, October 6, 1832., p. 402;

Ibid., January 10, 1929, p. 4; P. Chrysostomus Verwyet, *Life and Labors of Rt. Rev. Frederick Baraga*, p. 107; Milwaukee: M.H. Wiltzius & Co., 1900.

[43] Meline and McSweeny, *op. cit.*, Vol. 1, p. 222.

[44] Edw. D. Fenwick to Rev. Martin Kundig, Oct. 29, 1829, MBMBA.

[45] The Rev. Frederic Rese was born at Vieneburg, Germany, on February 6, 1791, and was ordained at Rome in 1822. After having met Fenwick on the latter's trip to Europe, he came to Cincinnati in 1824. He labored here for many years becoming the Vicar-General. In October of 1833, he was appointed Bishop of Detroit. In 1828, before his elevation to the episcopacy, Rese visited Vienna, Austria, where he was instrumental in forming the Leopoldine Society, an association for the propagation of the Catholic Faith in the American missions.

[46] *Catholic Telegraph*, November 19, 1891, p. 4.

[47] O'Daniel, *op. cit.*, pp. 69, 70, 79.

[48] *Ibid.*, p. 79.

[49] P. Chrysostomus Verwyet, *Life and Labors of Rt. Rev. Frederick Baraga*. Milwaukee: M. H. Wiltzius & Co., 1900.

[50] *Catholic Telegraph*, November 19, 1891, p. 4.

[51] O'Daniel, *op. cit.*, p. 370.

[52] Letter, Fenwick to Abbe Rigagnon, Feb. 25, 1830, UNDA.

[53] The cornerstone of the Athenaeum building was found in August of 1891 by workmen engaged in the work of tearing down the walls. The little leaden box contained a small faded document, and nothing else. The paper was a littler larger than an ordinary sheet of paper and had been folded down the center once, thence once, thence once again and rolled up and placed in the box. The color of the ink was deep brown and so effaced in places that it could not be deciphered, except to see the outline of what looked like cardinal's hat with the dangling tassels.

In the cornerstone was placed the document with this text written in Latin:

The cornerstone of this College, dedicated to St. Francis, was laid on the fourteenth day of the month of may, in the year of Our Lord 1830, by the Rev. James Ignatius Mullen, duly authorized by the Vicar-General of the Cathedral Church of Cincinnati. This college was begun under the auspices of the Most Rev. Edward Fenwick, the first Bishop of Cincinnati, in the seventh year of his Episcopacy, and is to be completed at his expense. The construction is entrusted to Mr. Alpheus White. Andrew Jackson is President of the United Provinces of America. Allen Trimble is Governor of the province of Ohio.

In testimony whereof, in the absence of the Most Reverend Bishop, with mine own hand, subscribe these letters and sealed with the seal of the Diocese. F. Rese, Vicar-General of Cincinnati.

Catholic Telegraph, August 8, 1891, p. 5. According to the article cited above in the *Telegraph*, the cornerstone and its contents were deposited and kept in the archives of Xavier University. At the time of the writing of this thesis neither the box nor the contents could be located there.

[54] O'Daniel, *op. cit.*, p. 372.

[55] *Ibid.*, p. 396.

[56] *Ibid.*, p. 395.

[57] Gilbert J. Garrigan, *The Jesuits of the United States,* Vol. 3, p. 162.

[58] *Ibid.*, p. 162.

[59] Garrigan, *op. cit.*, p. 163.

[60] Its total cost was $11,500. *Catholic Telegraph,* Nov. 14, 1926, p. 1.

[61] O'Daniel, *op. cit.*, p. 393, August 12, 1832. The Athenaeum building was torn down in July of 1891. *Catholic Telegraph,* July 9, 1891, p. 5.

[62] Lamott, *op. cit.*, p. 13.

[63] *A Dictionary of American English*, Vol. 1, p. 93. University of Chicago Press, 1938; *Encyclopedia Britannica*, Vol. 2. p. 602. Chicago: William Benton, 1958; *The Oxford English Dictionary,* Vol. 1, p. 534. Oxford: Claricordon Press, 1933; *Lexicon Horum Vocabulorum Quae Difficilius Latine,* Redduntur, (3rd ed.) by Antonii Bacci, Romae: Societae Libraria, 1955.

[64] *Oxford English Dictionary, op. cit.,* p. 534.

[65] *Catholic Telegraph,* October 22, 1831, p. 4.

[66] *Catholic Almanac,* 1833, pp. 71-73.

[67] O'Daniel, *op. cit.*, pp. 397-398.

[68] *Catholic Telegraph,* October 22, 1831.

[69] O'Daniel, *op. cit.*, p. 398.

[70] *Ibid.*, pp. 400-401.

[71] *Ibid.*, p. 402.

[72] Letter, Fenwick to Potier, Dec. 1, 1831, UNDA.

[73] O'Daniel, *op. cit.*, pp. 404-405.

[74] *Ibid.*, p. 408; *Catholic Telegraph,* Oct. 3, 1866, p. 4; *Ibid.*, Oct., 5, 1911; pp. 4, 5; *Ibid.*, July 9, 1831, Centenary Edition, p. 2, contains the only picture of Mullon on record.

[75] O'Daniel, *op. cit.*, pp. 409, 410, 417.

[76] *Ibid.*, pp. 409-410.

[77] *Catholic Telegraph,* May 5, 1832, p. 231.

[78] Letter to Fr. Peter Potier as quoted in O'Daniel, *op. cit.,* p. 410.

[79] O'Daniel, *op. cit.*, p. 418.

[80] Meline and McSweeny, *op. cit.,* vol. 1, p. 278.

[81] *Catholic Telegraph,* Jan. 12, 1833, p. 85.

[82] Shea, *op. cit.,* vol. 3, p. 618.

[83] *Catholic Telegraph,* Jan., 26, 1833, p. 102.

[84] This also happened in the early days at St. Mary's–Baltimore.

[85] John P. Foote, *The Schools of Cincinnati and its Vicinity,* pp. 122-123. Cincinnati: C.F. Bradley & Co., 1855.

[86] *Catholic Telegraph,* February 16, 1833, p. 127; Meline & McSweeny, *op. cit.,* vol. 1, p. 285.

[87] Letter, Mullon to Purcell, July 28, 1833. MSMSA.

[88] Purcell, John Baptist, Archbishop of Cincinnati, was born at Mallow, Ireland, 26 February 1800; he died at the convent of the Ursulines, Brown County, Ohio. His parents, Edward and Johanna Purcell, being industrious and pious, gave their children all the advantages of the education attainable at a time when the penal laws were less rigorously enforced. John displayed remarkable talent and mastered all the branches of the school curriculum before his eighteenth year. Entrance into the colleges of Ireland was an impossibility. He therefore decided to seek in the United States the higher education denied him in his native country. Landing at Baltimore, he applied for and obtained a teacher's certificate in the Asbury College. He spent about one year in giving lessons as a private tutor in some of the prominent families of Baltimore. His ambition was to become a priest, and this he never lost sight of while teaching others as a means of obtaining a livelihood. On 20 June, 1820, he entered Mount St. Mary's Seminary, Emmitsburg. His previous knowledge of the classics made it an easy task for him to take charge of important classes in the college, and at the same time prepare himself for the priesthood by the study of philosophy, theology, and other branches of ecclesiastical science. After three years study in the seminary, he received tonsure and minor orders from Archbishop Mareschal, of Baltimore, at the close of 1823. On March 1, 1824, in the company of Rev. Simon Gabriel Brute, on of the professors of the seminary, afterwards first Bishop of Vincennes, he sailed for Europe to complete his studies in the Sulpician Seminaries of Issy and Paris. On 26 may, 1826, he was one of the three hundred priests ordained in the Cathedral of Paris by Archbishop de Quelen. After his ordination he continued his studies until the autumn of 1827 when he returned to the Untied States to enter Mount St. Mary's Seminary as professor. He afterward became president, until his appointment as Bishop of Cincinnati, Ohio, to succeed the saintly Bishop Fenwick.

For an excellent account of Purcell's early life consult: Anthony N. Deye, "Archbishop John Baptist Purcell of Cincinnati, Pre-Civil War Years," unpublished doctoral dissertation, University of Notre Dame, 1959.

[89] *Catholic Telegraph*, May 11, 1833, p. 222.

[90] Meline and McSweeny, *op. cit.*, vol. 1, p. 308.

[91] *Catholic Telegraph*, July 6 1833, p. 286.

[92] Deye, *op. cit.*, p. 95; Journal, p. 241. MSMSA.

[93] Journal, p. 241, see note on Journal in Deye, *op. cit.*, p. 95.

[94] Purcell refused to accept O'Cavanaugh, who was suspended. O'Cavanaugh then went to Detroit on Feb. 11. Journal. MSMSA.

[95] Journal, MSMSA.

[96] Deye, *op. cit.*, p. 112.

[97] *Ibid.*, p. 113.

[98] Journal, MSMSA.

[99] James Conlon to Purcell, July 3, 1834, MSMSA.

[100] *Catholic Telegraph*, August 15, 1845, p. 299.

[101] *Ibid.*, p. 301.

[102] Badin to Brute, January 28, 1835. UNDA.

[103] Purcell to the Prefect of the Congregation Propaganda Fide. January 28, 1835, draft, UNDA.

[104] *Catholic Telegraph*, October 10, 1834, p. 365.

[105] Letter, Purcell to England, October 9, 1834, in *Catholic Telegraph*, 1898, p. 4.

[106] *Catholic Telegraph*, December 19, 1834, p. 365.

[107] *Ibid.*, July 3, 1835, p. 289.

[108] *Ibid.*, p. 292.

[109] Meline and McSweeny, *op. cit.*, pp. 307, 315-316.

[110] *Catholic Telegraph*, Jan. 21. 1836. The regulations for the Seminary Fund Association were (1)No subscription less than $1; (2)Life subscription $50; (3) Family subscription $100; (4) Right of presentation for one student $1000; (5) Solemn high mass twice a year for the members of which due notice will be given; and (6) Solemn high mass for the deceased members, once a year.

[111] *Catholic Telegraph*, March 10, 1836, p. 116.

[112] *Ibid.*, June 20, 1836, p 253.

[113] *Ibid.*, June 10, 1836, p. 259; *Ibid.*, July 2, 1836, p. 4.

[114] *Ibid.*, July 21, 1836, p. 269.

[115] Badin to Purcell, July 30, 1836, UNDA.

[116] *Catholic Telegraph*, September 22, 1836, p. 340.

[117] Purcell, wishing to come in touch with the learned and cultured men of Cincinnati became, a little before this, a member of the Ohio College of Teachers. At one of the meetings the discussion turned to religion and some remarks were made reflecting on the church. Bishop Purcell asked leave to reply to them. This permission could not be granted under the rules limiting speeches to ten minutes. In a spirit of fairness, a member, Dr. Wilson, offered the bishop the use of his church on Fourth and Main to reply. This offer was accepted and the Bishop delivered a fine discourse. The position and teaching of the Catholic Church were put before the people of Cincinnati clearly and forcibly. It stirred up a great deal of discussion in the community, so much so that Alexander Campbell, a Presbyterian Minister, felt called upon to take upon himself the defense of Protestantism. He sent a letter to the Bishop challenging him to a public debate. The Bishop accepted and invited Mr. Campbell to call at his residence on Sycamore Street The meeting took place at 2 p.m. Purcell, from these debates that followed, gained a wide reputation in the country and was thenceforth looked upon as the leading Catholic Bishop in the West.

A complete history of this debate is found in the *Catholic Telegraph*, January 7, 1937, p. 1.

[118] Deye, *op. cit.*, p. 206; Meline and McSweeny, *op. cit.*, vol. 1, p. 367.

[119] V.F. O'Daniel, *The Fathers of the Church in Tennessee*, pp. 381-382. New York: Frederick Pustet, 1926.

[120] *Catholic Telegraph*, February 3, 1881, p. 5.

[121] Right Reverend Josue Moody Marie Young, D.D., was born October 29, 1808, at Shapleigh, Maine. He was the co-founder of the *Catholic Telegraph*. On April 23, 1854, at Cincinnati, he was consecrated Bishop of Eric, Pennsylvania.

[122] *Catholic Telegraph*, October 12, 1837, p. 357.

[123] Stokes to Purcell, September 15, 1839, MSMSA.

[124] *Ibid.*

[125] *Catholic Telegraph*, September 19, 1839, p. 284. Deye, *op. cit.*, p. 216. *Catholic Telegraph*, August 22, 1839, p. 294.

[126] *Catholic Telegraph*, November 7, 1856, p. 1.

[127] *Ibid.*, March 21, 1840, p. 95

[128] Letters, Machebeuf to his father, Tiffin, Ohio, January 24, 1830, quoted in W.J. Howlett, *Life of the Rt. Rev. Joseph P. Machebeuf*, pp. 63-64, Pueblo Colorado; The Franklin Press, 1908.

[129] *Ibid.*, Monroeville, February 29, 1842, in Howlett, *op. cit.*, p. 101.

[130] *Catholic Telegraph*, March 21, 1840, p. 95.

[131] Garrigan, *op. cit.*, p. 165. Kelley and Kirwin, *op. cit.*, p. 1839. Garrigan, in following Kirwin, seems to have been mistaken in holding that the Athenaeum was not in existence during the year 1839-1840.

[132] Deye, *op. cit.*, p. 208.

[133] Garrigan, *op. cit.*, p. 165.

[134] Deye, *op. cit.*, p. 223.

[135] *Ibid.*, p. 223.

[136] *Ibid.*, p. 224.

[137] Garrigan, op cit., p. 167.

[138] Deye, *op. cit.*, p. 224.

[139] Garrigan, *op. cit.*, p. 170.

[140] Meline and McSweeny, *op. cit.*, vol.1 p. 408.

[141] *The History of Brown County, Ohio*. Chicago: W.A. Beers and Co., 1883. p. 326, says that he went to St. Martin's then to St. Patrick's Fayetteville and was Vicar-General of Covington, in 1849. He was later superior of the seminary in 1845.

[142] *Catholic Telegraph*, September 26, 1840, p. 4.

[143] Deye, *op. cit.*, p 225.

[144] Kelley and Kirwin, *op. cit.*, p. 19. *Catholic Telegraph*, Nov. 10 1832, p. 15; *Ibid.*, Aug. 17, 1833. *The History of Brown County, Ohio*, p. 324 *Fifty Years in Brown County Convent*, p. 57. Cincinnati: McDonald Company, 1895.

[145] The Rev. Claude Gacon was born in Rome, in the diocese of Clermont, France. In 1824 he was ordained as a Sulpician. In 1839, when the Archbishop visited France in search of Missionaries he, with Cheymol and Lamy, volunteered. He taught in the seminary at Brown County and died there June 2, 1865.

[146] Kelley and Kirwin, *op. cit.*, pp. 36-37. The Rev. William Cheymol was born near Clermont,

France, in April 1811. He was ordained a Sulpician in 1837, and also volunteered for the missions when Bishop Purcell visited France in 1839. He taught in the seminary at Brown County and died there on July 17, 1885.

147 *Catholic Telegraph*, May 20, 1841, p. 166.

148 *Ibid.*, October 9, 1841, p. 326.

149 *Ibid.*

150 *Ibid.*

151 *Ibid.*, May 28, 1842, p. 174.

152 *The Eudists.* St. Jean Eudes joined the Oratorian Fathers in 1623 and was an active member of that institute for twenty years. He withdrew when its superior general declined to permit him to found seminaries. Thereupon in 1643, he established the Congregation of Jesus and Mary (C.J.M.) which became known as the Eudists. Along with the Lazarists and Sulpicians, these communities had as one of their spiritual aims the administration of seminaries.

153 The Lazarists (or Vincentians) are known as the Congregation of the missions. It was founded by St. Vincent de Paul in France during the 17th century, and its original purpose was to engage in preaching and home missions to the poor. In this work, it was found that those who preach need special training. The Lazarists came to focus more of their activities on the conducting of seminaries. With the French Revolution, they came to the United States, and the group that we are now concerned with settled in Perry County, Missouri.

154 *Catholic Telegraph*, July 16, 1842, p. 231.

155 Charles Boglioli was born at Canjo, in the Duchy of Parma, on December 1, 1814. He came to American in 1841 and was ordained that year in New Orleans. He spent a short time in St. Louis and then was appointed to assist Fr. Burlando in the direction of the Diocesan Seminary at Brown County. He possessed and excellent mind and was a great scholar. Years later, Dr. Brownson is reputed to have said that he was the greatest philosopher in America. Later he was chaplain of the Confederate Army and died on July 22, 1882. Kelley and Kirwin, *op. cit.*, pp. 44-45.

156 *Ibid.*, pp. 238-43.

157 Deye, *op. cit.*, pp. 278, 290.

158 Purcell to Timon, March 9, 184, UNDA.

159 Burlando to Timon, April 3, 1845, UNDA.

160 Letter Senez to Purcell, April 18 1845. MSMSA.

161 *History of Brown County*, p. 325.

162 *Ibid.*, p. 326.

163 Kelley and Kirwin, *op. cit.*, p. 50.

164 *Ibid.*, op cit., p. 51.

165 Catholic Directory of 1847, p. 104.

166 *Catholic Telegraph*, March 27, 1884, p. 5. *Ibid.*, April 3, 1884, p. 5. *Ibid.*, April 10, 1884, p. 5., *Ibid.*, April 24, 1884, p. 5.

167 Kelley and Kirwin, *op. cit.*, p. 53.

CHAPTER TWO

The Early History of Mount St. Mary's Seminary at Price Hill (1851-1879)

INTRODUCTION

As noted in the preceding chapter, the first historical period of the seminary was indeed nomadic. No doubt, due to Bishop Purcell's preoccupation with the building of his cathedral, which was finished in 1845, the seminary received little attention during its days at Brown County. As pointed out there is some indication that Edward Purcell did not believe in being too generous to the seminary at this time. However, with the completion of the cathedral, Purcell now turned all this energies to the planning and construction of his seminary on a permanent basis. He accomplished this in 1851 in moving the makeshift seminary from the Episcopal residence to a beautiful and commanding site overlooking the entire city of Cincinnati. Even today, standing on the ruins of the old seminary on Price Hill, the view of Cincinnati from this vantage point is breathtaking. At this time Purcell changed the name of the seminary from St. Francis Xavier to Mount St. Mary's Seminary of the West. There is no doubt that he chose this name in memory of his old alma mater in the East.

In this era Purcell still faced many problems in regard to the seminary. The most important of these were the creation of a competent faculty and the establishment of solid financial support. By early 1860 Purcell had achieved both of these goals. From this time until the great financial disaster of 1879, Mount St. Mary's of the West enjoyed a period of success that was truly remarkable. The faculty of the seminary during this time was indeed an eminent one, and the reputation of the seminary as an institution of Catholic philosophical and theological learning had no peer in the Midwest.

During this time certain important questions were raised and settled: the matter of regional seminary; the question of the Mount being a Provincial Seminary; the right of the seminary to grant theological and philosophical degrees; and the matter of the seminary being raised to the status of a Pontifical Seminary.

In this very era of tremendous strength and vitality, the storm of financial disaster broke with terrible swiftness in the year 1879. The doors of the seminary were closed for a decade. One can only realize the extent of the debacle when one realizes the lofty and eminent position to which the seminary had risen in the years immediately preceding. This chapter traces these events.

EARLY PLANS FOR MOUNT ST. MARY'S SEMINARY (1847-1851)

On January 21, 1847, Messrs. John and James Slevin instructed Purcell that they would be ready to help financially in the work of building and constructing a new seminary.

Just a week later Messrs. Michael and Patrick Considine, not to be outdone by the Slevins, offered Purcell five acres of land in Price Hill upon which he could build his seminary. It was an ideal location for a seminary, and the bishop lost no time in accepting the generous offer.

It was right on the summit of Price Hill overlooking the entire city of Cincinnati, the Ohio River, and northern Kentucky around Covington.[1] Patrick Considine transferred the five acres of land to the bishop on May 29, 1847, for the consideration of one dollar.[2]

In that same spring, John and James Slevin began to build, at their own expense, a stone structure eighty feet square, with a height of four stories. The building cost them $22,166.05.[3] As one looks at the pictures of old Mount St. Mary's Seminary, it was the central structure. Two wings and a second building were to be added later. By the fall of 1847, the foundation of the central building were completed.[4]

On July 3, 1848, Purcell laid the cornerstone[5] for his new seminary now renamed Mount St. Mary's of the West in imitation of his old alma mater. Situated in Price Hill, it furnished, as Purcell said, "a delightful panoramic view of the city and its environments."

Once the seminary building was under way, Purcell began to plan the financing of the Seminary. For this reason he called a diocesan synod[6] in December, 1848. It was not the only reason for calling the synod, but it was perhaps one of the most important. The synod met on December 7, 8, and 9 of 1848. In the first session, in the sixth act, Purcell called attention to the need for providing permanent support in some fashion or another for the theological seminary. In the seventh act, the plans for the theological seminary were submitted and suggestion asked to avoid wasteful expenditures. In the second session, the support of the seminary was again discussed.[7]

From this synod came the land that was to be used in the future. On January 18, 1849, Purcell published a pastoral letter asking for financial support for the seminary through semi-annual parochial collections. This was the first such request that he had made, as reminded his flock, in his fifteen years as bishop. During this time he had not received as much as would support and educate a single seminarian from any of the altars at which he was destined to minister.[8]

When, therefore, we consulted with our venerable clergy, in the late synod, on the best means of accomplishing the object, it was suggested by them, that we should address to you this Pastoral, and invite you, in concert with your beloved pastors, to select any one or two Sundays of the year, which may be agreed upon, to have a collection made in every church and congregation throughout the diocese, for the support of the seminarists. One family, with a generosity which God alone can adequately reward, has undertaken to build for us the seminary. The foundation has been already built, and the materials for the super structure will be ready the moment Spring opens, and allows the work to be resumed. The Catholics of the diocese will, we doubt not, do the rest. The amount collected in every church will be published, to the honor of the congregation in the *Catholic Telegraph*. The names of annual, or life subscribers, will be sent to any of the clergy of the Cathedral, and all shall be faithfully preserved in our archives. The Holy Sacrifice of the Mass shall be offered once every month for the contributors to the fund which shall thus be realized, and the inmates of the seminary shall be exhorted constantly to pray for their temporal and eternal welfare.[9]

With the building of the seminary under way, and the plans for its financial support set in motion, Purcell now turned his attention to the problem of supplying a competent faculty. In view of his past troubles with the diocesan clergy in this area, he first turned to the religious orders of help in this regard. Actually he did not get them, and as a consequence, he was once more forced back upon the expediency of using his diocesan priest. This time, however, his use of the secular clergy for the staff of the seminary was to meet with eminent success and from the at time on they have always staffed the seminary in Cincinnati.[10]

However, in May of 1850, Purcell did write to the Visitor-General of the Sulpicians[11] then at Montreal, the Reverend C. V. Guitter offering charge of the new seminary to the priests of St. Sulpice, Paris. Father Guitter had to leave Montreal for Paris immediately upon the receipt of the letter, as he was called there upon the death of the Superior-General: but he promised Bishop Purcell to lay the matter before the new Superior-General. He did not hesitate to say that the first new house undertaken by the Sulpicians in the United States would be the one at Cincinnati. The new superior, Father Carrier, however, wrote to Bishop Purcell on June 6, that there were many difficulties which militated against them taking charge of the seminary at Cincinnati. The chief difficulty was the lack of men, and the consequent inability of the society to furnish and govern the two other establishments of the society then in America. Purcell then decided to go to Paris himself to see what he could do to alter this decision.[12]

On July 19, 1850, Purcell was made Archbishop and the See of Cincinnati was elevated to Metropolitan status. Hardly had this been accomplished, when Purcell left for Europe in January of 1851 to seek to convince the Sulpicians of Paris to take over his seminary.

Archbishop Purcell arrived at Paris on January 15, 1851, and made the house of the Sulpicians his center of activity for the next six or seven months, returning thereto after various side-trips to parts of France, Germany and Austria. But even his presence at Paris could not induce the Fathers to accept the charge at Cincinnati. He informed Father Decluol on July 7 that he had then lost all hoped of getting the priests. It seems that the archbishop wanted to establish a "mixed" seminary, i.e., a seminary proper and a college for lay students, in which he might foster vocations to the priesthood in the latter institution. To this Father Carrier objected, since all their institutions had to be put on the same footing as they were in France, namely seminaries for clerical students. At the end of July, archbishop Purcell left for England, a disappointed man.[13]

While Purcell was in Paris, the Sulpicians[14] as well as the Vincentians were asked to staff the seminary. They, too, declined because of the lack of priests.[15] In a letter to Bishop O'Connor, Purcell later rationalized this failure to obtain religious orders he wanted: "were you not all along rather opposed to our having our seminaries conducted by Sulpicians or any other Society? I could have got Oblates, Rosminians, and priest of the Saint Esprit, Paris, but declined accepting them."[16] It was a hard blow to the Archbishop who now saw himself obliged to revert to the system he had tried before on Sycamore Street and had found wanting—the use of the diocesan clergy for professors in the seminary. His new endeavor, however, was to be more glorious, one of the grandest works of the archbishop's later years was the assembling of a learned faculty for his seminary from his diocesan priest. No seminary in the country could boast of the faculty excelling or even equaling that which Purcell assembled at the Mount.[17]

THE OPENING OF MOUNT ST. MARY'S SEMINARY (1851)

Purcell returned from Europe in time to be present at the opening of his new seminary on October 2, 1851. Into the new seminary a small group of twelve seminarians moved.[18] In an address on the occasion he said:

> We place the seminary under the powerful protection of the Immaculate Mother of God, the Holy Angels and Saints now gloriously reigning in Heaven, who were distinguished on earth for the zeal and for the beauty of the sanctuary whose greatest ornament is the piety and the holiness of his ministers.[19]

HALLINAN, RECTOR (1851-1854)

In August of 1851, the Reverend Michael Mary Hallinan, D.D., returned home to Cincinnati from studies at St. Sulpice, Paris.[20] In October he was placed in charge of the seminary as rector.

The first rector of the new seminary on Price Hill was born near the town of Hallow, County Cork, Ireland, on September 29, 1827. Young Michael Hallinan attended grad school in his native Ireland and after decided to become a priest, he was sent to the little seminary of St. Sulpice in Paris. Here at the little seminary he acquired a thorough knowledge of French and was a leader in his class in the study in the Grand Seminary of St. Sulpice in Paris. While here at the Grand Seminary in Paris, he was introduced to Archbishop Purcell who was then on this way to Rome to receive the Pallium. The Archbishop, highly impressed with the brilliant young student, invited him to join the Cincinnati dioceses. After prayerful consideration he wrote to Purcell at Rome that he would like to accept the invitation. Purcell agreed, and instructed him to continue his course in theology and to strive to obtain a doctorate. Hallinan completed his theological course with high honors in 1851, and received the doctorate degree at the same time.[21]

After his ordination in June, 1851, he first visited his native country, and arrived in Cincinnati, in the latter part of August. As the seminary was not quite ready for occupancy at this time, Hallinan was stationed at the Cathedral. In October of 1851 he became the first rector of the seminary. He served in this capacity until 1854. [22]

Most of the students who studied under his held him in great respect; and those who attended his classes always held that he was a good teacher. In 1854, he went to Chillicothe, where he worked with one of his former student Father Ford, in trying to establish St. Peter's College. When this failed, he went to Dayton. Later on he became a priest of the diocese of Baltimore and Philadelphia. In 1868 he joined the diocese of Little Rock and in 1884 was appointed Vicar-General. He died on December 12, 1887.

During the tree years that he was rector, it seems that he worked hard, together with Purcell, in building a solid foundation for the spiritual and intellectual edifice that was to follow. He had, in retrospect, very little with which to do work. To be sure, he had a fine building, but he still did not have much of a faculty. He taught the classes in dogma and moral theology and David Whalen, also noting as treasure, assumed the classes in Sacred Scripture and church history. They were the only two. A young student, Jeremiah O'Connor, was commandeered to take over the classes in philosophy.[23]

Around the end of the year (perhaps some time in December) Francis Joseph Pabisch arrived in Cincinnati from the University of Vienna.

Later, he was to become rector of the seminary during one of its finest periods. At this time, however, he took over the classes in Sacred Scripture and Church History which Whalen had been teaching. At the end of the school year he asked to be allowed to engage in parish work and was sent to St. James in White Oak as pastor.

In January of 1852, Purcell had forty students studying for the Archdiocese of Cincinnati. Thirteen students were now studying at Mount St. Mary's of the West; three were studying at St. Sulpice in Paris; one at the College of Propaganda in Rome; three at Mount St. Mary's in Emmitsburg, Maryland; and twenty were studying at Mount St. Mary's Seminary, Perry County, Missouri.

At the end of this first school year, it is interesting to note the beginning of two customs which had been connected over the years with student life at the seminary while it was located in Price Hill. One was the unfailing custom of the seminarians attending and serving the devotions held at the Cathedral on Sundays and special fest days. The other was the custom of boarding out-of-town students in the rectories of Cincinnati Parishes during the period of summer vacation. Many a student later was to speak fondly of the time spent in such pastoral settings.[24]

When classes resumed in September of 1852, Hallinan again taught the classes in dogma and morality. Since Pabisch had left in the summer, Whalen again took over the classes in Sacred Scripture and church history.

Jeremiah O'Connor stayed on, after being ordained, to teach the classes in philosophy. On October 9 of that year, however, Sylvester Horton Rosecrans returned from studies at the College of the Propaganda at Rome and was assigned by Purcell to take over Hallinan's class in dogma.

Rosecrans was indeed an illustrious acquisition to the faculty of Mount St. Mary's Seminary. He returned from Rome to become professor of dogma. This post he held with great distinction for twelve years.[25] In 1855, he also became the first president of Mount St. Mary's College.

Rosecrans was born in Homer, a small village in Licking County, Ohio, on September 5, 1827. His parents, Crandall and Johann Rosecrans, were from Wilkes-Barre, Pennsylvania. They were both Protestant-Methodist. Stephen Hopkins, one of the signers of the Declaration of Independence, was a maternal ancestor. Young Sylvester gave evidence at an early age of possessing a very find mind. As a youth he entered Kenyon College, an Episcopalian institution. Sylvester's brother, General W. S. Rosecrans graduated at this time from West Point and soon after was appointed a professor at Kenyon. While here, General Rosecrans became a convert to the Catholic faith. His conversion led Sylvester to inquire into it also, and he himself became a Catholic in 1845. Leaving Kenyon College, he entered St. John's College, Fordham, New York, where he gradated with high honors in 1846.[26]

He then decided that he wanted to become a priest, and accordingly entered the diocesan seminary at Cincinnati which was then located in the bishop's quarters on Eighth Street. Bishop Purcell, perceived the talent of the young man, sent him to the College of the Propaganda in Rome. At the end of five years, July 16, 1852, he was ordained and received the degree of Doctor of Theology.[27]

When he returned home, he was made pastor of the Cathedral and began his long life of teaching dogmatic theology. While residing at the Cathedral, every morning they journeyed up the hill to the seminary on the public conveyance of the day which brought the people to Price Hill. Through the years Rosecrans made many friends in this fashion.

During these years he also was engaged with Edward Purcell in editing the *Catholic Telegraph*. In 1861, Purcell petitioned Rome for coadjutor. On December 23, 1861, Rosecrans became the auxiliary bishop of Cincinnati. He continued, however, to teach at the seminary until 1864. In 1868, he was made the first bishop of Columbus; he died in 1878.[28]

The number of seminarians studying for the diocese increased this second year to fifty; there were twenty at St. Mary's and the rest were scattered at St. Mary's County, Missouri; St. Joseph's College, Somerset; St. Mary's Seminary, Emmitsburg, and at St. Sulpice.[29]

In the second annual report of the seminary dated January, 1853, expenses exceeded receipts by $3,007.80. It had cost $5,508.50 to run the seminary, and the receipts amounted to only $2,500.70.

In September of 1853, Hallinan was again rector and taught morality; Rosecrans still taught dogma; Whalen taught Sacred Scripture and church history; and "Reverend Mr. Charles Shehan[30] a student in the last years of theology, had taken over the class in philosophy succeeding O'Connor. O'Connor had left because of ill health in January 1853.

At the end of this school year a report on the seminary appeared in the July 15 issue of the *Catholic Telegraph*:

> The annual examination of Mount St. Mary's Seminary of this Archdiocese took place on the 28th ult., and on the following day the seminarians left to spend the vacation with some one of the Reverend Clergy in the country, to recruit their health and strength, and to revive their spirits for the coming year.
>
> This institution, destined to supply our Diocese with priest in the future, and the hope and joy of all good Catholics, which their liberal support towards it best evinces, was opened some three years ago, and has in that short space of time already given seven priests to the Archdiocese. It numbers at present twenty-three students, five of whom are of the diocese of Pittsburgh, one belongs to the new diocese of Erie, and the remaining seventeen are of this archdiocese. Four of these are German, of whom two were ordained during the year. The number of seminarians has been constantly on the increase since it was first opened and will be con-

siderably augmented by new applicants the coming year, and the Rt. Rev. Bishop Baraga, Vicar Apostolic, of the Upper Michigan, also intends to place his seminarians there. The course of study lasts three years.

Considering the many difficulties which in the beginning every institution has to encounter, and the short period of its existence, the Seminary is advancing prosperously...May the blessings of the Almighty rest forever on the Institution.[31]

It will be noticed in the report that the Diocese at Pittsburgh and the Diocese of Erie were the first outside dioceses represented at Mount St. Mary's. The Diocese of Upper Michigan was the third. Representation from other dioceses began to grow; but these were the first.

It is also interesting to note the insertion of the element of nationalism at this time. The dominant element in the Cincinnati church up until this time was the Irish. They were to maintain their position of dominance for several generations. But it is interesting to note the increasing importance from this time forward of the German element in the affairs of the Church in Cincinnati.[32] For example, in the second annual report of 1853, there was this laconic item; "Three young men, Germans, were received into the seminary in September— but...they withdrew...[33] In this report of 1854, notice is taken of the words: "four of these are Germans."

In 1859 Purcell began to have trouble with the Ludwig Association in Germany concerning his German seminarians. He wrote to them:

The aim of the Seminary of Mt. St. Mary's near Cincinnati is to raise a pious clergy without distinction of language. It is no more for the Germans than for any other nationality, it is Catholic. It is a provincial seminary with the approbation of the Holy Father. Two-thirds of the students are German in origin. Never have the funds of the Ludwig Association been put to work more agreeable to God.[34]

Yet by 1882, thirty years later, it was found that:

Of the German-American priests born in this country the vast majority hail from this diocese or city and have been trained at Mt. St. Mary's Seminary...Cincinnati has three times as many German-American priests as any other in the United States. For instance, we head the list with forty-four. Baltimore comes next, falling off to sixteen, Louisville, four; Chicago, three; and Green Bay had two such priests.[35]

It should be noted also that in the report the course of study for philosophy and theology lasted for only three years with the philosophy course taking one year and the theology course two years. Some time in the 1860's the theology course was lengthened to three years. When reopened in 1887, the seminary had a course of two years of philosophy and three of theology. This again was the case in 1904 when the seminary was moved to Mount Washington. The four-year study of theology was initially begun in 1914.

It is important to realize, however, that during the years when there were only two (then three) years of theology instead of the four-year course which exists today, it was not as short a course as it first appears. The school year in those days lasted for ten full months, from early September to the last days of June. During the time when the seminary was in session, there were no vacation periods at Christmas and Easter. Taking into account the shortening of the seminary courses in later years to nine months, and the granting of a two-week vacation at Christmas and nearly one-week vacation at Easter, the old three-year program was, in the amount of time spent in the classroom at least, nearly the equivalent of the present day four-year program.

PLANS FOR A REGIONAL SEMINARY (1851)

In the fall of 1851, just as Mount St. Mary's was beginning, Purcell had the idea of making Mount St. Mary's of the West into a general or regional theological seminary.[36] Bishop O'Connor of Pittsburgh, who had been obliged to close his own seminary in the summer of 1851, began pushing this idea enthusiastically. From the latter part of October until the middle of November, Purcell and O'Connor were traveling together visiting the seminarians whom they had been studying at St. Mary's Seminary in St. Louis.[37] After meeting in Detroit, they traveled by way of Chicago to St. Louis. While no statement of Purcell was available concerning his plans for a general seminary at Cincinnati, the idea which O'Connor was pushing certainly discussed between them on this trip, especially since their object was to visit their seminarians and since Purcell had dedicated his new seminary just before leaving Cincinnati. While in St. Louis, O'Connor spoke at length with Peter Kenrick about accepting the Cincinnati institution as the seminary "for the entire western region." In view of the expenses of his own seminary, Peter Kenrick liked the idea.[38]

Shortly after Purcell returned to Cincinnati, he received a letter from Spalding, dated November 21, 1851. The postscript read: "What do you conclude about the project of a Provincial Seminary? Settled according to your Grace's plan it would do immense good for religion." [39]

In November of 1851, Purcell mailed the following letter to F. P. Kenrick as one of the propositions to be taken up at the coming 1852 Plenary Council at Baltimore: "Is it expedient and practicable to found a Catholic University? And if not, how shall we otherwise efficiently provide for the education of such clergy as the peculiar circumstances of the is country require?" Writing to Purcell on December 26, 1851, O'Connor expressed the willingness to let two of his priests, his brother and Father Heyden, and a German professor join Purcell's seminary faculty "with the understanding that the plan you proposed is carried out." O'Connor went on to explain that this could be done only if Mount St. Mary's became incorporated. O'Connor suggested that the government of the seminary be vested in a board composed of "the bishop and a priest, and a laymen of each diocese that would be connected with the seminary," and he proceeded with a lengthy explanation.[40]

This was probably more than Purcell had bargained for, because on February, 14, 1852, O'Connor wrote Purcell as follows:

I will say no more regarding the seminary. I have been, I fear, too forward, though I am not conscious of having suggested anything which may not be done not only without injury, but with advantage to your own diocese.[41]

Already the previous November, Archbishop Kenrick of Baltimore, in answer to this brother's expressed leaning toward a general seminary at Cincinnati, told him to keep his own seminary because every province should have one.[42] One of the decrees of the First Plenary Council of Baltimore, which met in May of 1852, recommended the formation of provincial seminaries for those bishops of the same province who had no seminaries of their own. Even provincial seminaries would be a step beyond the understaffed diocesan seminaries which had frequently had a precarious existence in Episcopal residences at the temporary quarter. But certainly O'Connor, and apparently Purcell also, had the idea of a western seminary in the Queen City which would serve more than an ecclesiastical province. Unfortunately Purcell's letters on this subject are no longer extant. For the present, the seminary which Purcell dedicated in 1851 would be merely diocesan.

However, the idea of a regional or central seminary, once even larger than the provincial seminary, had always been an idea or proposal advocated by certain once concerned with arch-diocesan seminary administration and the apparent duplication of facilities and faculties in America. Certainly this is another instance of the farsighted ideas of Purcell. In 1896, John Talbot Smith wrote on this subject the following words which could be applied even in our own day:

> The central, not the diocesan seminary, is the institution best suited to the times, the nation, and the general purse. The man of intelligence is today the world's citizen. Intercommunication is so easy, news is spread so thoroughly and cheaply, that a man is not educated unless his acquaintance with the earth is large. The mere living in certain localities is an education...the central seminary, not confined to the students of one or two dioceses, located in a social center, patronized by clerics of all sections, is in line with the present tendency...as a consequence their colleges will get the best students in numbers, and can give them the best possible training. The narrowness of diocesan seminaries is a certain and ineradicable as the narrowness of a country town. The professors and superiors may have the best intentions, wide experience, liberal views...nevertheless their diocesan seminary will be narrow in fact if not in intention or method. And if the time could be conceived when this country would have a seminary in each of two or there hundred diocese, the fancy might easily grow confused, manufacturing two, hundred, special atmospheres to surround the said seminaries.[43]

THE PROVINCIAL SEMINARY AND PONTIFICAL DEGREES (1855)

Among the most forward-looking legislation passed by the American bishops in the years of the mid-century was that of the various councils of the Province of Cincinnati. When Archbishop John B. Purcell presided at the opening session of the First Provincial Council in his See city in May, 855, Mount St. Mary's Seminary of the West was nearly four years old.

At this council the bishops of the province determined to make this seminary a provincial one with a board of five bishops appointed for the administration. But the Cincinnati bishops went beyond this when they petitioned Rome to erect Mount St. Mary's of the West into a pontifical institution with the right to confer the doctorate in philosophy and theology.

The Council was held from Sunday, May 13, to Sunday, May 20. On Saturday May 12, a preliminary meeting was held fro the purpose of making immediate preparations. The officials of the Council were selected at this meeting and various appointments were made.

Two of the most important topics taken up at the Provincial Council in May, 1855, were very much interrelated; the matter of establishing an American College in Rome, and the matter of setting up the Provincial Seminary in Cincinnati. As to the latter, it was certainly true that Purcell at this time was finding the financial burdens of the seminary quite taxing. This is very easily seen in the early financial reports on the seminary. There was a continuing string of deficits. But it seems that Purcell was motivated by stronger consideration then financial burdens in stressing the idea of a provincial seminary. Purcell wanted his seminary on Price Hill to be the ecclesiastical center of the Midwest, and he firmly believed that he could make it such. Therefore, it is easy to see that he would not be too receptive to the idea of establishing such a center in the city of Rome.

The idea of having a Roman College for American students stemmed from the suggestion of Cardinal Bedini when he visited the United States in 1853. He suggested that it would indeed be appropriate that he United States have a seminary in Rome similar to those maintained by other countries. He proposed this to the Propaganda in his report of July 12, 1854. There seems to be evidence that when Purcell first heard of this (almost a year before the convoking of the council) his reaction seemed favorable. By the time the council opened, however, his attitude had changed.

One of the significant reasons for this change of attitude seemed to be the attitude of the committee of theologians of the First Provincial Council of Cincinnati. After much discussion, they reported against the foundation of the Roman College. The assembled bishops accepted this report as the full expression of their own views on the subject of a Roman College and forwarded the decision to Rome.

At the same council the bishop's accepted Purcell's Mount St. Mary's of the West as a provincial major seminary, and Spalding's St. Thomas Seminary as a provincial minor seminary. They passed official decrees (Decrees VI and VIII) to that effect. They also petitioned (Decree VII) the Holy Father to grant the major seminary pontifical status with the privilege of conferring the degrees in philosophy and theology. The proposed provincial status of Mount St. Mary's and St. Thomas was immediately published in May 26, 1855, issue of the *Catholic Telegraph,* "subject, of course, to the decision of the Holy See before which they cannot have force."[44]

On June 2, 1855, Purcell had the following comments to make on the decision of the Provincial Council regarding the matter of the Provincial Seminary:

We understand that the appointment of a Rector and Faculty is to rest with the Bishops of the Province, and that they will act in the matter in the early part of July, so that studies may commence in September...this step we consider one of the most important for the good of religion that could have been taken...Another advantage we expect form this project is, that seeing an institution in our midst, established on a respectable basis, and calculated to exert an immense influence for good...Hithertofore, there has been much apathy on this subject, much supine reliance on aid from abroad in the shape of priests from Belgium, Ireland, France, and Italy.[45]

In the September 8, 1855, issue of the *Catholic Telegraph* appeared this item:

The provincial Seminary erected by the Bishops at the late council opened on Monday. The students from the suffragan sees, Louisville expected, have not yet arrived. We regret that we neglected to announce earlier than last week, the time of commencement of studies.[46]

Twenty-one months later, in February of 1857, the authorities in Rome asked to consider further the proposals of the council. Around the VII and VIII Decrees, the authorities said that they wished to defer an answer for the present moment as to whether the Provincial Seminary of Cincinnati should be declared Pontifical, and as to whether it should have the power of conferring academic degrees.[47]

Rome, however, finally did not agree to the conferring of Pontifical status nor to the conferring of degrees in philosophy and theology. Pius IX, in a letter to Archbishop Barnabo of the Propaganda, pointed out that Rome was just then establishing the American College at Rome and American students should be sent there for the purpose of obtaining the desired degrees.[48]

Archbishop Purcell, though, did not give up the point. In 1861, while in Rome, he again personally petitioned for the privilege. As to remedies for the church in Ohio, he suggested the only one to which the bishops of the province in Council had all agreed three years before: "That the provincial seminary be empowered to grant degrees in philosophy and theology. This would improve the seminary and yet allow the better students to go to Rome.[49]

Thus, although Rome did not take kindly to the petition for the privilege of granting theological and philosophical degrees, Purcell also never took too kindly to the idea of a Roman College. As late as January of 1871, he wrote in a letter that under the present conditions, he did not like a college in Rome. He believed he had a great seminary in Cincinnati whose professors were as learned as any in Rome.[50]

THE INCORPORATION OF THE SEMINARY (1855)

At a meeting held at Mount St. Mary's Seminary on May 21, 1855, the Mount St. Mary's Seminary Association was incorporated as a body corporate under an act of the State of Ohio entitled "An Act to enabled the trustees of Colleges, Academic Universities and other institutions for the purpose of promoting education to become bodies corporate." This act was passed April 9, 1852, and also two acts supplemental to it were passed on March 11 and 12, 1853.[51]

Trustees for the term of three years were elected. They included: John B. Purcell, Peter P. Lefevere, Maurice de St. Palais, Amodeus Rappe, Martin Spalding, George A. Canell, Frederick Baraga, Edward T. Collins, James Slevin, Reuben R. Springe, John Sleven, Patrick Considine and John L. Quinse. Edward T. Collins was elected clerk.[52] There names indicate two things: the Bishops of the Province were all represented, and Catholic laymen were also represented.

This meeting and subsequent recording in the records at the County Court House constituted the charter of the Mount St. Mary's Seminary Association. By reason of this it was empowered to grant degrees according to its by-laws. Later Mount St. Mary's College actually did grant the degree of Bachelor of Arts for the several years of its existence. However, there is no record that this association functioned after the Civil War.

QUINLAN, RECTOR (1854-1859)

At the beginning of the school year in September of 1854, Hallinan was succeeded as rector of the seminary by the Reverend John Quinlan. John Quinlan was another Irishman born in the little village of Cloyne in County Cork on October 19, 1826. His name is still there on the parish register. He was sent as a youth to the fine classical school at Middleton. At the age of eighteen he came to the United States with his widowed mother. Desiring to become a priest, he approached Purcell and was admitted to the small group of students studying in the attic of the Episcopal residence. Purcell, just as in the case of Rosecrans, noticed Quinlan's talents and decided to send him on for further studies at Mount St. Mary's Seminary, Emmitsburg. In 1852, he and Richard Gilmour finished the courses in philosophy and theology. He served after ordination at Piqua, and at St. Patrick's Church in Cincinnati. In 1854 when he was almost twenty-eight years of age, he was made rector of Mount St. Mary's Seminary. With Rosecrans teaching dogma, he taught the course in moral theology along with the course in philosophy. At the first Provincial Council of Cincinnati, he was appointed the theologian of Archbishop Purcell. In 1859, he was appointed Bishop of Mobile. He proved himself to be a true southerner during the days of the Civil War. In 1882, he visited Rome and died while there of the campagna fever.[53]

John Quinlan was a man possessed of a clear, strong, logical mind together with wide breadth of learning. In retrospect, it certainly seems that from the beginning the seminary was blessed with able men. Hallinan, Rosecrans, and Quinlan gave to the seminary the healthy impetus it needed. During the days of Barry and Pabisch, the faculty of Mount St. Mary's Seminary was to flourish and develop to such an extent that it had no peer in the Midwest. But it was men of the caliber of Quinlan who gave it the initial healthy thrust.

Quinlan took over Hallinan's classes in moral theology. Rosecrans continued to teach dogma, and the Reverend A. Toebbe[54] succeeded Whalen as treasure of the Seminary. Toebee also taught Whalen's classes in Sacred Scripture and church history and Shehan's classes in philosophy.[55]

The old custom in the seminary of a Solemn Pontifical Mass on St. Sylvester's Day for the benefactors of the seminary was instituted during Quinlan's time as rector.[56] It was a custom which was practiced for many years in the seminary. Since there was no long Christmas vacation at the time, the practice of celebrating this day for the welfare of the seminary's benefactors was made possible until the removal of the seminary from Price Hill in 1904.

It is interesting to note the various texts which were then used at the time in theology and philosophy. The textbook used in dogmatic theology was Perrone.[57] Perrone's manual was the fundamental text used by both Rosecrans and Hecht as Mount St. Mary's. Other texts used at the time were Dixon[58] in the introduction to Sacred Scripture: Dherdt[59] in liturgy; Ferrante[60] in canon law.

From 1851 until 1866, Liguori[61] was the text used in moral theology. In 1868, at Mount St. Mary's Seminar, Gury[62] was introduced as the text in moral. Gury, revised by Ballerini[63] was introduced in 1872, and continued to be the text used until the seminary closed in 1879. When the seminary returned in 1887 to Price Hill, Gury, revised now by Sabetti[64] became the official text in moral.

In regard to church history, the text used at St. Mary's from 1866 on was Alzog's[65] church history. The manual of Universal Church History by the Reverend John Alzog, Professor of Theology at University of Freiburg, was translated from the ninth and the last German edition by the two professors at Mount St. Mary's Pabisch and Byrne. [66]

In 1878 they had published all three volumes of the book in English having worked together for six years on the translation. According to the authors of the translation, they sought not merely a translation, but a church history attached to the requirements of this country. At this time it was highly praised and widely received. Purcell gave his hearty endorsement to the work upon its completion.

It was indeed a scholarly work and was used widely for many years as the official textbook of this seminary and many others. In retrospect, however, the book was written in a heavy German style, and come to be considered too ponderous. John Talbert Smith had this to say about this and other church history textbooks of the day:

> So little importance has been attached to the study of history in our seminaries that we do not possess the proper textbook or series of textbooks suited to clerical training in this country. Alzog (the one translated by Pabisch and Byrne) was too large and heavy and too condensed; Darras is too light and sketchy and Brueck is simply a help to memory. There is need of a series of historical textbooks to cover the six years of seminary life. While waiting for it, the seminary professors are doing their best arrangements of their own in the shape of lectures from which the students take copious notes.[67]

It would seem that Smith's criticism is still pertinent. There is still no church history text designed specifically for American students in American seminaries.

In regard to textbooks used in Catholic seminaries in the United States, there was a conspicuous absence of American authors. The contribution of Byrne and Pabisch at this time was a beginning. But the production of textbooks then, as now was not great. John Talbert

Smith in 1896 spoke of this very same difficulty, but the overall picture even up to this time warrants the same criticism. There are no manuals used as texts in the ecclesiastical sciences written by Americans for American seminaries.

Up to and including the year 1866, Franc. Rothenflue, S.J. was the text that was used in teaching philosophy. His *Institutes of Theoretical Philosophy* were widely used up until this time in the teaching of Catholic philosophy. Rothenflue was a professor who taught philosophy in the College of St. Michael in Freiburg, Switzerland.[68]

Sometime between 1856 and 1870, Tongiorgi[69] became the text in philosophy used at Mount St. Mary's Seminary. Tongiorgi was an Italian and was disciple of James Balnes. Balnes, a Spanish philosopher of the nineteenth century, is important because of this effort to revive Thomism before the statement of Leo XIII in Encyclical *Aeterni Patris*.[70] The use of Tongiorgi as a text in philosophy continued until the close of the seminary in 1879.

The report of the seminary published in the *Catholic Telegraph* in February 23, 1856, submitted by John W. Quinlan, President, gives as the total amount of receipts $4,648.60

> There are at present in the Seminary eighteen students, thirteen of whom belong to the diocese. Besides, there are sixteen at St. Thomas near Bardstown; three at Mt. St. Mary's, Maryland; two at N, France; and one at St. Charles near Baltimore.
>
> During the past year substantial improvements have been made on the Seminary ground. A two story brick house, with cellar has been erected, cisterns have been built, and the students employed many of their recreations in the healthful and useful exercise of contracting and beautifying terraces, planting trees, cultivating kitchen, gardens, etc.[71]

MOUNT ST. MARY'S COLLEGE (1856)

A Catholic college in connection with the seminary was soon recognized to be a necessity. True, St. Xavier's College in the city had sent many youths to study at Mount St. Mary's. St. Mary's of the Barrens, Missouri, had also done yeoman service in the education of the seminarians for the Mount. The provincial Preparatory Seminary of St. Thomas had contributed a number of youths to Mount St. Mary's. But Purcell was a "Mountain" man and throughout his life, he remained convinced that the best possible education set-up for a Catholic seminary in this country was a an education arrangement begun and practiced at Mount St. Mary's of the East, and at so many of the other early seminaries—the seminary-college combination. It was an arrangement that gave the seminary of source of income. But, it was also an arrangement whereby the diocesan clergy provide for itself a splendid recruiting ground. In the Spring of 1856, ground was broken for a southern wing for the seminary which was to be used as a collegiate department. The Catholic residents of Price Hill demanded a convenient place of worship, and the Archbishop resolved to annex the Chapel, destined of the use of the Catholics of the neighborhood and for the seminarians and students of the new college, to the extremity of the southern wing. One of the generous citizens presented the Archbishop with $5,000 and another with $1,000 to aid him in the completion of the new Chapel.

On June 22, 1856, the cornerstone[73] of the new Chapel of St. John the Baptist was laid by the Reverend James F. Wood.[74] Although the day was intensely hot, quite a large number of people assembled to witness the ceremony. All the seminarians assisted, chanting the songs, antiphons, and litanies of the ceremonies.[75]

When news was received in Cincinnati in the summer of 1856 that the college in Chillicothe had failed, Purcell had the work speeded up on the south wing. He now determined to open his college the coming September. Thus, it was that on September 15, 1856, Mount St. Mary's College in Price Hill was formally opened. It was patterned after Mount St. Mary's at Emmitsburg in its connection with the seminary, and in its administration and spirit. Two courses were offered: the classical and scientific. The classical curriculum consisted of philosophy, Latin, Greek, mathematics, geometry, algebra, French, German English, History, arithmetic, English grammar, ancient history, bookkeeping, modern history, geography, writing, rhetoric, and catechism. The scientific (sometimes referred to as the commercial) course consisted of mathematics, surveying, civil engineering, bookkeeping, and business education, together with chemistry, and many of the courses from the classical program.[76] Each course lasted for eight years, covering the four years of high school and college in modern education.

On September 13, 1856, the following prospectus appeared in the *Catholic Telegraph*:

> This institution will be opened on Monday, the 15th of September, 1856. It is situated on one of the hills overlooking the city of Cincinnati, in a position unrivalled for healthy air and beautiful scenery. Its object is to afford to pupils a thorough education under Catholic influences. The regular classical and scientific course is eight years, though students from other institution will be allowed to enter the more advanced classes upon satisfactory examination. The connection of the college with the Cincinnati, Provincial Seminary, affords ample facilities for thorough instruction of the pupils in the ancient classics, as well as the German, French, and Italian languages. The discipline of the College will be paternal but vigilant...the student being always under the eye of the Prefect of Professor. The domestic arrangements of the Institution are under the superintendence of the Sisters of Charity. The auspices under which this college is placed, and the cordial approbation extend to it by the Most Reverend Archbishop and the clergy of the diocese, are sufficient to warrant the confidence that it will deserve a high rank amount Catholic institutions of learn, and amply reward to patronage which no doubt it will receive from the parents and guardians of youth.[77]

When the college was started, Rosecrans was appointed its first president. In this instance, the administrative organization was again exactly patterned after Mount St. Mary's Emmitsburg. The arrangement of Price Hill was again the seminary-college combination. Each has its own separate administration, but each was dependent upon the other.

It is important to point out that the college in this case was again "mixed," that is, the college was considered, a school for students preparing for entrance into the major seminary, as well as a regular college for lay students. Here at Price Hill, Purcell in the first years relied quite heavily on the help of the seminary, as well as a regular college for lay students. Here at Price Hill, Purcell in the first years relied quite heavily on the help of the seminary in supply in the faculty for the courses in the college. By 1858, however, he had assembled a faculty second to none in the region for both the seminary and the college.

The faculty for the seminary in September 1855, was the same as the previous year: Quinlan, Rosecrans, Toebbe, and Shehan. In the next year, Toebbe and Shehan Left. Quinlan took over the classes in Sacred Scripture and church history, and young William Barry, a student, took over the classes in philosophy.[78]

On June 24, 1857, the first Annual Commencement of Mount St. Mary's College took place. On the same day the chapel of St. John the Baptist was dedicated. It was estimated at the time that new wing with the chapel and the library had cost close to $60,000. The chapel was in Gothic style. The interior painting was done by Mr. Lanthrop of Cincinnati. Bishop Leogh of Pittsburgh delivered the dedication speech on the subject of the church and education.[79]

In 1857, the faculty was Quinlan, Rosecrans, and Pabisch. Pabisch had volunteered to come back to teach the course in church history and Sacred Scripture. Barry had been sent to Rome, and Quinlan most likely took over his course. It is also known that in this year the enrollment rose to a total of forty students. In November, a new organ, built by Mr. Schwab of Cincinnati, was placed in the seminary chapel.[80]

Then in February of 1858, Xavier Donald MacLeod,[81] one of the most brilliant members of the faculty in the entire history of the seminary, arrived Cincinnati from St. Louis, and was appointed by Purcell to teach at Mount St. Mary's.

MacLeod was born in New York City on November 17, 1821. His father, Alexander MacLeod, a native of Scotland, emigrated to America in 1792, and soon thereafter joined the Reformed Presbyterian Church, and entered Union College. He later became an ordained minister. He gave to his young son, Donald, the best educational advantages possible. Graduating from Columbia, Donald took up the study of law. This he did not like, and he turned to the study of theology. "Much to the regret of his family," says the *Encyclopedia of American Biography*, 1901, "he took orders in the Episcopal Church, 1845, and was for five years rector of the country parish."

Desiring to investigate the religious claims of the Episcopal Church, he then journeyed to Europe. He remained there two years, and before coming home, he became a convert to the Catholic Church.

Upon his return to the United States, MacLeod joined the cultured literary clubs of New York City. He made friends with such eminent men of letters as George Bancroft, Washington Irving, and N. P. Willis. Works which came from his pen at this time included the following: *The Life of Sir Walter Scott*: *Pynnhurst*: and *Bloodstone*. In 1857, he published his important work, *The Biography of Mary, Queen of Scots*.

In 1857, McLeod journeyed to Panama. He returned to start a lecture tour throughout the United States. Settling down in St. Louis he became the editor of the *Shepherd of the*

Valley, a publication there. Finding it difficult to support a religious newspaper, he wrote to Archbishop Purcell to remind the bishop of this offer to help if he (MacLeod) ever needed him.

The kindly Purcell kept his word, and in 1858 MacLeod arrived in Cincinnati, and was immediately sent to the seminary to teach. While he was teaching there, MacLeod studied theology privately. Three years later he was ready for the examination, and was ordained a priest by Purcell on October 15, 1861, in the seminary chapel.

During these years he taught English, French, and Latin. He also began a course of lectures on English literature. While at the seminary he devoted himself also to contributing columns to the *Catholic Telegraph,* and writing such varied productions as a fantastic tale called the *Pre-Adamite Sultan*; a review of Carlyle's *Frederick the Great* (published in the *Telegraph*); *Haroun al Raschid*; and a small volume of collected poetry entitled *Our Lady of the Litanies.*

In accordance with the decree of the previous council, the second Provincial Council of Cincinnati was opened on the fourth Sunday after Easter, May 2, 1858, and lasted until the following Sunday, May 9. On May 6, 1858, the Fathers of the Second Provincial Council visited the seminary and a "scholastic" debate was held for them. [82]

On August 21, 1858, in a letter to Purcell, Quinlan asked to be relieved of the duties as rector. He felt that his course in theology at the "Mountain" had been too limited. Apparently Purcell felt differently about it, for Quinlan continued on as rector.[83]

In September of 1858, the faculty of the seminary was composed of the following men: Quinlan was the rector of the seminary and taught morality and liturgy: Rosecrans was president of the college and taught dogma: F. Doetz now taught the class in church history and German: O'Leary[84] was the principal in the classical department and taught chemistry and geology; Scammon[85] was the principal of the mathematics department; MacLeod was the principal of rhetoric and belles-letters; Henry Safge taught music and David Walker was the treasurer.[86]

The faculty was thus composed of four priests and four laymen. Father F. Goetz replaced Pabisch who was departing for Europe to pursue further studies. It also was announced that Charles O'Leary had purchased some new "philosophical apparatus" (scientific equipment). [87]

In the same year (1858) there were ninety students at Mount St. Mary's. Purcell had forty of them studying for the diocese here: some were at Mount St. Mary's, Emmitsburg; some were in France; and some were at St. Thomas in Bardstown.

The following comment was made about the course of studies:

Not only is the course a very full one, but the pursuit of it is very thoroughly made. The professors, unfiltered by traditional rules, unswayed by any perhaps worn-out system, conserved simply because it was our grandfather's, have for their main object the communication of knowledge well digested and not the triumph of any set manner of teaching. The results of this were noticed in the classical and philosophical examinations here. [88]

BARRY, RECTOR (1859-1863)

The *Catholic Telegraph* announced on October 29, 1859, that Quinlan had been chosen Bishop of Mobile.[89] The appropriate farewells were made to Quinlan by the faculty, seminarians, and collegians.[90] He had indeed been a good rector, and had been loved by all.

Father Barry, though only twenty-five years of age, succeeded Quinlan as rector. He thus became the third successive Irish rector of Mount St. Mary's. William James Barry was born in the city of Cincinnati on October 13, 1834, of saintly Irish parents. After attending grade school at St. Peter's Cathedral, in 1845 he was student in the old Athenaeum on Sycamore Street, now the College of St. Francis Xavier. Upon the graduation, he went to Mount St. Mary's Seminary at Emmitsburg. Here he studied under William H. Elder, the future Archbishop of Cincinnati. William James Barry in many ways was indeed a remarkable and brilliant young man. During his stay at the "Mountain" he showed not only great learning, but also fineness in character. It seems that he was liked and loved by all who knew him. It was said that had he lived longer than the three years that were yet allotted to him, he would have ranked high among the distinguished men in the history of the Catholic church in America.

On June 6, 1857, he was ordained by Purcell, and celebrated his first Mass in the seminary chapel. In September of 1857, he was sent to Rome. While there, he was a correspondent for the *Catholic Telegraph*. In 1858, he returned to the seminary and took up the classes in church history and philosophy. Upon becoming rector, he had assumed Quinlan's classes in moral theology.

It was unfortunate, however, that this brilliant mind was housed in a very weak body. On December 8, 1862, he suffered a hemorrhage while saying Mass in the seminary chapel. Through the winter and into the spring his condition grew worse, and on April 20, 1863, he died.

He had written quite a bit. His principal work was the *Sacramentals of the Church or Flowers from the Garden of the Liturgy*. He composed several hymns, among them a hymn for Mount St. Mary's Seminary.

During his tenure of office the seminary grew as never before. In fact, it might be said that in reading the accounts of these days, one concluded that the fine spirit prevailing at the seminary was its most remarkable characteristic. It was a deeply religious spirit, extremely priestly; nevertheless, a spirit possessed of a certain kind of robustness—or flamboyancy—which remained with it until the time of the great financial failure in 1879.

In September 1860, Barry was teaching moral theology and philosophy. The rest of the faculty remained the same. It was also mentioned that the tutors of the collegiate department were some of the advanced students of the seminary. Cincinnati had forty students studying for the diocese.[91]

In April of 1861, before the school year was over, the Civil War had begun. It affected the seminary and college in two ways: first some of the laymen and the faculty were to go off to the war; and second, it so sharply curtailed the number of students entering, that the college finally ceased operation in 1863.

On April 28, 1861, the Third Provincial Council of Cincinnati was solemnly opened. It was held throughout the ensuing week and closed Sunday, May 5. Three solemn sessions and four public and five private congregations took place. A great number of topics were discussed by the prelates, but few of them gave rise to legislation. Only twelve decrees were enacted. The eleventh part of the pastoral dealt with ecclesiastical seminaries. It merely urged their support and said that St. Thomas Preparatory and Mount St. Mary's were in good condition. It also had a word of commendation for the American colleges in Rome, Louvain, and all-Hallows in Ireland. [92] On April 28, 1861, the bishops assembled at the Third Provincial Council of Cincinnati visited the seminary and seemed to be well satisfied with it.[93] In the pastoral of the Third Provincial Council of Cincinnati in 1861, it was noted that it cost $2,000.00 to educate one student for the priesthood.[94]

On December 23, 1861, Reverend Sylvester Rosencrans, President of the College, was made coadjutor of Cincinnati. Barry succeeded Rosencrans as Presidnet of the College. Walker was still treasurer.

In September of 1861, there were forty-six students at Mount St. Mary's twenty-six of whom were theologians. Purcell had forty students studying for the diocese at Mount St. Mary's, the American College, Rome, and St. Thomas near Bardstown.[95]

Semi-annual examinations were held the last of June, 1862. Students were examined on metaphysics and theology. Following is a student's account of these examinations, giving a fine picture of the day.[96]

The half-yearly exams of the theologians of Mt. St. Mary's took place on the third of February, 1863. As it was to be held in the presence of more numerous and distinguished spectators than usual, the preparation for it were unwontedly active. For some days beforehand weak points in theology were carefully strengthened, breaches in Scripture and Church history were repaired, arguments were tested as nicely as a Toledo or Damascus blade, the armory of the schoolmen was ransacked for invincible syllogisms, infallible soritae, and other weapons of less formidable name and nature; stubborn facts and steadfast dates were refurbished and made to do service; and to many it seemed that these were inexpugnable in the superlative degree, and their mail as unimpressible as the gorget of King Henry III.

The youngest theologians displayed the rash confidence natural to their age, but the older and more wary ones were less exultant, for they know how often an unaccountable fear and trembling came upon the very bravest, when confronted with the examiners, even as a panic seizes the soul of the swift footed warrior and turns him backwards on his course.

On the morning of the day of examination—the day big with the fate of many high blown hopes—some might be seen carefully turning over the leaves of their books, as if riveting what they had already studied and learned, some "cramming" energetically, despairingly, frantically, some moving about with an unquiet feverish look, and some sitting, standing, walking with the easy unconscious air of the vacant wayfarer in the presence of a robber.

About nine o'clock the prelates and priests began to come in, the Most Reverend Archbishop and Rt. Rev. Bishops Spalding, Luers, and Young arriving first, Bishops Carroll,

Juncker and Wood soon afterwards. Among the priests present were Very Rev. B. Spalding, V.G.; Very Rev. Jos. Ferneding, V.G.; Rev. Fathers Weniger, Sopranis and Murphy, of the Company of Jesus; F. Grander of the Order of Servites of May; E. Stehle, J.F. Goetz and V. R. Mr. Heneweg, O.S.F. At about five minutes past nine the bell tolled for the theologians to march to the place of examination. In a few seconds they entered the hall in order with blanched faces and an uneasy twitching about the mouth, but still stouthearted.

But little time was spent in the arrangements of preliminaries, ere the work began. The theologians looked with astonishment, envy and despair upon the imperturbable coolness of the examiners, and their admirable concerted plan of attack. A striking difference was now observable in their deportment and mine. They who, erewhile, were confident and elate, were now disconcerted and chest-fallen; whereas, those who had a few days ago been reserved and seemingly fearful, now stood stiffest in the stow.

Yet did all carry themselves right bravely. Some, it is true, were overwhelmed by the ruins of their battered strongholds, and others were unhorsed and smothered, or hopelessly encumbered in their fall by the panoply wherein they were right, but all did their devoir like gallant knights.

At the close of the examination, which was about four-o'clock in the afternoon, a monument to patience and the interest with which the bishops and priests regarded the progress of the seminarians, the following address was presented by them to the assembled clergy:

"Most Rev. Archbishop, Right Rev. Bishops, Reverend Fathers: Your presence among us today would be another proof, if proof were needed, of the deep interest you feel in our welfare. Yet it is but one more added to a long series of kindnesses and favours, so precious as to shame the poverty of our acknowledgements. It were not a return worthy of you, and it would be unfilial in us, to endeavor or wish to repay them with the cheap gratitude of words. But we are encourage to hope that your graciousness and the sincerity with which we will say our humble mite is offered, may give to it, in your eyes, and value not its own.

We have just presented to you the fruits of our studies during the last half-year, and we have been abundantly recompensed by your kind words and smiles of approval.

And now to give us new strength for our coming labours, whereby we may deserve still farther marks of your approbation, we beg your blessing."

At the conclusion of the address, the Archbishop gave the Seminarians his blessing, and spoke to them a few words of advice and encouragement to persevere in well-doing.

On April 20, 1863, after a long period of suffering, the young and brilliant Barry died. He was only twenty-eight years old.[97] Pabisch over his classes in Moral, and Corcoran[98] became rector for the remainder of the year.

PABISCH, RECTOR (1863-1879)
In September of 1863, Francis Joseph Pabisch became rector of Mount St. Mary's Seminary. He was the first rector of Mount St. Mary's Seminary of German descent, and held this office

longer than any other rector in the history of the seminary. He was a man who had already distinguished himself for great intellectual abilities. It might be said in all truth that from every aspect, Mount St. Mary's Seminary in Price Hill reached its highest point of development while he was rector. In 1887 when the seminarians returned after the financial failure, the seminary did enjoy a great measure of success, but did not seem to be able to recapture the spirited days of Barry and Pabisch.

Pabisch was born in Zlabling, Moravia, on May 30, 1825. On August 3, 1850, after years of studying philosophy and theology at the University of Vienna, he was ordained a priest by Cardinal Rauscher.

On a visit to Vienna in 1850, Purcell met Pabisch and was impressed with him. Invited to come to Cincinnati, Pabisch arrived here in 1851, and was immediately given the task of teaching Scripture and church history at the new seminary. However, at the end of the year he asked permission to engage in parochial work, and was sent to St. James in White Oak. In 1857, he was recalled to the seminary to again teach Sacred Scripture and church history. The next year, however, in October 1858, he asked permission to go to the Dominican College Minerva in Rome for further studies. After four years of study, he returned to Cincinnati in the summer of 1863 and succeeded Corcoran as rector of Mount St. Mary's Seminary. During his long tenure as rector (sixteen years), the seminary did indeed prosper. He himself was a scholar, and he gathered around him and maintained an excellent group of professors. He himself worked incessantly in the field of church history and moral theology, the two subjects, which he taught during his long stay in the seminary. [99] In a sense it was more than just a translation since it was corrected and enlarged with his own learning. It was one of the few textbooks produced for American seminaries in the ecclesiastical sciences. Today, of course, it is obsolete, but it was a manual which was used for many years.

In June of the year 1879, he was forced to resign as rector of the seminary. His physical constitution, which was never too strong, was overburdened by work and by the mental anguish of great financial failure which descended upon his great friend and superior, the Archbishop of Cincinnati.

In later years the students would say that had anyone possessed the sanctity of a Barry, the logical mind of a Rosecrans, the elegance of a MacLeod, and the general knowledge of a Pabisch, he would be, in the natural and supernatural orders, a perfect man.

Of Pabisch, one of his pupils later wrote:

A priest for a quarter of a century leaving as the sweetest recollection a noble life; a spotless name; a true Israelite without guile, a Christian Gabriel, at whose feet hundreds of priests of many dioceses have learned the lessons of wisdom; a rarely gifted teacher of the divine science, whose erudition would have made him a loved pupil of the Angel of the Schools whose writings were his daily food and highest earthly pleasure; an intellectual giant, even among men of gifted minds, yet a child in the innocence of life. [100]

At the entrance of Mount St. Mary's Seminary on the first floor just before entering the chapel, there is a marble plaque in his memory. It was erected by his students at the time of his death, and in the early days stood at the entrance of Mount St. Mary's in Price Hill.

At the beginning of Pabisch's first year as rector of the seminary (September, 1863), very few students returned to the college. It seems that a goodly number were from the southern states. At least two of the lay members of the faculty had gone off to the war and, under the circumstances, it was impossible to find replacements for them. Thus, it was decided to close the college. The seminarians who were studying for the diocese of Cincinnati were kept on, but were now called "preparatorians." Up until the close of the seminary in 1879, these "preparatorians" were housed in the old college quarters on Price Hill. After the war Purcell never attempted to reestablish the "mixed" college. One explanation of this might be the fact that the number of seminarians greatly increased during the post-war period, and he just did not have room to start the college again.[101]

On October 20, 1863, while some men were making roof repairs, they neglected to take down with them their fire-pot when they went for dinner. The roof caught fire and the students, coming out for their recreation, were horrified to see the building ablaze. The chapel, with its famous painting of St. John the Baptist, was destroyed, as well as half the adjacent wing, which contained the library, one of the finest in the world at the time. The students tried to save the books, but a number of priceless volumes snatched from the fire were practically ruined by being hurled from the windows.[102]

The fire of 1863 also deserves a place in the lore of the seminary because of the heroism of one Barney McCabe, the seminary busman. It is related that at the height of the fire in the chapel wing, the flames had leaped to the cupola at the top of the central structure, and threatened to engulf the entire seminary. Two companies of firemen (who arrived one and one-half hour after the discovery of the blaze) were unable to make their way through the dense smoke to reach the stairs leading to the cupola. Then Mr. McCabe took over. As the seminary chronicle reports it:

> It was at this critical moment that Barney McCabe, the busman, his quick eye which had so often directed the ship with unerring accuracy over the backs of the old steeds that brought the young men from the city, taking the situation in at a glance, his true Celtic heart nerved to desperation at the imminent danger which threatened the home of the young "soggarths," snatched up the hose from the firemen, dashed through the black smoke, up the corridor and cupola until he emerged breathless and begrimed, amid the cheers of all, upon the blazing roof. [103]

He extinguished the fire and thus saved the remaining part of the building.

Later that fall, Pabisch and the seminary suffered another great loss in the resignation of two of the ablest members of the faculty, Rosecrans and MacLeod. Bishop Rosecrans, because of the press of duties as auxiliary of Cincinnati, found it now impossible to make the daily trip to the seminary. MacLeod took over a little parish in Sedamsville. Almost two years later, June 30, 1865, he was killed while crossing the tracks of the Ohio & Mississippi and Indianapolis

& Cincinnati Railroad in his parish. He had been called that day to the bedside of a dying parishioner. Turning into the street which crossed the tracks, he was halted by a train. Standing on the tracks at a sharp bend in the road, he failed to hear the warning of another train coming from the opposite direction. The Cincinnati newspaper printed glowing tributes to the character, scholarship, and great personal charm of the former linguist, philosopher and poet of the seminary.

About December of the year 1863, O'Regan took over the class in dogmatic theology which Rosecrans had taught for so many years. Daniel O'Regan had been ordained the previous May in the Church of St. John the Lateran in Rome. There he had earned his degree in theology. Returning home in September, he was put in charge of the college section until it was decided to close it, at which time he was put in charge of the preparatorians. Kerwin, in his history of Mount St. Mary's, mistakenly lists him as one of the rectors.[104]

In September of 1864, Pabisch was the rector and was teaching the course in moral theology and canon law. O'Regan was the vice-rector and was teaching the course in dogma. Two new acquisitions to the faculty were Fathers Joseph Fitzgerald and James F. Callaghan,[105] both of whom had arrived in the latter part of the previous school year. Fitzgerald was procurator, and Callaghan taught English.

In this year of 1864, the student body of the seminary consisted of fifty-six students, twenty-four of whom were theologians and thirty-two preparatorians. Later that year, December 8, 1864, the new chapel of the seminary was dedicated and placed under the patronage of St. John the Baptist. The Archbishop officiated at the ceremony and was assisted by the faculty and seminarians, together with a large delegation of priests from Ohio and Kentucky. The new altar of the chapel was built by Mr. J. Marienfeld of Cincinnati.

At the opening of the new school year in 1865, O'Regan left the faculty and was replaced by Joseph Richter who took over the class in dogma. Patrick Quinn was appointed the procurator of the seminary that year also, succeeding Fitzgerald. Rosecrans returned to reside at the seminary.[106]

Henry Joseph Richter, Born April 9, 1838, was a student at Mount St. Mary's of the West from 1857 to 1860. After ordination, he was sent to Rome where he obtained his doctorate in theology in 1865. He then returned to Cincinnati and immediately was assigned to teach dogmatic theology in the seminary. He took Father O'Regan's place. In 1869, he became pastor of St. Lawrence Church in Price Hill and continued to teach at the seminary. In 1883 he was appointed the first Bishop of Grand Rapids. He died on December 26, 1916.[107]

The other new member of the faculty that year was Patrick Quinn. He was born in the county of Tyrone, Ireland, on August 28, 1828, and came to Cincinnati in 1853 as a Christian Brother. He taught in the Cathedral school for five years and was known as "Brother Moses." In 1858 he entered Mount St. Mary's of the west as a theological student. There he remained as procurator until he was ordained by Rosecrans on February 24, 1870. He was then stationed at Greenville; the Cathedral; Urbana; St. Joseph's Orphan Asylum; Glendale; Hamilton; and Chillicothe. He died April 5, 1890, at St. Martin's Brown County, and was buried in the little cemetery where Archbishop Purcell was laid to rest.

In the annual report published in the *Telegraph* for the period July 1, 1865 to July 1, 1866, the total receipts for the seminary amounted to $17,859.45. The expenses amounted to $19,106.30. It was noted that the cost of board and educate each student was $267.25.[108]

In September of 1866, it is interesting to note that the *Telegraph* made mention of the fact that three professors on the faculty (Pabisch, Rosecrans, and Richter) were men who were educated and who had received their degrees in Rome.[109]

In was indeed noteworthy because this did mark the beginning of a trend for the seminary. Previous to this, the philosophical and the theological learning in the seminary had been largely Sulpician and in the spirit of Mount St. Mary's, Emmitsburg. The learning and the degrees were in the future to be Roman in increasing measure. Callaghan and Quinn were the other members of the faculty.[110]

In September of 1866, no doubt due to the ending of the war and the period of reconstruction, there was a marked increase in the total number of students at Mount St. Mary's. There were now eighty students at the seminary: eighteen theologians; eight philosophers; and fifty-three "preparatorians." All but two of these were students studying for the Archdiocese of Cincinnati.[111]

In this year, 1866, the authors used in the various texts were: Rothenflue in philosophy; Perrone in dogmatic theology; Gury in moral; Alzog in church history; Dixon in Scripture; and DeHerdt in liturgy.[112]

In October 1866, the Second Plenary Council of Baltimore opened. The Council devoted an entire chapter of its legislative enactments to the organization and administration of seminaries and to curriculum. In the curriculum, chief stress was laid on dogmatic and moral theology, canon law, exegesis, and homiletics.[113] It called for the financial support of seminaries.[114]

This Second Plenary Council of Baltimore commended the seminary in Cincinnati for having public examination, and gave this as one good reason for the establishment of provincial seminaries:[115]

> We are glad to see the system of public examinations adopted by the learned rector of Mt. St. Mary's of the West, the well-known theological seminary in the archdiocese of Cincinnati. It is but lately that we saw in the Cincinnati paper a public notice of the examinations to be held in the above seminary; a schedule also of the matter of examination and a list of the textbooks employed by the students were added, and an invitation was extended to the priests of the city and vicinity to assist at the examinations.
>
> Many of our small diocesan seminaries, it is but too true, could not very well suffer the light of day to shine upon their examinations. They are but poorly supplied with competent professors, their means being insufficient to enable them to provide for all the requirements belonging to a well-constituted seminary.
>
> It has, moreover, only too often happened that the professors of these small seminaries were , as the Fathers of Baltimore term the, "sacerdotes vagabundi," wandering from diocese

to diocese, and who began to teach theology as a last resort, when all else had failed. Hence the position of a professor of theology was looked upon by the rest of the clergy with mingled feelings of commiseration and contempt. Yet all this cannot be attributed to any personal fault on the part of the various rectors of such institutions. The chief mistake lies perhaps in a mis-apprehension of the proper status due to a professor of theology.

The discipline will naturally suffer under these circumstances. All these defects are easily remedied in provincial seminaries, where a good staff of professors can be engaged, and discipline properly enforced.

As therefore, in many parts, means are wanting to maintain diocesan seminaries, provincial seminaries as ordered by the Council of Trent and recommended by the American prelates would seem to be of all others best calculated to train candidates for the priesthood in this country.

In the financial report of June 7, 1867, the receipts and expenses of the seminary remained just about the same as the previous year. Receipts were listed as $16,277.17 and expenditures amounted to $16,540. In the following year, 1868, the enrollment of the seminary increased by one-third over the enrollment of the previous year. One hundred and thirty students poured through the gates off Warsaw Avenue. For this reason, Purcell decided to add the north wing to the building. Mr. and Mrs. R. R. Springer gave eleven thousand dollars to the bishop so that he might begin construction. It was not until two years later that the corner-stone was laid. The new structure was completed in the summer of 1870, and it was estimated that it had cost forty thousand dollars. The building was four stories high, like the opposite wing, and the thenceforward to be used as a refectory, library, lecture hall and for the private rooms of the students.[116]

In September of 1867, the faculty was composed of Pabisch, Richter, Bonner, Callaghan, and Quinn. Rosecrans had left to take charge of parish in Columbus. In March of 1868, he was appointed the first Bishop of Columbus, Richard Gilmour came in April, 1868. He was born in Glasgow, Scotland, on September 28, 1824. He was ordained in Cincinnati in 1852. After serving in various parishes of the diocese for sixteen years, he was appointed to teach at Mount St. Mary's. He taught the remainder of that year and the entire following year. After that he became pastor of St. Joseph's Church in Dayton and ultimately the Bishop of Cleveland in 1872.[117]

In this year of 1868, Pabisch, Richter, Bonner, Callaghan, Gilmour, and Quinn were still on the faculty. It was in this year also that Bernard Henry Engbers came to the faculty. Engbers was born October 11, 1845, in Dalen, near Meppen in Hanover, Germany. He came to this country in 1866 and settled in Cincinnati where he entered the seminary. During his last years as a student he taught Latin. He was ordained on February 6, 1868, and was appointed a full-time professor. It was the beginning of a long and brilliant career of service in the work of the seminary. He continued to teach the Latin classic until the seminary closed in 1879. He then taught the classics at Mount St. Mary's of the East at Emmitsburg for one year. He then returned to Cincinnati and became pastor of St. Rose Church in Fulton, which is now the East End of Cincinnati. Chapter Five considers the important roles he and Richter played in the founding of St. Gregory's Seminary in Mount Washington.[118]

The annual report for Mount St. Mary's was made in the *Catholic Telegraph* of May 12, 1869. It had cost $22,830.00 to operate the seminary in the fiscal year then ending. Receipts, on the other hand, amounted to $21,051.52, leaving a deficit of $1,778.38. The tuition charge was then $150.00 for the ten-month session.[119]

When school took up in 1869 there were one hundred nineteen students; thirty-four theologians, twelve philosophers, and seventy-three preparatorians. The diocese of Cincinnati had eighty-eight students, and the remainder were from the following diocese: Fort Wayne, Columbus, Little Rock, Alton, Covington, Nashville, and Providence, Rhode Island.[120]

In September of 1869 the faculty was composed of Pabisch, Cusack, Richter, Byrne, Quinn, Hecht, Engbers, Geyer, and Mr. J.M. Murray, M.D. Doctor Murray taught the classes in chemistry. Callaghan had been asked by the brother of the bishop, Edward Purcell, to help in the work of the diocesan newspaper, the *Catholic Telegraph*. Callaghan was a capable writer and in the remaining years before the financial trouble of 1879, he did some very fine work on the paper's staff.

The first newcomer this year was Thomas Sebastian Byrne. He was born in Hamilton, Ohio, on July 29, 1841 and was ordained to the priesthood on May 22, 1869. Father Byrne served as procurator and subsequently as professor in the College Department of Mount St. Mary's of the West until the year 1879. When the seminary was reopened in 18887, Elder appointed Father Byrne the new rector. On July 25, 1894, he was consecrated Bishop of Nashville. Bishop Byrne aided Doctor Pabisch in translating Alzog's three volumes of church history. He himself did a great deal of translating form the Italian and the French. He died in Nashville on September 4, 1923, and was buried in the cemetery at Mount St. Joseph on the Ohio.[121]

The other important addition to the faculty that year was the Reverend Edward Hecht, D.D., D.C.L. Father Hecht was born in 1836, at Ruffach, near Colmar, in Alsace, of pious and wealthy Catholic parents. His native birthplace, the Rubacum of the Romans, was an old historical town of about 4,000 inhabitants. Near this famous town was the castle of Egisheim where Pope Leo IX was born. Westward were the Vosges Mountains from which a magnificent view of the fertile plains of upper Alsace, the valley of the Phine and the far distant plains of upper Alsace, the valley of the Rhine and the far distant mountains of the Black Forest, Ruffach was in the olden times a favorite residence of the Kings of the Merovingian Line.[122]

Edward Hecht was baptized and made his First Communion in St. Arbogast Church, a basilica of the Roman style of architecture, completed in the twelfth century. He first attended the schools of hi native town and, then afterwards, attended the gymnasium. A lamentable accident that occurred about this time had a great influence on the young man. Two of his fellow-students were drowned while bathing in the little stream that flowed near the town, and the principal of the college narrowly escaped death while attempting to rescue them. This sad event turned the thoughts of the young student to serious thoughts of priesthood.

Completing his classical studies, Edward went to the Preparatory Seminary of Strasbourg, and, under the able teaching of the Reverend Chasine Reich, he completed his philosophy. This seminary in the 20's and 40's had an unequaled staff of professors. Among them were Reverend Beautain, the bishop of Rouen; the Reverend Meratin, afterwards principal of the college of Tuilly; and some celebrated converts from Judaism. At the end of the year Hecht passed with success his examination, and was admitted into the grand seminary.[123]

At the Grand Seminary in Strasbourg, Hecht spent the next four years in the study of theology. While in the seminary at Strasbourg, he began his lifelong interest and study of dogmatic theology. Coming home, he was then appointed professor in the Preparatory Seminary of Strasbourg and there he remained until 1865. At this time, at the invitation of Bishop of Hungary, he assumed the chair of dogmatic theology in his seminary. In 1869, while Purcell was traveling through Europe, he had the occasion to meet Hecht and liked him very much. At the request of Purcell, who always kept a sharp lookout for capable professors for his seminary, Hecht came to America and for ten years taught the class in dogma at Mount St. Mary's Seminary. After the closing of Mount St. Mary's Seminary in 1879, Bishop Gilmour offered him a like position in the Cleveland Seminary where he remained until August, 1887, when he returned to teach again at Mount St. Mary's.[124]

He died on June 9, 1888, at Mount St. Mary's. The plaque located in the main corridor of the seminary at present was given by the alumni as a memorial to him. He was indeed one of the all-time great teachers of Mount St. Mary's.

In the middle of the year, Pabisch became ill and was not able to teach his classes. In a letter to the Archbishop, he wrote of the good conditions at the seminary, and asked for permission to have Hecht take over his classes in morality.[125]

The *Telegraph* noted in the latter part of the summer that there were now six professors on the faculty who had been educated in Rome; five of them—Pabisch, Cusack, Richter, Hecht, and Geyer—had received the Doctor of Divinity degree, and one, Engbers, had a doctorate in philosophy. It was with good reason that the Archbishop could at this time boast that:

> We know not if the American College in Rome will be continued or reopened or whether it will be worthwhile to send students any more to foreign seminaries. But it is gratifying to reflect that we have no longer any need to seek elsewhere for what our domestic training so amply affords.[126]

This, undoubtedly, was the reason there were no great or significant changes in the faculty for the next six years. Richter and Murray left at the end of the school year in 1871. But the names of Pabisch, Hecht, Cusack, and Byrne formed the nucleus of the faculty up until 1876.

During the winter of 1871, it had become painfully evident that the chapel constructed after the fire of 1863 was in danger of collapse. After the fire of 1863, the walls were left standing and were used to support a new roof. In 1871, it was quite evident that this had been a mistake. The fire and the water had done too much damage to the foundation. With the first break of spring, the old chapel was then torn down, new foundations were sunk, and work on the new chapel was started. The work proceeded very rapidly all through the summer and into the fall. On December 14, the new chapel was dedicated, again under the patronage of St. John the Baptist.[127]

It was of the pure and chaste Gothic style architecture, the ceiling groined and immaculately white. The walls were blocked off into the different colors of rough Irish and Scotch granite. The windows were of ground glass with stained borders. The floor of the chapel was eighty-seven feet long and twenty-nine feet wide. The chapel was thirty-one feet long and twenty-nine feet wide. The sanctuary contained besides the altar and the seats for the sacred ministers, the Archbishop's throne and forty-four stalls for the professors and theologians. The ornamentation of the choir and the organ corresponded with the rest of the Gothic interior. The entire work in the chapel was done by William Cameron & Son of Cincinnati.[128]

The examination of June, 1871 show that Perrone was still used in dogma; Gury[129] was used in moral; Darras was used in church history; Dixon was used in Sacred Scripture; and DeHerdt in Liturgy. Ferrante was now used in canon law, and Tongiorgi was still used in philosophy.[130]

In September of 1871, the only new member of the faculty was the Reverend J. Kristoffey. Father Kristoffey was born in Hungary, ordained there, and received a doctorate in theology after completing studies in Rome. He was a man of wide culture, acquainted with many oriental languages, and held in great esteem by those who knew him in Hungary. He left the faculty, however, in 1873.

In this year, it seems there was an unusually large number of students, well over the one hundred and twenty-six of the previous year. For the first time in the history of the seminary, two examination boards were set up for the examinations in February. One board examined the preparatorians on Latin, history, English, and German; the other board examined the students on Greek, mathematics, natural sciences, and French.

The school years of 1872, 1873, and 1874, passed very quickly. The seminary seemed to have finally stabilized itself. It had an excellent faculty which was equal to that famous group which had taught in the days before the war. This was the second high point in the history of the seminary at Price Hill. Later it would come close to duplicating the superb faculty of these days, but not the before being transferred to Mount Washington.

In 1875, C. S. Kemper, Florence Bruggs, and J. F. Feldman came. Father Kemper remained for only two years. The others, Bruggs and Feldman, remained until the close of the seminary in 1879. Later Father Kemper returned to teach the classics as St. Gregory's Seminary. The older priests of the diocese, who knew him from his days as St. Gregory's claimed that he was a very learned man and a fine teacher. For the last part of his life he was an invalid and resided at St. Francis Hospital. He died there in April, 1920.[131]

On February 5, 1866, the new library in the new north wing of the seminary was formally opened. Engbers began the difficult task of putting order into the chaotic situation which had grown over the years. With the help of such students as John Feldman, William Manning, and George Houck, he began the difficult task of cataloging all the previous acquisitions.[132]

In 1876, Cusack, the vice-rector, left and in the following year, 1877, Byrne and Kemper left. IN 1876, John Femotti replaced Cusack. The following year, he in turn was replaced by Henry Moeller (the future Archbishop of Cincinnati.)[133]

In this year of 1876, the attendance at the seminary had dropped to ninety-seven students. Twenty-two of these were theologians, fifteen were in philosophy, and sixty were preparatorians. The students attending at this time were from the dioceses of Cincinnati, Columbus, Fort Wayne, Detroit, Covington, Alton and Little Rock.

In the middle of this school year, it seems that Byrne and Pabisch began to have differences of opinion as to the quantity and quality of discipline both for the students in philosophy and theology, and for the students in their preparatory years. Pabisch was not a strict disciplinarian; Byrne certainly was. Perhaps it was inevitable that the two would clash. At the close of this school year in 1877, it was apparent that the word of the clash had reached the ears of the Archbishop.

This is the reason that before he left the seminary in 1877, Byrne wrote a memorandum to the Archbishop in answer to the Archbishop's request that he "set down in writing what you think deficient in the present system of government and studies at the seminary."

In regard to discipline, Byrne proposed that the discipline of the house be handled by one person, distinct from the rector of the seminary. He proposed that such a person "promulgate all the rules and such cautions as time and circumstance require, that he punish of his own authority any infraction of rules; that he correct of himself any abuse that may come under his notice; in short, that he have complete and entire control of the discipline." For this office he proposed the name of reverend W. M. Carey. Bryne suggested that he be given the name of rector, and should be in full and complete charge and control of discipline and the classes of the preparatory departments.[134]

In regard to studies, Byrne felt that professors should be selected in a better way than in the past. He suggested the Reverend Mr. Ahern to succeed the Reverend Engbers, who was leaving. He also suggested that the rector should endeavor to "draw out a curriculum of studies, determine the classbooks belonging to each grade and year of the course, settle on the number of professors requisite, and in this way have something fixed definite and satisfactory, and not be changing year after year."[135]

The last faculty at Mount St. Mary's, before the storm struck, consisted of Pabisch, Hecht, Engbers, Bruggs, Feldman and Moeller. With the run on the bank in December of 1878, financial failure beset the diocese.

Pabisch overworked for many years and closely associated with the Archbishop in all his work, found the strain of the financial collapse too much. It broke him physically and mentally as well. In June of 1879, he was forced to resign, and Doctor Hecht was appointed rector of the seminary for the remainder of the year. Pabisch died the following October 2, 1879. He was mourned by the Archbishop as one of his truest friends and wisest counselors, and by the many students whom he had so ably prepared for the work of the priesthood.

The history of the library at Mount St. Mary's Seminary begins[136] on Sycamore Street at the old Athenacum. Purcell gave his personal collection of books to the seminary in those days. Having served as president of Mount St. Mary's Seminary at Emmitsburg, his collection was quite extensive. Because of the vicissitudes of the days at Brown County, the Jesuits scholasticate and the Episcopal residents, the seminary's library did not fare too well. The books which were left after all of this traveling, were placed in the library reading room located on the second floor of the new seminary on Price Hill. Purcell was greatly interested in enlarging and furthering the development of the library. In 1853, a valuable collection of books from the Reverend L. Navarron was added. It contained about two hundred volumes. At the same time, eighty volumes were received from Reverends Michael Kennedy and Whittler.

The fire of 1863 which destroyed the chapel and southern wing of the seminary looked like it was going to make its way to the library. To save the books in this crisis, they were pitched out windows by the students. The loss which resulted due to books being lost, mutilated, torn, and damaged by water was very extensive.

In the autumn of 1865, Purcell gave the seminary another collection of five thousand volumes. In August of the same year, Reverend Edward Collins, Vicar-General of the Archdiocese, and a former teacher at the old Athenaeum on Sycamore Street died. He bequeathed to the seminary his entire library valued between twenty and twenty-five thousand dollars and numbering forty-eight hundred volumes.

In 1870 the north wing of the seminary was erected at the cost of fifty thousand dollars. In it was housed a truly magnificent library for the times. Pictures of the library clearly attest to its extensiveness and completeness.

However, the administration of the library seemingly was not handled with any degree of success until 1873, at which time it came under the supervision of Engbers, who supervised for many years the laborious task of cataloguing the books.

Other gifts to the seminary library at this time included five hundred and seventy three volumes donated by Edward Purcell, and three hundred and forty volumes donated by David Walker.

The new library was formally opened on February 5, 1876, and at that time contained fourteen thousand one hundred and sixty-eight volumes.

In 1876 Edward Purcell donated four thousand more volumes from a special collection of Mr. J. J. Rickey. In 1879, when the seminary closed, the care of the institution and old library was placed in the hands of caretakers. They did not take good care of either the building or the library. During the period the seminary was closed there was a great deal of vandalism and looting, and in the process the seminary lost many of its books.

THE DECISION TO CLOSE THE SEMINARY (1879)

The Purcell financial failure was the collapse of a financial structure which had been built up over a period of forty years by Father Edward Purcell, the Archbishop's brother. The

Archbishop, who never attempted to conceal his own lack of sagacity in monetary matters, had entrusted the diocesan finances to his brother from the time of the latter's ordination in 1838. At this time the diocesan funds included a certain sum which several Catholics had deposited with Bishop Purcell for safekeeping during the national depression of 1837. Subsequent financial panics and bank failures in 1842, 1854, and 1857, and especially the great panic of 1873, induced other Catholics to turn their savings over to Father Edward Purcell, who seems to have conducted what amounted to an informal savings and loan company. It is estimated that in the forty years in which the "company" operated, Father Purcell handled receipts in the excess of thirteen million dollars.

The entire structure collapsed late in 1878 after a series of unwise investments and bank failures. There was a run on Father Purcell's "bank" and at one in December, 1878, a crowd of depositors clamored at the Cathedral doors for their money.

No one ever questioned the honesty of Father Purcell or of the Archbishop Purcell in this matter. In the opinion of the diocesan trustees, who investigated the failure, the collapse was due to the "large amount paid in interest, bad investments, shrinkage in value, misplaced confidence and unbusinesslike management."

The creditors, numbering more than three thousand, sought to attach Catholic parish and institutional property to cover their losses, but the Cincinnati District Court, after a protracted review of the case, decided that they had a legal claim only upon the few churches and diocesan institutions which had been directly aided by funds from Father Purcell's Bank. The Ohio Supreme Court upheld the decision.[137] The seminary was one of these obligations.

Some of these obligations were met by means of gifts, bazaars, donations from bishops and priests, but only a fraction of the deposits, which at the time of the failure totaled close to four million dollars was returned.

The failure led to considerable bitterness, and resulted in some defections from the faith. The material advance of the diocese was halted for almost a generation.

On July 18, 1879, the decision was made to close the seminary. In announcing the decision, Purcell wrote the following letter:[138]

Beloved Catholics of the Archdiocese of Cincinnati: We are under the painful necessity of informing you, that with the advice of our esteemed and trustworthy council, we have come the conclusion to close, for at least one year, the Archdiocesan Seminary, Mt. St. Mary's of the West. Our reasons for this conclusion are several:

First—During the thirty-one years of its existence, whilst it accomplished great good, we had to struggle hard to support it, and to incur heavy debts which we find it difficult to liquidate. The present stringency of the times forbids the hope of immediate payment of these debts.

Second—Another reason for closing the seminary at the present time is the absence of any pressing need of priests for the mission of the diocese. We have all that the diocese requires. There are three students in European seminaries concluding the ordinary course of philosophical and theological studies before ordination; for these we have no vacant missions or parishes.

Moreover, the closing of the seminary will give us five priests, members of the faculty, to be otherwise employed.

Third—The temporary closing of the seminary will be a diminution of the burdens which the Catholics of the diocese are now striving to carry with so much good will and devotion to the cause of religion. The seminary has been placed as diocesan property in the hands of the assignee. He would be compelled by law to charge rent for its occupation until the financial difficulties for the diocese are settled. This rental would amount to a sum which our generous diocesans would not be able to pay in addition to the current expenses of the seminary.

We might give as another reason, the illness of the late president, the Rev. Dr. Joseph Pabisch, the most learned and devoted ecclesiastic, who has seriously injured his health by overwork as professor, and by excessive study. It will be months before he has recovered his wasted strength of mind and body. His constant occupation during the period of four years, in translating Alzog's History, which he enriched with elaborate notes and learning additions, has sadly enfeebled him, and compelled him to give up the position which he filled for fifteen years with the highest honors to himself, and with incalculable benefit to the diocese. Under these distressing circumstances we bow to the adorable will of God.

With the announcement, an era came to a close. The students left that summer and were told that they would have to go elsewhere at least for the coming year. The professors were given other assignments, and the doors of the seminary were locked. It was thought then that it would be for only a short time. But no one, even in July of 1879, realized the full extent of the calamity. The doors of the seminary were to remain closed for almost a decade. It, indeed, was a sad day in the history of the Church of Cincinnati!

SUMMARY

This chapter has covered the history of the seminary of Mount St. Mary's from 1851, the date when it was established on Price Hill, to 1879, the year it was closed because of the financial failure of Purcell. Purcell's early plans for the seminary on Price Hill and his proposals for financing the institution were considered. The seminary opened in 1851 with Hallinan as rector. In its very early years Purcell had ideas about making his seminary on the hill into a regional seminary. During the First Provincial Council of Cincinnati, pontifical status and the power to award degrees was asked for, but ultimately denied by Rome. In 1855, the seminary was incorporated as an educational institution, under the then existing laws of Ohio, with the power to grant degrees. During the tenure of Quinlan, Mount St. Mary's College opened in the southern wing of the seminary under the direction of Rosecrans as president. In 1859, the brilliant Barry became rector and was succeed in 1863 by Pabisch. Because of the war, the college existed only 1863. In 1879, the seminary was closed because of the financial failure of the archdiocese.

In the particular period discussed, the seminary was blessed with a fine group of pious and learned men as rectors. One is amazed at the energy Purcell must have expanded over the years to acquire such a group. Hallinan, Quinlan, Barry, and Pabisch had no peer in the entire country. They were totally committed to the work of the seminary and to its spiritual and intellectual development. They had all done graduate work in their respective fields and were well qualified.

The faculty members during this era produced many books in their respective fields, and it seems that had not the financial failure come along when it did, many more works would have been forthcoming.

During this time the study of theology and philosophy was greatly improved. For one thing, there was a great deal of stability in the faculty during this period and, on the whole, quality of the highest order was maintained. Emerging from this period was the "core" curriculum of future years; in theology, the big five—dogma, moral, Sacred Scripture, church history, and canon law; in philosophy, the emphasis was placed upon a well-rounded course of two years. On the other hand, the seminary's classical course reached an extremely high point of development. The scholars who taught in this field were men with eminent educational backgrounds from the colleges of the East and from Europe.

In this era, the enrollment of the seminary had climbed steadily. From the figures available, the number of students reached well past the one hundred thirty mark in total annual enrollment. For seven successive years, close to ninety of these students were studying for Purcell's diocese alone.

The exuberant spirit of Mount St. Mary's Seminary during its youthful days on Price Hill must have been marvelous to behold. The enthusiasm, the dedication, the devotion, the work, the deep feeling of comradeship, and the great sense of mission shared by both the faculty and the students as they went about the task of preparing for the great work of the vineyard was indeed tremendous. These days wrote a splendid page in the history of the institution, and were never again to be duplicated at Price Hill. They bring into sharp focus the wrenching misfortune and the calamity of the financial failure.

NOTES
[1] *Catholic Telegraph*, January 31, 1982, p. 4.
[2] Deed, Patrick Considine to J. B. Purcell, recorded in Book No. 129, p. 470. It should be noted this Considine title was later found defective and involved Purcell in some later litigation. *Catholic Telegraph*, October 4, 1884, p.1.
[3] *Ibid.*, June 3, 1852, p. 4.
[4] Kelly and Kirwin, *op. cit.*, p. 61.
[5] This was apparently lost when the building was torn down in 1962.
[6] A synod is a meeting of the priest of a diocese, preside over by the bishop, which adopts legislation affecting the Church within the diocese.
[7] Deye, *op. cit.*, p. 344.
[8] Deye, *op. cit.*, p. 345.
[9] In the years ahead, Purcell was also to ask every clergyman of the diocese to contribute ten dollars annually to the support of the seminary. Lists of the clergy and the laity who con-

tribute were generally published in the *Telegraph*. *Catholic Telegraph*, May 22, 1855, p. 4. Letter, Reverend J. A. Kelly to Purcell, April 25, 1859, MSMSA.

[10] It will be seen later that the there was a time just before the reopening of Mt. St. Mary's in 1887 that Archbishop Elder contemplated using religious to staff his seminary.

[11] Letter, Guitter, Montreal, May 21, 1850, to Purcell, Cin., UNDA.

[12] The Sulpician Fathers were founded by H. Olier, in 1643 as a society of secular priests in France devoted exclusively to the training of men for service on seminary faculties. They derived their name from the Church of St. Sulpice in Paris near which this institute was founded. The Sulpicians were identified with the seminarians the United States from the very beginning, having founded the first seminary of Mount St. Mary's in Baltimore, and Mount St. Mary's at Emmitsburg. Since these two institutions exerted such a far-reaching influence on the spirit they almost totally colored the philosophy of clerical training until approximately 1875. They still have a great influence on the training of priest in the United States.

[13] Journal of Father Decluol as quoted in Lamott, *op. cit.*, p. 291.

[14] Letter, Bodin, Cincinnati, to Purcell, Cincinnati, April 2, 1851, UNDA.

[15] Letter, Moeller to Purcell, October 9, 1851, UNDA.

[16] Purcell to O'Connor, February 16, 1853, as quoted in Deye, *op. cit.*, p. 345.

[17] Lamott, *op. cit.*, p. 291.

[18] *Catholic Telegraph*, November 1, 1851, p. 4.

[19] *Ibid.*, November 1, 1851, p.4.

[20] *Catholic Telegraph*, August 16, 1851, p. 3.

[21] Kelley and Kirwin, *op. cit.*, p. 105.

[22] Kelley and Kirwin, *op. cit.*, p. 106.

[23] *Catholic Telegraph*, June 30, 1853, p. 5.

[24] *Catholic Telegraph*, January 26, 1852, p. 4.

[25] Kelley and Kirwin, *op. cit.*, p. 74. He resigned in January, 1853 due to bad health.

[26] *Ibid.*, p.75.

[27] Kelley and Kirwin, *op. cit.*, 76.

[28] *Ibid.*, p.77.

[29] Catholic Directory of 1853, pp. 81, 82, 87.

[30] *Catholic Telegraph*, January 8, 1853, p. 4. He was ordained on October 15, 1853.

[31] *Ibid.*, July 15, 1854, p. 5.

[32] Thomas T. McAvoy, *The Great Crisis in American Catholic History: 1985-1990*, pp.23-24. Chicago: Henry Reynery Company, 1960.

[33] *Catholic Telegraph*, January 4, 1853.

[34] Purcell, Cincinnati, to Archbishop Gregory von Scherr, Munich, Germany, March 4, 1859. UNDA.

[35] *Catholic Telegraph*, June 1, 1882. p. 1.

[36] Consult McDonald, *op.cit.*, pp. 60-63, for earlier discussions of this problem at Baltimore.

[37] *Catholic Telegraph*, October 25, 1851, p. 4.

[38] Deye, *op. cit.*, pp. 345-346.

[39] Spalding to Purcell, November 21, 1851, UNDA. On November 27, 1851, Spalding wrote to Purcell (UNDA): "I hope most sincerely that the project of a general theological seminary (sic) will succeed."

[40] O'Connor to Purcell, December 26, 1851, UNDA. Deye, *op.cit.*, p. 347.

[41] O'Connor to Purcell, February 14, 1852, UNDA.

[42] F. P. Kenrick to Peter Kenrick, November 24, 1851, as quoted in Deye, *op. cit.*, p. 347.

[43] John Talbot Smith, *Our Seminaries, An Essay on Clerical Training*, pp. 51-59. New York: William H. Young and Company, 1896.

[44] *Catholic Telegraph*, May 26, 1855, p.1.

[45] *Catholic Telegraph*, June 2, 1855, p. 4.

[46] *Ibid.*, September 8, 1855, p. 4.

[47] *Acta et Decreta Quatuor Conciliorun Provincialium Cincinnatensium*, p. 41.

[48] Pius X to Purcell, June 14, 1858, UNDA.

[49] Purcell, American College, Rome, to Pius, IX, UNDA.

[50] *Catholic Telegraph*, September 29, 1870. p. 4.

[51] See Appendix A.

[52] Recorded in Church Records Book I, Page 131, Recorder's Office, Hamilton County, Ohio. See Appendix B.

[53] Kelley and Kirwin, *op. cit.*, p. 84.

[54] Augustine Toebbe was born on June 17, 1829. He went to the Mt. St. Mary's Seminary 1852, 1853, and 1854. He was ordained on September 14, 1854. He was stationed at St. Boniface Church and St. Philomena, Cincinnati. On January 9, 1870, he was made Bishop of Covington. He died on May 2, 1884. *Catholic Telegraph*, May 8, 1884.

[55] Kelley and Kirwin, *op. cit.*, p. 77.

[56] *Catholic Telegraph*, January 7, 1860, p. 4., *Ibid.* January, 8 1960, p. B-1.

[57] Joannes Perrone, *Pralectiones Theologicae*, Third Edition. Paris: A. Vouby, Bibl and Roger, 1870.

[58] Joseph Dixon, *A General Introduction to the Sacred Scriptures*. Baltimore: John Murphy and Company, 1853. pp. xv-271.

[59] P.J.B. DeHerdt, *Praxis Pontificialis Ceremonialis Episcoporum*, Three Volumes. Lovanii: Valinthout Fratres, 1863.

[60] Joseph Ferrante, *Elementis Juris Canonici*. Editio Secunda. Roma: Leonardi Oliveirei, 1872, pp. 172.

[61] Alphonsus Liguori, *Theologicae Moralis*, Three Volumes. Fourteenth Edition. Bassari: Rondinini, 1837.

[62] P. Joannis Gury, *Compendium Theologicae*. Ratisbonae: Joseph Mans, 1868. Gury was later criticized by John Talbert Smith as a moral book that was not adaptable to American life. He said: "The new social condition were the tremendous changes in our industrial system; the great advance in science call imperatively for the new Moral Theology,

written by an American of natural ability and approved scholarship. The textbooks now in use simply exasperate those who depend upon them; the oracles of Egypt are not so dumb as that upon American problems. Smith, *op. cit.*, p. 56.

[63] P. Joannis Gury, et Antoni Ballernini, *Compendium Theologicae Moralis*. Rome: Polyglotta, 1872.

[64] Aloysius Sabetti, *Compendium Theologicae Moralis*. Ratisbonae: Pustet, 1898. pp. 896.

[65] Johannes Alzog, *Handbuck der Patrologiae oder de Altain christilicken Literargeschickte*.

[66] F.J. Pabisch and Thos. S. Byrne, *Manual of Universal Church History*. Three Volumes. Robert Clarke and Company, 1978.

[67] Smith, *op. cit.*, p. 310.

[68] Franc. Rothenflue, S. J. *Institutiones Philosophiae Theoretica* Lugduni, Two Volumes. Prisse: Fratres, 1854.

[69] Salvatoris Tongiorgi, *Instituiones Philosophicae*, Three Volumes. Bruxellis, H. Goemaere, 1864.

[70] F.J. Thonnard, *A Short History of Philosophy*, Tournai: Desclee, 1955. pp. x, 1074.

[71] *Catholic Telegraph*, February 23, 1856, pp. 4 & 5.

[72] Kelley and Kirwin, *op. cit.*, p. 87.

[73] Cf. Chapter IV, p. 196. This was apparently lost in 1962.

[74] *Catholic Telegraph*, April 28, 1932, p. 4. Later Wood became Archbishop of Philadelphia.

[75] Kelley and Kirwin, *op. cit.*, p. 87. *Catholic Telegraph*, June 25, 1931, p. 1

[76] *Catholic Telegraph*, August 21, 1858, p. 6.

[77] *Ibid.*, September 13, 1856, p. 5.

[78] *Catholic Telegraph*, September 13, 1856, p. 4

[79] *Ibid.*, June 20, 1857, p. 4; *Ibid.*, June 27, 1877, p. 4.

[80] *Ibid.*, November 21, 1857, p. 4.

[81] Kelley and Kirwin, *op. cit.*, p. 160.

[82] *Catholic Telegraph*, May 15, 1858, p. 4.

[83] Letter, Quinlan to Purcell, August 21, 1858, MSMSA.

[84] Kelley and Kirwin, *op. cit.*, p. 197. Dr. Charles O'Leary was the author of a Greek Grammar. He became a surgeon in the armies of the North in the Civil War.

[85] E.P. Scammon was a native of Maine. He graduated from West Point. He taught mathematics there for seven years. After leaving the seminary in 1861, he received from President Lincoln a commission as Brigadier-General in the Union Forces.

[86] *Catholic Telegraph*, April 9, 1859, p. 4.

[87] *Catholic Telegraph*, August 14, 1858, p. 4.

[88] *Catholic Telegraph*, January 29, 1859. p. 4.

[89] *Ibid.*, October 29, 1859, p. 4.

[90] *Ibid.*, December 3, 1859, p. 4.

[91] *Catholic Telegraph*, September 15, 1860, p. 7; *Ibid.*, February 2, 1861, p. 7; Kelley and Kirwin, *op. cit.*, p. 180.

[92] *Catholic Telegraph*, May 11, 1861, p. 4.

[93] Kelley and Kirwin, *op. cit.*, p. 197.

[94] Acta, *op. cit.*, p. 153.

[95] *Catholic Telegraph*, May 14, 1862, p. 156. Kelley and Kirwin, *op. cit.*, p. 199.

[96] *Catholic Telegraph*, June 23, 1862, p. 28.

[97] *Catholic Telegraph*, April 29, 1863, p. 141

[98] Father E. P. Corcoran was born in Dayton, Ohio, March 26, 1832. He was ordained by Purcell in 1856 at the Mount. His first work was the missions in Glendale, Sharon, Pisgah, and Marion. He was in the 61st Regiment of the Ohio volunteers as a Chaplain. He served with Fremont, Pope, and Hooker at Cedar Mountain, Chancelorsville, and Second Bull Run. Health broken, he returned to the Seminary. He died December 29, 1866.
Catholic Telegraph, January 24, 1867, p. 4.

[99] Kelley and Kirwin, *op. cit.*, p. 210.

[100] Kelley and Kirwin, *op. cit.*, p. 213.

[101] *Catholic Builders of the Nation*, Vol. 5, p. 180. *Ibid.*, December 12, 1912, p. 1.
Ibid., September 16, 1863, p. 300.

[102] *Catholic Telegraph*, December 12, 1912, p. 1. *Ibid.*, October 21, 1863, p. 340. Kelley and Kirwin, *op. cit.*, p. 213-217.

[103] Kelley and Kirwin, *op. cit.*, p. 213.

[104] Kelley and Kirwin, *op. cit.*, p. 211.

[105] *Catholic Telegraph*, May 4, 1864, p. 148. *Ibid.*, June 26, 1959. pp. 1B-1. Emily A. Callaghan, Memoirs and Writings of James F. Callaghan. Cincinnati: The Robert Clark Company, 1903.

[106] Kelley and Kirwin, *op. cit.*, p. 221.

[107] *Ibid.*, p. 304.

[108] *Catholic Telegraph*, July 11, 1866, p. 4.

[109] *Ibid.*, June 27, 1866. p. 4.

[110] *Ibid.*, February 6, 1967, p. 4.

[111] *Ibid.*, June 26, 1867, p. 5.

[112] *Catholic Telegraph*, June 16, 1867, p. 4. *Ibid.*, June 22, 1868, p. 2. *Ibid.*, June 16, 1869, p. 4.

[113] McDonald, *op. cit.*, p. 27.

[114] *Catholic Telegraph*, November 14, 1866, p. 2.

[115] S. Smith, *Notes on the Second Plenary Council of Baltimore*, 1874, pp. 137-139. New York: P. O'Shea. 1896.

[116] *Catholic Telegraph*, May 31, 1894, p. 1.

[117] *Catholic Telegraph*, September 29, 1879, p. 4.

[118] Cf. Chapter V, p. 204.

[119] *Catholic Telegraph*, May 12, 1869, p. 5.

[120] *Ibid.*, May 12, 1869, p. 5.

[121] Kelley and Kirwin, *op. cit.,* p. 405.

[122] *Ibid.,* p. 372.

[123] Kelley and Kirwin, *op. cit.* p. 372.

[124] *Ibid., op. cit.* p. 374.

[125] Pabisch to Purcell, December 19, 1869.

[126] *Catholic Telegraph,* September 29, 1870, p. 6.

[127] Kelley and Kirwin, *op. cit.,* p. 280.

[128] Kelley and Kirwin, *op. cit.,* p. 281.

[129] *Catholic Telegraph,* June 23, 1873, p. 4.

[130] *Ibid.,* June 8, 1871, p. 5.

[131] Kelley and Kirwin, *op. cit.,* p. 290.

[132] *Ibid.,* p. 290.

[133] Kelley and Kirwin, *op. cit.,* p. 291.

[134] Memorandum in Archives, MSMSA.

[135] *Ibid.,* MSMSA.

[136] Kelley and Kirwin, *op. cit.,* p. 355.

[137] *Catholic Telegraph,* January 20, 1950, p. 3.

[138] *Ibid.,* July 24, 1879, p. 4.

CHAPTER THREE

Reopening of Mount Saint Mary's Seminary on Price Hill

INTRODUCTION

When the seminary closed its doors in 1879 it was thought that they would reopen in a very short time. No one thought that almost a decade would pass before the seminary would reopen. In the meantime, Archbishop Purcell had been succeeded by Bishop Elder who began to unravel the knotted financial affairs of the diocese while the seminary was closed, Leo XII issued his letter on prescribed study of the philosophy of St. Thomas in Catholic seminaries and the Third Plenary Council of Baltimore had drawn up a completed and detailed course of study for American seminaries. John Lancaster Spalding had proposed that Mount St. Mary's be the site for graduate school in theology. When this proposal failed, Elder worked during the middle part of the 1880's to reopen the seminary. This he accomplished in 1887 and the students returned to the Hill. Thomas S. Byrne was appointed rector. It was like starting over again, except for the construction of the buildings. In 1894, when John Murray became the rector, the seminary almost reached the level of its former development prior to the financial disaster. It almost did. But in 1904 calamity struck. It was decided to move the site of the seminary to Mount Washington. The glorious days of the seminary on Price Hill were brought to a close.

HISTORIC TRENDS (1879-1904)

Two things vitally affecting the seminary and seminary life happened in the years during the closing of the seminary.

The first of these was the encyclical letter of Leo XIII, entitled *Aeterni Patris*, which prescribed the study of the philosophy of St. Thomas. At the beginning of the century scholastic philosophy seemed to be quite dead. The distaste for metaphysics on the part of modern contemporary philosophers, and the lack of understanding of the advances of modern sciences on the part of scholastics, had led to the decadent condition of scholasticism during the seventeenth and eighteenth centuries.[1] At the beginning of the nineteenth century, and prior to this, most Catholic seminaries taught a brand of philosophy that was an eclectic mixture of Descartes and Malbranch.[2] What there was of philosophy was more of what we would speak of today as the first part of experimental psychology, with a great deal of emphasis placed on sense perception in varying degrees. At the beginning of the century, however, there began a scholastic revival, set in motion by the encyclical of Leo XIII, prescribing the necessity of Thomistic philosophy in the training of clerical students. For most seminaries, including Mount St. Mary's, this meant a new and distinct orientation for the philosophical curriculum.

Twenty years later, in a letter to the French clergy, Leo XIII reiterated the necessity of teaching Thomistic philosophy. He also gave schematic outlines of the essential core subjects of theology. They were to be dogma, moral, Sacred Scripture, church history, and canon law.

He urged that the scholastic method of theology also be used in the seminaries, and that the catechism of the Council of Trent be a definite textbook. He gave explicit directions to the professors who taught each one of these subjects.[3] The second major and minor seminaries put into effect by the Third Plenary Council of Baltimore. This council met in November of 1884 and definite steps were taken to establish a curriculum which would serve as a model for ecclesiastical institutions all over this country. To clarify still more the position of the Council on seminary education, a committee of bishops was appointed to work out a curriculum designed for American seminaries.[4] The Committee of Buffalo, as it was called, met in 1886 and, in essence, outlined the courses of study for major seminaries.

There were to be at least two years of philosophy. In the first year the student was to take philosophy for six hours, natural philosophy for two hours, archaeology for one hour, Hebrew grammar for two hours, Latin for two hours, Greek for two hours, and chant for one hour, for a total of sixteen hours. In the second year there were to be six hours of philosophy, one hour of archeology, two hours of Hebrew. Latin and Greek were eliminated and in their places were put three hours of debating and one hour of Hermeneutics, for a total of eleven hours.[5]

In theology the course was to last for four years. In the first year, dogma was to be taken for six hours, moral for six hours, church history for three hours, Scripture for three hours, debating for one hour, introduction to Sacred Scripture for one hour, and chant for one hour. In the second year of theology the very same courses with the same allotted hours were to be taken except with different tracts. Both first and second years took twenty-one hours per semester. In the third year there were six hours of dogma and six hours of moral, one of debating and one of chant. However, in the third year, church history and Scripture were dropped and were replaced with three hours of canon law, two hours of liturgy, one of homiletics, and one hour of ascetical theology, for a total of twenty-one credit hours. In the fourth year, dogma and moral were reduced to three hours each and the rest of the course remained the same for a total of fifteen credit hours.[6]

Thus, in essence, the orientation and schemata of the seminary curriculum was fairly well delineated when the doors of Mount St. Mary's Seminary reopened in 1887. During the course of the years this is one aspect of seminary education which has hardly changed at all. Not only what subjects were to be taken but the manner in which they were to be studied and the amount of time to be allocated to each were quite firmly fixed. The seminary was free to better prepare its professors and the administration of the seminary might grow and develop, but the curriculum was at this time set and from henceforth it was not to be modified.

ELDER IS MADE BISHOP OF CINCINNATI (1980)

In the midst of the financial disaster, William Henry Elder came to Cincinnati in April of 1880 to assume his duties as coadjutor and administrator of the diocese. The diocese had hit upon difficult times. In regard to the seminary, Elder later wrote that the old archbishop asked him to open it as soon as possible, this always remained a cardinal aim of his early administration.[7] Deep personal sanctity was the outstanding attribute of Archbishop William H. Elder, who guided the Archdiocese of Cincinnati for more than twenty-one years as its Ordinary. Named coadjutor bishop to Archbishop Purcell on January 20, 1880, he succeeded Purcell on July 4, 1883. William Henry Elder was born in Baltimore, Maryland, on March 22, 1819, the son of Basil Spalding Elder and Elizabeth Snowden. He was one of the thirteen children, three of whom died in infancy. The eldest sister, Eleanora, became a Sister of Charity.[8]

His early education was received in a private school in his native city, and he entered Mount St. Mary's College, Emmitsburg, Maryland, for his high school work. At the time of his entrance Father John B. Purcell, later to be Elder's predecessor as archbishop, was president of the school. Elder remained at Mount St. Mary's for his collegiate and philosophical courses. After this he was sent to Urban College in Rome, Italy, for a four-year study of Theology which preceded his ordination in the chapel of the college on March 29, 1846. [9]

For the next eleven years Father Elder was professor of dogmatic theology at this alma mater in Maryland. He was named Bishop of Natchez in Mississippi, and was consecrated in the Cathedral of Baltimore on May 3, 1857. The Diocese of Natchez embraced the entire state of Mississippi but numbered only a few poor, widely scattered missions administered by nine priests. Father John Lamott in his *History of the Archdiocese of Cincinnati* writes as follows of the trials of Bishop Elder:

> Traveling to the various missions was extremely difficult and could only be done in private conveyances or on foot. The labors of the Bishop soon won the hearts of the faithful, and an abiding love and simple trust in their Bishop were harbored by them upon the outbreak of the Civil War.[10]

An incident took place during the struggle between the North and the South which sheds some light on the character of the bishop. As spiritual leader of a territory which was hotly contested in the war, the bishop was confronted with the problem of caring for the spiritual well-being of both Union and confederate soldiers. The natives for the most part had taken the side of the South. During the time of occupation by the Union Army, a Union Army official took it upon himself to issue a decree that prayers should be offered in all churches for the President of the United States, and for the success of the Union arms. Bishop Elder at once saw that this request could not be met for to comply would be an insult to the people among whom he labored. The fact that a government official was attempting to dictate what the worship of the church should be was a point not taken lightly and not to be granted. Despite threats of violence from the military, the courage of the gentle bishop eventually won out.[11]

Although he was appointed coadjutor to Archbishop Alemany of San Francisco in 1878, Elder never filled the assignment. At the time the appointment came from Rome, the Diocese of Natchez was still suffering from the effects of the plague. Bishop Elder replied to the Prefect of the Propaganda that in his judgment it would be disastrous to religion for him to leave the diocese at that time. This was not a refusal to go to San Francisco. Rome answered that he should remain at Natchez until conditions permitted the change. [12]

After some months Bishop Elder wrote to the Cardinal-Prefect, and in reply he was directed to go to Cincinnati as coadjutor to Archbishop Purcell. Upon his arrival in Cincinnati on April 18, 1880, he immediately took up the task of straightening out the financial failure of the two Purcells. The next thirteen years, spent in attempting to make order out of the chaos which was the Purcell failure, taxed him severely, but the Archbishop was earnest and sincere in his efforts to pay off even the large debt. Although he had been counseled that the job was an impossible one, he did not spare himself in his attempts to clear the church of any stigma that might be attached to it by reason of the failure.[13]

Archbishop Elder's greatest task was reorganizing the administrative branch of the archdiocese. Primitive ways were still being pursued in the various channels of Episcopal and parochial administration. To remedy this situation required prudence as the reformation and changes had to be instituted among those who knew the privilege of authority. Gradually he systematized the inner workings of the archdiocese by setting up an office of chancellor, insisting on annual reports from the clergy and from the parishes, and establishing the various courts and counseling bodies for arbitrating ecclesiastical matters. [14]

He appealed for a coadjutor because the infirmities of the old age were making it increasingly more difficult for him to carry on the work of the archdiocese. Bishop Henry Moeller of Columbus was appointed coadjutor on April 27, 1903, with the right of succession. Upon the arrival of Bishop Moeller the following June, Archbishop Elder practically relinquished the administration of the See, though he continued to be active to the day of his death. Archbishop Elder died October 31, 1904.[15]

Proposal of John Lancaster Spalding

It was the Cincinnati financial disaster which prompted John Lancaster Spalding to propose, in August of 1880, that the site of old Mount St. Mary's be used to realize his cherished dream of school of higher education for the American Catholic clergy. It was at this time that the Bishop of Peoria broached the subject to the new Bishop of Cincinnati.

> I have been thinking of late that possibly the troubles in the finances of Cincinnati might offer an opportunity to make a beginning towards founding a Catholic University; and I hope you will pardon me for inquiring whether you will be forced to sell your Seminary Property. If so, might not the Bishops of the U.S. buy it in and start there a Theological High School for the best students among those who have already made the three years course of theology in the different seminaries of the country. In this high school they would go through what is called the profound course of theology. I see no other way by which we can hope to raise the standard of Clerical Education and you know better than I how difficult it is to find priests who have the learning which bishops ought to have; and as our dioceses are becoming so numerous it seems to me to be necessary to set about doing something in earnest by which we may raise up a class of men in the priesthood who will become the ornament and the strength of our holy faith. If you think there is any thing in this suggestion, I would be glad to cooperate

in order to help carry out some such plan.[16]

Unfortunately the personal correspondence of Bishop Spalding seem to have been lost or destroyed and it is impossible to ascertain the exact answer which Elder gave to this communication. It must have been generally favorable because about a week later Spalding again wrote Elder as follows:

> I felt sure that you would gladly cooperate in any feasible plan to raise the standard of Clerical Education. All the bishops of this country, I suppose, agree in admitting the urgency of our need; but what is everybody's business receives the earnest attention of no one. Several bishops have urged me to take a special interest in this matter, an since no one else seems at present to think of the work, it can surely do no harm to try to get at the real thought of some of the leading bishops of the U.S. on this point. To begin, I should think it unwise to entrust such an institution to a religious order. Omne animal generat simile sibi, and secular priests alone to get the services of this or that learned man among the orders for a time, to act as professor. There will I think be little difficulty in finding suitable Professors; and Father Vandenhende, the first President of Troy seminary, and one of the most experienced and able priests of Belgium, would I have reason to believe, be willing to accept the direction. The great difficulty is that of deciding on a location, and unless some preponderant reason determines the point, there is danger here. It is for this reason that I think of Cincinnati. The diocese is in great trouble. The bishops sympathized with the archbishop and yourself; and by agreeing to locate the theological University there they would add dignity to the See, inspire courage in the people and by buying your Seminary property, help in some slight measure to lighten your financial burden. If you intend to continue the Seminary as a diocesan institution, then of course my suggestion need not be considered; but if you have no such intention, then I feel confident that tow or three bishops could be induced to canvass the country to raise funds to found there and endow the Theological University of the U.S. Only those who had finished a three years' course of Theology would be admitted to this institution. As many dioceses are now supplied with priests, a considerable number of bishops would be able to allow their best students to continue their course of learning. What is greatly needed and never acquired in foreign seminaries and universities is a thorough knowledge of English language and of English literature. A competent professor of Sacred Eloquence would give these Theologians an insight into this subject. Then we cold induce men of ability to give short courses of lectures on special subjects. I have not written to the Cardinal or to any one on this subject but yourself. I wish to know before taking any further step whether my ideas with regard to Cincinnati meet your approval. I am sorry to trouble you and have only good intentions to offer as an excuse.[17]

After receiving another favorable response from Elder, Spalding wrote to him again about ten days later. In this letter he went into more detail concerning the proposal. Text of the letter is as follows:

Your letter encourages me. I have frequently spoken with Bishop O'Connor on the subject of a Theological High School. He himself has no hope of being able to do anything either with Philadelphia or Woodstock.

You are perfectly right in saying that if Cincinnati is to be chosen, the impulse and agitation should come from others, not from you. All that my plan contemplates is your consent and cooperation. The institution would have to be under the supreme direction of a Board chosen by the Bishops of the Country and representing their authority. I beg you therefore to mention the subject to the archbishop, as you suggest, and to any others whom you may care to consult. I should also alike to get a rough estimate of what you think we ought to pay for the property, together with a statement of the amount of ground and some general description of the buildings. When I have a tangible proposition of this kind I shall try to enlist the Cardinal, the archbishop of Baltimore and others in the work. Bishop of Grace of St. Paul has begged me to undertake some such work; at least to make the attempt; and as he is a holy man I have thought it might be the will of God. It will be time to discuss many details when influential persons have approved of the general idea. The Holy Father would I am confident be delighted with the project and we could rely upon his encouragement.[18]

Having received approval of his plan from the coadjutor Archbishop of Cincinnati, Spalding then tried to enlist the support of Cardinal McCloskey, Archbishop of New York. The proposition of a Catholic University was not new to McCloskey. Spalding's uncle (the archbishop) had attempted fourteen years before to secure his cooperation in a similar enterprise at the time of the Second Plenary Council. Now Archbishop Spalding's nephew had tried his hand with New York's Cardinal and apparently achieved no more success than his uncle. On October 23, 1880, Spalding wrote McCloskey as follows:

There is another subject which I beg permission to submit to your consideration. There is, it seems to me, urgent need of a Theological High School in the U.S. Something like the Dunboyne in Ireland or the Theological Faculty of Louvain; where a few of the best students, after finishing the elementary courses, could get a more thorough training in Philosophy and Theology.

This is not given in the colleges at Rome or Louvain; it will never be given unless we create a home institution. The Seminary property at Cincinnati would be suitable for such a purpose and Bishop Elder with whom I have corresponded on the subject, heartily approves of the idea. The plan would be to have the bishops of the U.S. purchase this property, for the purpose of a Theological High School for the whole country. It would be under the direction of a board appointed by themselves. Only the best students, who had finished the ordinary course in the various seminaries, would be admitted. Such an institution at Cincinnati would encourage the disheartened Catholics of that diocese; it would be able to build a body of men who in time would bee able to fill our episcopal sees with honor. If you Eminence and the archbishop would propose such an undertaking, I doubt not but several of the younger Bishops would offer their services to appeal for funds.

For my own part I should be willing to devote my whole life to such a work, for I am persuaded that in no other way shall we able to meet the demands which the near future will make upon us. Your greater wisdom and experience will enable you to pronounce whether such a project may be entertained. If you do not think favorable of it, I shall at once put it out of mind. Apologizing for this long letter, I am with great respect, your Eminence's humble servant.[19]

The cardinal's reply was not favorable and Spalding apparently knew just where to turn to win the support he needed. Two weeks after writing McCloskey, the Bishop of Peoria wrote Elder again.

I enclose a letter which I have just received from the Cardinal. This, I fear, shows that the project (sic) in regard to the seminary cannot be carried out. Please return the Cardinal's letter to me. Could you suggest anything? I have thought that Mr. Springer might be induced to buy the property and present it to the Bishops of the United States provided that (they) would agree to found there a Catholic University.[20]

In spite of the fact that he told Cardinal McCloskey he would drop the question if the latter disapproved, Spalding kept up the agitation. He continued writing Elder in the fall of 1880. If he had not lost heart entirely, it was evident that he was growing provoked at the failure to win approval of his proposal. On November 14, he again wrote Cincinnati's coadjutor.

I most sincerely hope that something may still be done, by which we may establish a Theological High School in Cincinnati. Nothing that I can do shall be omitted. I would be willing even, for a few years, to become a teacher in such an institution. It could be founded, without the smallest shadow of doubt, within a year, if the Bishops of the Country had the will. Nothing else is needed.

Those who urged me to stir up the matter are unfortunately, like myself, in new or small dioceses. The impulse must be given by those higher up. When I see the blindness with which we allow opportunities to pass us by, I almost lose heart. What you say of Provincial Seminaries is my own conviction. Those bishops who have no seminaries, will choose the place for their students, and will rarely unite in support of a provincial seminary. A High School would raise the standard of instruction at once in all our seminaries. It would be well I think if you were to sound the Archbishop of Baltimore and others on the project. I shall be delighted to beg, work, (?) or do anything as the servant of the bishops if they will but unite in saying let us make the effort. Would it not be well to have the Holy Father get the bishops to meet in some sort of Council?[21]

That Archbishop Elder was well disposed towards the proposal of the Bishop of Peoria is known from a letter written to Archbishop Gibbons a few days after Spalding had made the suggestion outlined above. Elder wrote Gibbons as follows:

Bishop Spalding wrote to me of a suggestion made to him—of letting our Seminary here be purchased to establish in it a Theological College of a superior course of studies. In that form it would be doubly beneficial to us here. But apart from the selecting of this place, the project of having such an institution I think a most important one, and one that ought not to be delayed a year longer than necessary. His Eminence of New York seems to think the time is not yet come. But my conviction is that with such exertions as could be made, it might be instituted in a year or two. Even if begun on a small scale it would begin to produce fruit at once, and it would be certainly grow larger.

One chief factor of success is to have a person able and willing to work for it. This we have in Bishop Spalding himself, and another time such a person might be hard to find. He himself may be advanced to some position demanding all his attention.

Please consider and consult and use your influence to push it without delay. I would very much like that our building be taken for it, but wherever it is, I would like to see it begun speedily.[22]

Although Elder favored the plan, John McCloskey of New York vetoed it and the proposal came to nothing.

PRELIMINARIES TO REOPENING THE SEMINARY (1879-1887)

The task of reopening the seminary was a primary concern of Elder. As early as 1882 he had written to Father Byrne asking him to make necessary arrangements with Father John Mackey, pastor of St. Patrick's church, to "begin collecting money for the 'Mountain' after the New Year."[23]

The Archbishop then wrote to Father Mackey directly, informing him that his services had been requested for obtaining money for the financial restoration of the seminary. Here one admires Elder's sense of loyalty to his predecessor. To the old archbishop, who was now in retirement at the Ursuline Convent in Brown County, such activity could not help but bring a smile of satisfaction.[24]

In May of 1885 the financial pall really began to lift from the seminary. In a bequest announced during this month Ruben Springer had again come to the financial rescue of the diocese. He left $100,000.00 to the Archdiocese of Cincinnati. Elder then announced that the reopening of Mount St. Mary's was certainly brought nearer.

In the diocesan synod of 1886, the question of reopening Mount St. Mary's Seminary was one of the matters under discussion. At this time Elder stated that although he was anxious to see Mount St. Mary's in operation again, when this could be accomplished he did not know. It is interesting to note that at this time he was thinking of turning the seminary over to the direction of a religious order. The cycle of events had come back once again to the problem which had plagued Fenwick and Purcell: the difficulty of obtaining, training and developing a faculty from the ranks of a secular clergy.[25]

On April 28, 1887, Archbishop Elder addressed a letter to Reverend Aemilian Sele who was then studying in Rome. He mentioned the possible reopening of the Cincinnati Theological School the following September, and asked Sele to return and assume a professorship there. "Once again, philosophy and theology will be offered along with the branches of theology will be offered along with the branches of theology, i.e., Sacred Scripture and church history. We will occupy again the old Mount Saint Mary's of the West in the hills west of the city."[26]

In the spring of 1887 a force of carpenters, plumbers, and painters was put to work to prepare the buildings for the students who were to arrive in the fall. There was work to be done everywhere; from the cellar to the garret, from the chapel to the library. Everywhere the hand of time or the work of vandals had produced some sad effects. It had been idle for eight years and the once neat and well-ordered institution was now in a wretched and miserable condition. The plaster in many places was torn from the walls; the windows were very much in need of repair; the old desks were torn from their fastenings and defaced; chairs, tables, and beds were damaged. Everything connected with the institution was either destroyed or damaged to such an extent as to be rendered useless.[27]

With clean-up work well under way at the old seminary, Elder expressed his joy of heart at the long-looked-for consummation of his hopes and desires as follows:

A diocesan seminary is the nursery, we might say, for all other institutions of religion. Churches, schools, asylums, hospitals, whilst these are the work of all the faithful, still they only become realities when there are priests to lead the way. And the sacraments, the great channels through which God's grace is given to us…religious teachings, and all the other helps appointed by the Almighty for the sanctification of our souls, God has been pleased to entrusted to his priests.

While the education of priests can be effected in any other seminary outside the diocese, yet it is desirable that each diocese should have its own seminary when this is practicable. Even if we saw no sufficient reason for this ourselves, we have the testimony of the Holy Ghost, expressed through the ordinance of Church in the Ecumenical Council of Trent. The Council demands that each diocese should have its own seminary under the care of its own Bishop; and if this cannot be done, that at least in each ecclesiastical province there should be a seminary.

But, we can see at least some of the reasons why the Church has made this enactment. The Bishop is responsible for the care of the souls of his diocese. And the priests exercise this care under the direction of the Bishop. It is important, therefore, that he guide the preparation of the young men, whom he is afterwards to direct in this sacred ministry. It is also a great advantage to have most of the students educated in the diocese, because the chief body of the pastors will have an opportunity of seeing them, forming thus a family and brotherly spirit with them, and becoming more identified and acquainted with the local wants of the people, among whom they are one day to exercise the sacred ministry.

Then the recollection connected with our venerable seminary makes it a work of love and gratitude to have it restored to its original purpose. It is a monument of the labors, the virtues and the zeal for education and religion, which have made so dear to our whole community and to our church, the holy and learned first Archbishop of Cincinnati. It also reminds us of the learning and virtues of so many illustrious priests and prelates who have given fame to it by their teachings and their studies. And it speaks so loudly of the noble liberality of distinguished benefactors, of the active charity of the whole body of Catholics, by whose contributions it was established and conducted.

For these and other reasons which need not be mentioned, we feel that all of you, both clergy and laity, have an earnest desire to see its halls again devoted to the implanting of ecclesiastical science and priestly virtues in the minds and hearts of those who are preparing for the sacred priesthood.[28]

Elder now busied himself with the task of recruiting professors. He wrote to the Reverend Gmeiner at the Seminary of St. Francis de Sales in Milwaukee. For reasons unknown Gmeiner did not come.[29]

In a letter to Reverend Hecht at the seminary in Cleveland, he urged his return with these words: "We have to make a good many sacrifices to provide the seminary with an efficient body of Faculty and Directors. We must all do hard things to get to heaven. I know you are resolved there; so you will be well-disposed to take your share of hardships in the Providence of God." It is worthy of note that Hecht did return only to die in January of the first scholastic year.[30]

In May of 1887 Elder happily announced the reopening of the seminary in these words, "We are preparing to re-open our own Diocesan Seminary, Mt. St. Mary's of the West. This has long been the desire of my heart. The very first time that I presented myself to the late venerable Archbishop when I came to assist him, he requested me to try to have the seminary opened as soon as possible. And in my subsequent visits he spoken oftener about this than any other point of diocesan administration."[31]

Over the summer months $18,000 was spent in repairing the buildings. When all the work was completed, opening day was set for September 12. The small but impressive faculty consisted of the Reverend Thomas Byrne as rector; and under his direction were the Reverend J. Hecht, D.D., Reverend E. Aemilian Sele, D.D., Reverend Henry Brinkmeyer, and Reverend Joseph Pohlschneider. The scholastic year began with a spiritual retreat for seven days. On September 20 the archbishop officially welcomed the seventeen new students by celebrating a pontifical high mass.[32]

BYRNE, RECTOR (1887-1894)

When the seminary reopened in 1887 Thomas S. Byrne was appointed rector. He was born in Hamilton, Ohio, July 19, 1842. In 1860 he entered St. Thomas Preparatory Seminary in Bardstown, Kentucky. He finished his college course at Mount St. Mary's and, after one year of philosophy, was selected by Purcell to study theology at the American college in Rome. He remained there for three years and returned to Cincinnati in October of 1868. For one year, while a student, he served on the faculty and held the office of procurator. He was ordained in May of 1869. In succeeding years, until the closing of Mount St. Mary's Seminary in 1879, he took charge of the various classes in physics, chemistry, mathematics, Latin, English and geology. In 1887 he took charge of the parish of St. Vincent de Paul and lived at Mount St.

Joseph's. In 1887, while rector of the cathedral, he was made rector of the seminary.[33]

As rector of the seminary, Byrne was an extremely able administrator and stern disciplinarian. Perhaps this was what the seminaries needed at this time. There is some evidence to indicate that he was a little too strict. During his years as rector the seminary lacked the lustrous spirit which prevailed before its closing and during the subsequent tenure of Doctor Murray.

On May 22, 1894, Byrne celebrated his Silver Jubilee. A year previous to this he had received from Rome the title of Doctor of Divinity. Poor health had prevented his receiving it in 1868 before he left Rome. On the occasion of conferring the Doctorate, Archbishop Elder presented Byrne with an amethyst ring. It was the very same ring which the Emmitsburg students had given to Elder when he was made Bishop of Natchez. This ring is now part of the archives of Mount St. Joseph College.[34]

Arriving to serve the faculty in its first year was Aemilian Sele, a native of Triesenberg, in the little principality of Liechtenstein. He was born on January 17, 1847. At the University of Innsbruck he received the degree of Doctor of Theology. Coming to America at the invitation of Bishop McCloskey, Doctor Sele taught at the Seminary of Preston Park, Louisville, and later became its rector. In 1887 he received the Doctor degree in canon law at the Gregorian University in Rome where he had gone to pursue a special course. He taught chiefly dogmatic theology, Sacred Scripture, and Hebrew at Mount St. Mary's of the West. The astounding erudition of Doctor Sele was due in great measure to his quick and tenacious memory. Doctor Sele was a humble and retiring disposition and was very appreciative of the kindness and friendship of the priests and students. Doctor Sele was one of the towering figures in the history of Mount St. Mary's Seminary. He worked incredibly hard, and was a man of vast learning in the fields of dogma and Sacred Scripture. He taught for many, many years at the seminary and his death on January 29, 1918, was a sad loss felt by all. He is most worthy of the plaque commemorating him, which is located in the main floor corridor, outside of the chapel.[35]

In this first year, 1887, Byrne taught the course in moral; Hecht taught the course in dogma and liturgy; Sele taught the course in Sacred Scripture and Hebrew; Pohlschneider taught the course in canon law; DeCoursey taught chemistry and physics; and philosophy was taught by Brinkmeyer.[36]

The first year back on Price Hill passed uneventfully, except for the death in January of one of the seminary's great professors, Doctor Hecht, and the conferral of the degree of Doctor of Divinity upon the rector. In February of 1888 the archbishop informed Byrne of this honor with the following words: "It will be an additional means for you to give glory to God."[37] At this time G. Wuelffing succeeded Hecht in teaching the course in dogma.

In a pastoral letter of May 1888, the archbishop referred to the seminary as follows:

Priests and laity all through the diocese are rejoicing the reopening of our diocesan seminary; the venerable Mount St. Mary's of the West. It cheers our hearts and revives our energies, to see the lights of science and piety again burning in those halls, consecrated by the labor of the apostolic first Archbishop, of the illustrious and holy men, who as professors or as students, hallowed the place with happy traditions and enriched the diocese with the knowledge and love of God. In this first year of reopening it is already bearing good fruits. There are now twenty-seven students of Philosophy and Theology in the Seminary...[38] (Fifteen were from the diocese of Cincinnati and twelve were from five other dioceses.)

In 1888 the faculty of the seminary remained the same as the previous year (Byrne, Whelffing, Sele, Brinkmeyer, and DeCoursey) with the exception that Matthew O'Brien now replaced Pohlschneider. O'Brien began his brilliant career in the teaching of church history.[39] The enrollment in the seminary this year increased to sixty-one students.

For the years 1889 and 1890 the faculty and the subjects they taught remained the same. Byrne was rector and taught moral; Wuelffing taught dogma and liturgy; Sele was professor of Sacred Scripture and Hebrew; Brinkmeyer taught philosophy; O'Brien, church history; and DeCoursey taught chemistry and physics.[40]

During the spring of 1890, the Alumni of the seminary generously contributed to the fixing up of the handball courts, the gymnasium, the bowling alleys, and donated money for the purchase of musical instruments for the famous concert band of Mount St. Mary's For the remaining days at Mount St. Mary's on Price Hill the school concert band was a much talked about organization, and contributed a great deal of enjoyment to the students and faculty.[41]

The faculty at the beginning of 1891 was the same as the previous two years with the exception that Bernard Leubberman replaced Brinkmeyer as teacher of the course in philosophy. Brinkmeyer left at this time to take a place on the faculty of the new minor seminary just built at Cedar Point (now Mount Washington). As will be seen in the following chapter, he filled the position of rector the following year, a post he held until the close of that seminary in 1907. Luebberman had been a member of the faculty of St. Meinrad's in Indiana where he also had taught philosophy.[42]

In December of 1891 the student body had grown to a total of sixty-eight students. By April of 1982 the number had reached seventy. Slowly but surely the students from the various dioceses were returning to Mount St. Mary's. In April of this year it was proposed that the seminary go back to its famous practice of holding public examinations. This was voted down by the faculty "with the reservation that it would be a tried in the presence of the faculty first before being adopted."[43]

The faculty for 1892 was the same as the previous year with the exception that Bernard Feeney replaced Matthew O'Brien who went to St. Gregory. The makeup of faculty for this year was Byrne, Sele, Wuelffing, Lueberman and Feeney.[44]

Bernard Feeney was a native of Ireland and was educated at the Seminary of Maynooth. He was ordained there on September 15, 1867. He was the author of some works like *Home Duties, Studies in the Passion,* and *How to Get On.* He taught moral theology and church history the first year he was at Mount St. Mary's. His most famous work, however, was his *Manual of Sacred Rhetoric,* the first fully original, homiletic textbook in English.[45]

In this year of 1892 the student body increased to ninety-eight students. Twenty-two dioceses throughout the country were therein represented.[46] The following is a description of the seminary at this time (1892-1893) by one of its former students:

> The seminary is situated on a beautiful hill within the corporate limits of Cincinnati, and overlooks the city from the west. Surrounded by magnificent trees, the venerable structure, embowered in their dense foliage, has the appearance of an ancient castle. The grounds cover ten acres. The main building, constructed of while limestone, now darkened with age, is about three hundred feet long, and includes two imposing side wings. On the east side is the main entrance, reached by stone steps from the graveled carriage-way. The main section has four floors, with a basement. On the first floor are the rooms of the faculty, while the three upper floors are given up to the student's apartments. The basement is used for the domestic service, and also contains the large refectory, kitchen, laundry, etc. The interior of the building is elegantly fitted up, having all modern accommodations and improvement. The north wing is seventy-five feet long and is occupied almost entirely by the valuable library which contains, it is estimated, 30,000 volumes. In the south wing which is ninety feet long is the oratory and chapel—the former used for the daily private devotions of the seminarists, the latter for the solemn ceremonies on Sundays and festivals. Both oratory and chapel are enriched with the sacred paintings of the lamented Rev. D. Pabisch, the former beloved rector of this seminary. For the physical culture of the students, there is a well-equipped gymnasium and two asphalt-floored ball-courts. The seminary this year has eight-five students, who represent twenty dioceses.[47]

On March 29, 1894, plans were made for the $35,000 addition to Mount St. Mary's on the north side of the property. The new building was to be forty-eight feet in length, one hundred and sixty-six feet wide, and four stories high. At the first break in the weather work was started on the foundation. Giannini and Moorman were the architects, and P. Hazen was the contractor on the job. The new building confirmed very much in appearance to the old structures and was constructed of the same kind of limestone.[48]

In August of 1894 it had been announced that due to increased seminary enrollment it was now necessary to double its former capacity. Commenting on the expansion, the Telegraph wrote that "Each student will have his own room and no pains will be spared to proved for his health and comfort." the new addition was finished March 7, 1895, at a cost of $40,693.00. This cost included a new laundry which was installed at this time.[49]

On May 20, 1894, announcement was received from Rome that Thomas Byrne, the rector, had been elevated to the post of Bishop of Nashville. Bishop Byrne was consecrated at St. Joseph Church in the city of Nashville on July 25, 1894. Archbishop Elder was the consecrator. Many of the Cincinnati clergy, it was reported, attended the ceremony.[50]

MURRAY, RECTOR (1894-1904)

The man chosen by Elder to succeed Byrne was the kindly and saintly John B. Murray. Murray was born near Martinsburg, West Virginia, March 15, 1841. At the age of thirteen he entered St. Thomas Preparatory Seminary near Bardstown, where he remained for four years.

In 1858 he entered Mount St. Mary's to pursue his classical and theological course. On October 24, 1863, he was ordained by Purcell. He was assistant at St. Patrick's in Columbus, and pastor at St. Mary's, Chillicothe, for seventeen years. In 1883 he became pastor of St. Mary's in Urbana, Ohio. In 1889 he was made pastor of St. Edward's, Cincinnati, and in July 1984, became rector of Mount St. Mary's, succeeding Byrne.[51]

Monsignor Murray Differed from his predecessor. He was an older man and during his tenure of office exhibited none of the strictness of Byrne. It is true that the discipline of the seminary was very much relaxed during this time in contradistinction to the era under Byrne. However, the spirit of the seminary was excellent, and the faculty for the times was extremely able.

At the meeting of the faculty in September of 1894 (the first meeting under the new rector), the professorships were distributed among the faculty as follows: Murray took the class in liturgy; Sele taught exegesis, church history, canon law, and Hebrew; Wuelffing taught dogmatic theology, introduction to Sacred Scripture, Latin, German, and Sacred Eloquence; Feeney taught moral theology and the Senior English Sacred Eloquence Class; and Kuhlmann taught philosophy, the Junior English Sacred Eloquence Class, and plain chant. At this meeting the faculty decided that the class in Greek would be dropped.[52]

Bernard F. Kuhlmann, D.D., the new professor of philosophy was born in Cincinnati, January 31, 1866, and was educated at St. Xavier's College in Cincinnati and the American College in Rome. On July 27, 1890, he was ordained in the Eternal City by Cardinal Parocchi. Upon returning to Cincinnati, he became an assistant at St. Joseph's here in the city, then became pastor of the parish in Taylor Creek, Ohio. He was very successful in parish work. He came to St. Mary's in 1894 and remained there for nine years. He then left the Soldiers' Home in Dayton and remained there for thirty-two years.[53]

On March 7, 1895, there was the solemn dedication of the new seminary building located on the north side of the property. The newspaper of the day carried the following account of the event:

> The great grey massive structure of the chiseled stone, that crowns the wooded summit of Price Hill, was profusely decorated with flags and banners, making a mass of vivid color against the dull, wet sky. At nine o'clock the seminary bell rang out jubilantly and the sound of many approaching feet, told the little group of visitors assembled in the chapel, the hour of dedication had arrived. The procession was formed in on of the large halls and as it would through the lofty corridor to the chapel it presented a spectacle to stir the heart. First came the long line of seminarians in black cassocks and snowy surplices their studious faces alight with enthusiasm; following them were the younger priests, whose years since leaving their cherished alma mater are easily numbered; then came the older pastors, grave, and dignified, whose names are honored and revered throughout the Archdiocese.[54]

The dignitaries present on this occasion were Very Reverend J. B. Murray, rector of St. Mary's Seminary; Reverend Henry Brinkmeyer, of St. Gregory's Seminary; Reverend A. J. Burrowes,

S. J., president of St. Xavier's College; the Chancellor of the Archdiocese, Reverend Henry Moeller; the Vicar-General, Very Reverend John Albrinck; the Vicar General of the diocese of Nashville, Very Reverend Bernard Feeney (in the earlier part of the school year he had been asked by his friend and former rector, Byrne, to come to Nashville); the Provincial of the Fathers of the Precious Blood, Very Reverend Henry Drees; Bishop Byrne, Bishop Maes; and Archbishop Elder.[55]

Through the new addition to the seminary in 1895 it was now possible to provide single rooms to about one hundred and fifty students. Considering the times this was a very substantial physical plant for a seminary.

The faculty of the seminary for the school year 1895 was composed of Murray, Sele, Feeney, Kuhlmann and Louis Nau. Louis Herman Nau was a new addition to the faculty. He taught moral theology and sometimes church history. He was admitted by all to have possessed a very brilliant mind and to have been a very fine teacher. While a member of the faculty he wrote numerous historical and sociological essays, an important work on moral theology, and a dogmatic treatise entitled "Mary, Mediatrix of All Graces." With brief intermissions, spent in studying abroad, he taught at the seminary until 1910. He then left to take up parish work at St. Augustine and St. Lawrence Churches in Cincinnati. In 1924 after an absence of fourteen years, he was recalled to the seminary to serve as rector. In this same year he was made Domestic Prelate.[56]

In a faculty meeting held on November 29, 1895, the subject of Latin and its use in the seminary came up for discussion. At the meeting it was decided that in the examinations conducted in the fields of dogma, moral and canon law, each student should be able to answer one of the questions in Latin. This was to be the desideratum. The faculty noted, however, that if this could not be done by any one of the students, he would be permitted to answer in English.[57]

At a meeting of the faculty held at the beginning of the new scholastic year in 1896 (with archbishop in attendance), it was decided that dogmatic theology should be taught six times a week the same as moral theology. It was also decided to go a step further and require that the courses in dogma, moral, and canon law be taught in Latin. A new history textbook was needed and suggestions were proposed. The custom of granting two half holidays, instead of the one whole free day, began at this time. Tuesday and Thursday afternoons were decided upon. In regard to the matter of the dates for the conferring of the various major and minor orders, it was decided that tonsure would be given at the end of second philosophy; the first two minor orders would be given at the end of first theology; the last two minor orders would be given during the season of Lent in second theology; the subdeaconate would be given at the end of second theology; the deaconate would be given during the Lent of third theology; and the priesthood would be conferred at the close of the third year.[58]

The faculty for the next seven years (1896-1903) remained fundamentally unchanged consisting of Murray, Sele, Kuhlman, Feeney, and Nau. In 1897, Mr. Butala came to teach music. (In the year 1897 one hundred and fifty-two students were enrolled at the seminary.) Feeney left the faculty in 1899 and was replaced by Timothy Deasey. During these years Murray continued to teach liturgy; Nau taught the course in moral and church history; Slee, the classes in dogma, Scripture, and Hebrew; Kuhlmann, the classes in philosophy; and Deasey, the classes in Sacred Scripture, sacred eloquence, English and chant.

On April 23, 1900, a notice was sent out to all former students that an Alumni Association was to be formed, and that the first grand reunion would be held on May 16 of that year.[59]

The Golden Jubilee (1901)

Fifty years after the first students entered the seminary in the days of Archbishop Purcell, Mount St. Mary's celebrated with great gusto its Golden Jubilee. The memorial given out on the occasion read as follows:

Mt. St. Mary's of the West celebrated with pomp and splendor, its Golden Jubilee as a Theological seminary on Tuesday October 22, 1901. Preparation had been actively going on for some time to make the occasion a memorable one, and nature seemed to add its charms in gracing the festive days of the jubilee with the smile of most enchanting Indian summer weather.

The great part of the week, October 20-27, was given to the festivities. Besides the Golden Jubilee exercises, the Alumni Association of the Seminary held its annual meeting, and the rector, Rt. Rev. John B. Murray, was invested with the dignity of the Monsignorship. The venerable institution was decked in a gala attire, the national shields and bunting being tastefully interwoven with the softer shades of the papal standard, while from the tower and turret flags threw out their folds to catch breezes whose gently murmurings blended with the chorus of praise and alleluia.

The central driveway was lined on either side with varicolored festoons. At the entrance was a triumphal arch, on which were inscribed, in letters of gold, the words, "Our Golden Jubilee," with the dates, "1851" and "1901." A little farther on was another arch with the design, "Welcome, Alumni." Over the main entrance to the seminary was an awning, in which strips of bunting of different colors were exquisitely blended, the whole surmounted by a papal shield bearing the welcome, "Introite ejus Portas." The decoration of the interior of the building, especially, in the chapel and the refectory, bore evidence of skill and taste on the part of the students. The floral designs were the gift of the Rev. Dr. John Schoenboeft, of Cincinnati.

The guests began to arrive on Sunday evening, October 20, and from all parts of the United States came priests and prelates...from the plains of the West, from the busy marts of the East, from the shores of the Mexican Gulf, and the fertile slopes of the Northern States...to do honor to the Seminary and tender best wishes to her, their beloved alma mater.[60]

The formal opening of the jubilee festivities took place on Tuesday morning, October 22. At the time there were assembled one hundred and fifty priests and six bishops. A Pontifical Requiem Mass was celebrated by Bishop Richter, the former professor, for the deceased prelates, priests, students, and benefactors of the seminary. The remaining bishops and representatives of seminaries and colleges occupied places of honor in the sanctuary. At the end of Mass, John Murray, the rector, was elevated to the dignity of Domestic Prelate. He thus became the first rector to become a monsignor. Then the Reverend James Henry of St. Patrick's Church, Cincinnati, delivered an address on the history of the seminary. At eleven o'clock the priests and seminarians assembled in the Theologian's Hall for the reading of two papers, on by Mr. J. A. Dollard, and the other by Mr. Jeremiah Roach, both seminary students and members of the Newman Literary Society. On Wednesday morning Archbishop Elder celebrated the Pontifical Jubilee Mass. The Right Reverend John L. Spalding preached the sermon. In part, the sermon was as follows:

> Since last I stood within these historic walls, forty-three years have gone by, and yet amid all the changes, the memory of this seminary has ever remained with me. I have always regarded this institution as my Alma Mater. I am proud of my connection with it, and I look with pleasure to the time when I entered here as a student desirous of acquiring a portion of that learning and zeal for which the professors who were then placed over Mt. St. Mary's were justly famous. I myself owe a great deal to those saintly men who were here in 1858. It was here in this seminary that I resolved to become a priest, and to fashion my life after the pattern of those men of '58; and now when I look back over the years that have passed since then, I thank God fervently for that vocation. The Catholic Church in America has made gigantic strides of progress during the past half century, and its work has been assisted and strengthened in a meritorious manner by the seminary whose golden anniversary we celebrate today.[61]

At the beginning of the school year in 1902 Murray, Sele, Kuhlmann, Nau and Deasey comprised the faculty. At the start of the year stained glass windows which had been ordered by the Alumni Association from Munich, Germany, were placed in the seminary chapel. The five new windows were dedicated to Purcell, Rosecrans, Pabisch, Hecht, and Engbers.[62]

It is interesting to note on October 7 of this year the faculty's engagement of the students in a baseball game. Perhaps this was the forerunner of the present custom of the annual faculty game played at Fort Scott. The account of the game in the *Telegraph* said that "thirteen innings were required before the decision fell to the seminarians by the marginal score of 4 to 3."[63]

MOELLER, COADJUTOR (1903)

The Cincinnati diocese was in existence for more than eighty years before a native son was appointed to administer it. He was the Most Reverend Henry Moeller, a Cincinnatian, who became coadjutor bishop of Cincinnati on April 27, 1903, and archbishop upon the death of Archbishop William H. Elder on October 21, 1904. The fourth ordinary of the diocese was born in Cincinnati's West End on December 11, 1849, only a few years after his parents, Bernard Moeller and Teresa Witte Moeller, had immigrated to the United States from Germany. The family was to give the other sons and a daughter to religion. Ferdinand entered the Society of Jesus and Bernard, as a diocesan priest, eventually became chancellor of the diocese. The daughter, Anna, joined the Sisters of Charity of Mount St. Joseph's.[64]

After Henry Moeller attended St. Joseph's elementary school and St. Xavier's College, Archbishop John B. Purcell sent him to Rome for seven years of study the American College where he distinguished himself as a theology student. He was ordained in Rome on June 10, 1876. Shortly after his return to Cincinnati he was placed in charge of St. Patrick's church, Bellefontaine, where he remained for one year. Then he was named professor at Mount St. Mary's Seminary.[65]

Meanwhile, his former rector at the American College, the Very Reverend Silas M. Chatard had become bishop of Vincennes, and he asked the young priest to serve as his secretary. Father Moeller was granted leave of absence, but spent only a few months in Vincennes. Bishop Elder became coadjutor bishop of Cincinnati and he recalled the priest and made him his own secretary in July, 1880. In this position, and especially as chancellor of the diocese which he became in 1886, Father Moeller became the archbishop's right hand man in the administration of the diocese.[66]

His long association with Archbishop Elder was interrupted in April, 1900, when he was appointed Bishop of Columbus. He received his Episcopal consecration from the hands of Archbishop Elder in St. Peter's Cathedral on August 25 of that same year. The Diocese of Columbus was beset by such a grave financial crisis at this time that church authorities were considering the possibility of dividing that diocese between Cincinnati and Cleveland. But the new bishop, in his regime of less than three years, managed to weather the storm and to place his diocese on a strong financial foundation.[67]

Archbishop Elder, now in his eighties, found it increasingly difficult to administer the Cincinnati diocese and asked for a coadjutor bishop. Bishop Moeller was appointed to this position on April 27, 1903. It seems that with Moeller's coming, Elder assumed fewer duties in the diocese. This was even more noticeable in the case of the seminary. During the last few years of his life Elder had ceased to concern himself with any of the affairs of the seminary. Moeller was in virtual charge of the diocese at the time of the archbishop's death on October 31, 1904. Cardinal Gibbons bestowed the Pallium, the insignia of the archbishop's office, on Archbishop Moeller on February 15 of the following year.[68]

Since the diocese no longer faced the pioneering problems which had confronted it in earlier years, Archbishop Moeller's main task was administration. It can be said that, along with Archbishop Elder, he was a key figure in bringing the diocese back to its former eminent position. During his long service as secretary and chancellor to Archbishop Elder, the two churchmen collaborated closely in producing what was the outstanding achievement of the Elder administration, the organization of the administrative structure of the diocese. During his term as chancellor Father Moeller also had shared with his superior the burden of coping with the effects of the Purcell's administration's financial failure.[69]

In 1902 the seminary now boasted a concert band. The following men were members of this first concert band: Lawrence Denning, E. Werle, A. Kistner, Herman Leising, George Meyer, H. Hoestman, C. Schneider, Nicholas Schneider, James Falls, H. Scrypinski, E. Berry, John Sialar, L. Brinker, and W. Schaffer.[70] It is said that the band enjoyed a fine reputation among the Catholic residents on the "Hill."

The faculty for the school year 1903 was again Murray, Sele, Nau and Deasey. In this year Father William Clarke came to the staff to replace Kuhlmann who had left for the Soldiers' Home in Dayton. William Clarke, the newcomer, was born in Springfield on February 2, 1887. He attended St. Raphael's school there and St. Xavier's College in Cincinnati. After deciding to study for the priesthood, he entered Mount St. Mary's and was ordained in June, 1901, by Archbishop Elder. He served at the cathedral for two months and was then sent to the Catholic University at Washington for two-years of post-graduate work. He returned to the diocese in 1903 and was appointed professor of Sacred Scripture at the seminary, a position he held for eight years. In July of 1911 he left the seminary for pastoral work in the diocese. He died in early March of 1942.[71]

In the fall of this year Elder, accompanied by Moeller, attended the faculty meeting held at the seminary. The archbishop asked that a printed code of rules be drawn up. A draft was made and submitted to the faculty. At a meeting held on February 4, 1904, the rules of discipline were formally adopted.[72]

DECISION TO MOVE

Early in January of 1904, it became apparent that a move was on foot to transfer the location of the seminary from Price Hill. At the time the proposal was made Archbishop Moeller had asked for the opinions of the priests of the diocese concerning the change. There were strong opinions stated both for and against changing the location of the major seminary.

On March 22, 1904, the final decision of Archbishop Moeller was stated in the *Catholic Telegraph* as follows:

No doubt you are aware that Mt. St. Mary's Seminary has been sold to the Sisters of the Good Shepherd, Bank Street, for $126,000 plus street assessment of $3,000 on condition that the houses on Bank and Baum Streets be closed. This sale was rendered necessary for the following reasons:

1. To put the grounds and the buildings in proper condition to meet modern requirements, such as laundry, bathrooms, approaches, grading, enclosures, cement walks and steps, retaining wall, etc., is estimated to cost at least $50,000 for which expense there are no available funds.

2. Even were such funds available, Mt. St. Mary's is at present so surrounded by dwellings that the privacy needed for an Ecclesiastical Seminary could no longer be maintained.

3. The expense of maintaining two separate institutions as boarding schools entails too great a burden to the Diocese. We feel that both the fair name of the Archdiocese of Cincinnati—the Catholic Metropolis of the middle west—and the love of our priests for their Alma Mater call on us to preserve and support with might and main old Mt. St. Mary's of the West, although it has become necessary to transplant it to a new location.

In order to accommodate the students in outside dioceses who have supported Mt. St. Mary's so loyally in the past, it is suggested that alterations and additions be made at Cedar Point, to which Mt. St. Mary's has been transferred. The cost of the improvements will not exceed $40,000. This will provide one hundred and twenty-five single rooms for students. It is the experience of all seminaries that an increase in the number of students means a per capita decrease of expenses. This is evident for light, fuel, general repairs, service, etc., are nearly the same for one hundred students as for fifty students. An increased number of boarders in a hotel decreases the per capita cost of guests.[73]

In 1959 it was announced that the Good Shepard Sisters were vacating the property on Price Hill and were moving to North Bend Road. The Telegraph on the occasion of the announcement wrote as follows:

The *Telegraph* on the occasion of the announcement wrote at follows:

What will become of Mt. St. Mary's, has not been decided. Although part of it is more than a century old, it deserves a better fate than demolition. Carrying its years well, it is a sturdy memorial to the hundreds of young levites who studied and prayed there. And it is still, in Archbishop Purcell's words, "a monument to the liberality and zeal of the pioneer Catholics of Cincinnati."[74]

Although it did deserve a more benign fate than demolition, demolition was its sad fate. In the summer of 1962 wrecking crews entered the premises and, by the fall, the old building was completely torn down. Not knowing that the old seminary had been torn down, this author was extremely disappointed on a trip to the site in the fall of 1962 to find everything was gone. To one who had visited the old seminary site only once before, but how had read enough about it to feel a sort of nostalgic charm for its rather flamboyant days, it was indeed a sad and melancholy scene.

The sale and demolition of the old Mount St. Mary's Seminary building on the brow of Price Hill in Cincinnati was the result of a decision made by the Cincinnati Planning Commission, the Good Shepard Sisters had announced. The Sisters, who had owned the property since 1904, said a real estate developer had agreed to purchase the building if the planning commission would permit the erection of a large apartment house on the site. The seminary building would be razed to make room for the apartment project which developer James L. Brown said would cost about $2,000,000.[75]

Archdiocesan authorities, as well as the Good Shepard Sisters, said every attempt had been made to salvage the building for use by some religious or charitable organization before deciding to sell the property. It had been suggested that the building be transformed into a home for the aged, a novitiate, a hospital, a school, or a similar institution. Several religious communities were invited to take over the building. In each instance, however, investigation proved the cost of conversion to be prohibitive.

SUMMARY

In this chapter the events in the history of Mount St. Mary's Seminary between the years of 1879 and 1904 have been reviewed. With the closing of the seminary in 1879 due to the diocesan financial failure, an attempt was made to reopen the seminary as an institution of higher learning for the secular clergy. This proposal of Spalding's did not meet with success, and Elder began preparations for the reopening of the seminary for the diocese. This was accomplished in September of 1887, and Byrne became the new rector. During his administration, which emphasized discipline, the seminary slowly sought to return to its former higher standards. With the coming of John Murray as rector in 1894, the seminary came very close to achieving that aim. Perhaps if the decision had not been made to change its location, the former glory of the seventies would have been recaptured. Nonetheless, the seminary did reach a high standard of achievement during Murray's time.

The spirit of the seminary was excellent and the faculty for its day was extremely able.

In regard to the curriculum, due to the influence of Leo XIII on philosophy, and the Committee of Buffalo, the course of studies for American seminaries was fairly well defined and standardized for the future. Development, if any were to take place, would have to be in the area of professional standards of the teachers and the sharpening of the administrative organization.

NOTES

[1] F. J. Thonnard, *A Short History of Philosophy*, pp. 991-992. Translated, revised and corrected edition by Edward A. Maziarz. Tournai: Desclee & Cie, 1955.

[2] *Ibid.*, p.992.

[3] *Catholic Telegraph*, November 2, 1899, pp.1-4.

[4] McDonald, *op. cit.*, p. 29.

[5] Appendix C.

[6] Appendix D.

[7] *Catholic Telegraph*, April 15, 1880, p. 4.

[8] Lamott, *op. cit.*, p. 86.

[9] *Ibid.*, p. 86.

[10] *Ibid.*, p. 87.

[11] *Ibid.*, p. 87.

[12] *Ibid.*, p. 88.

[13] *Ibid.*, p. 90.

[14] *Ibid.*, p. 91.

[15] *Ibid.*, p. 92.

[16] Letter, J. L. Spalding to William H. Elder, Peoria, August 29, 1880 as quoted in Ellis, John Tracy, *The Formative Years of the Catholic University of America*, p. 68. Washington: American Historical Association, 1946.

[17] Letter, J. L. Spalding to William H. Elder, Peoria, September 7, 1880, as quoted in Ellis, *op. cit.*, pp. 69-70.

[18] Letter, J. L. Spalding to William H. Elder, Peoria, September 16, 1880, as quoted in Ellis, *op. cit.*, pp. 70-77.

[19] Letter, J. L. Spalding to John McCloskey, Peoria, October 23, 1880, as quoted in Ellis, *op. cit.*, pp. 72-73.

[20] Letter, J. L. Spalding to William H. Elder, Peoria, November 6, 1880, as quoted in Ellis, *op. cit.*, p. 74.

[21] Letter, J. L. Spalding to William H. Elder, Peoria, November 14, 1880, as quoted in Ellis, *op. cit.*, p. 74.

[22] Letter, William H. Elder to James Gibbons, Cincinnati, November 19, 1880, as quoted in Ellis, *op. cit.*, pp. 74-75.

[23] Letter, Elder to Byrne, November 29, 1882, p. 306. MSMSA.

[24] Letter, Elder to Mackey, January 3, 1883, MSMSA.

[25] *Catholic Telegraph*, October 28, 1886, p. 4.

[26] Letter, Elder to Sele, Cincinnati, July 17, 1887, MSMSA.

[27] Kelly and Kerwin, *op. cit.*, p. 366.

[28] *Ibid.*, *op.cit.*, pp. 367-368.

[29] Letter, Elder to Gmeiner, Cincinnati, August 3, 1887, MSMSA.

[30] Letter, Elder to Hecht, Cincinnati, August 11, 1887, MSMSA.

[31] *Catholic Telegraph*, May 26, 1887, p. 4.

[32] Kelly and Kerwin, *op. cit.*, p. 366.

[33] Kelly and Kerwin, *op. cit.*, p. 405.

[34] Sister Mary Agnes McCann, *The History of Mother Seton's Daughters*, p. 273. New York: Longmans, Green and Company, 1923. Three Volumes.

[35] *A Gateway to the Priesthood*, p. 59.

[36] Kelly and Kerwin, *op. cit.*, p. 373.

[37] Letter, Elder to Byrne, Cincinnati, February 13, 1888, MSMSA.

[38] Pastoral of Elder, Cincinnati, May 1888, MSMSA.

[39] Kelly and Kerwin, *op. cit.*, p. 374.

[40] *Catholic Telegraph*, October 2, 1890, p. 5.

[41] Kelly and Kerwin, *op. cit.*, p. 375.

[42] *Catholic Telegraph*, July 16, 1891, p. 5.

[43] Faculty Minutes, April 28, 1892. MSMSA.

[44] *Catholic Telegraph*, September 15, 1892, p. 5.

[45] Joseph Michael Conners, "Catholic Homiletic Theory in Historical Perspective," p. 341. Unpublished Doctor's Dissertation, Northwestern University, 1962.

[46] *Catholic Telegraph*, September 15, 1892, p. 2.

[47] *Ibid.*, May 11, 1893, p. 4.

[48] *Ibid.*, March 2, 1894, p. 5.

[49] *Ibid.*, April 25, 1895, p. 1.

[50] Kelly and Kirwin, *op. cit.*, p. 406

[51] *Catholic Telegraph*, September 20, 1894, p. 1.

[52] Minutes of Faculty Meeting, September 1894. MSMSA.

[53] *Catholic Telegraph*, July 12, 1940, p. 1.

[54] *Ibid.*, March 7, 1895, p. 4.

[55] *Ibid.*, March 17, 1895, p. 4.

[56] Cf. Chapter Seven.

[57] Minutes of Faculty Meeting, November 29, 1895. MSMSA.

[58] Minutes of the Faculty Meeting, August 16, 1896. MSMSA.

[59] *Catholic Telegraph*, April 26, 1900, p. 1.

Ibid., May 17, 1900, p. 1.

[60] Memorial of the Golden Jubilee, p. 3. MSMSA.

[61] Memorial of the Golden Jubilee, p. 26. MSMSA.

[62] *Catholic Telegraph*, September 4, 1902, p. 5.

[63] *Ibid.*, October 9, 1902, p. 5.

[64] Lamott, *op. cit.*, p. 92.

[65] *Ibid.*, p. 94.

[66] *Ibid.*, p. 94.

[67] *Ibid.*, p. 95.

[68] *Ibid.*, p. 96.

[69] *Ibid.*, p. 96.

[70] *Catholic Telegraph*, June 26, p. B-1.

[71] *Ibid.*, September 24, 1903, p. 4.

[72] Minutes of the Faculty Meeting, October 8, 1903. MSMSA.

[73] *Catholic Telegraph*, March 22, 1904, p. 4.

[74] *Ibid.*, March 7, 1959, p. 4.

[75] *Catholic Telegraph*, April 22, 1960, p. A-3.

CHAPTER FOUR

The Founding of St. Gregory's Seminary

INTRODUCTION

This chapter will deal with the founding of the Preparatory Seminary of St. Gregory at Cedar Point (now Mount Washington). It is important to keep in mind that the diocese had a preparatory seminary long before the founding of St. Gregory's. The first students in the little seminary begun in 1829 listed among their members some "preparatory" students. This remained the almost unbroken tradition of the diocese during the days at the Athenaeum, at the seminary at Brown County, at the Episcopal residence, and certainly during the days of Mount St. Mary's College and the days of the "Preparatorians" on Price Hill. But as the years went on, the status of the original preparatory seminary began to change. In the early sixties, the idea of a "mixed" college for educating both clerical and lay students was abandoned, and it was decided that clerical students in the preparatory years should be separated from the clerical students in the major seminary. At this juncture, St. Gregory's was founded as a preparatory seminary for clerical students, separated entirely from the locale and administration of the major seminary. St. Gregory's was founded in 1890. Reverend J. C. Albrinck was the first rector. In 1892 he was succeeded by Reverend Henry Brinkmeyer who remained the rector of the seminary until it closed in the year of 1907. During these years it grew and prospered. The administration was excellent. The professors of the time were generally well educated and prepared for their work. The curriculum was very thorough and well designed.

Due to the moving of the major seminary to the same site in 1904, the preparatory seminary moved to West Seventh Street in downtown Cincinnati. Here again a modification in the plan of the minor seminary was tried. It was thought that it would be best to allow those in the preparatory years to remain at home and attend the seminary as any day student would. For many reasons this plan did not work, and the minor seminary ceased operation in 1907. It did not resume its work again until 1924. This chapter will deal with these events.

EVENTS PRECEDING THE FOUNDING (1829-1890)

As explained in Chapter II, the first preparatory seminary in the diocese actually had its beginning in 1829 in the little frame seminary which had been prepared by Fenwick. Clicteur wrote, "there were then four seminarians studying theology and six young men who were taught Latin."[1] Thus the preparatory seminary goes back in history to the very beginning of the seminary in Cincinnati. Thus the preparatory seminary goes back in history to the very beginning of the seminary in Cincinnati.

In 1831 when Fenwick built his Athenaeum, it was a "mixed" college, that is, it was designed to prepare students for the ministry as well as for secular vocations. The Athenaeum, for all intents and purposes, ceased functioning as a "mixed" college when taken over by the Jesuits in 1840.

From our meager information, apparently there were preparatory seminarians among the small group of students at Brown County from 1840-1845. This seems also to have been the case with respect to the seminarians who lived at the Jesuit Scholasticate in 1845 and 1846. It is certainly true that there were seminarians taking their classical studies at the Bishop's residence from 1847-1851.[2]

During this time, and for many of the succeeding years, Purcell sent some preparatory seminarians to St. Thomas Seminary in Bardstown, Kentucky, or to St. Mary of the Barrens, Missouri. St. Thomas Seminary in Bardstown was proclaimed the Provincial Preparatory Seminary at the First Provincial Council of Cincinnati.[3]

In 1855 a college of St. Joseph was begun at Chillicothe by Hallinan who had been the first rector of the seminary on Price Hill. Hallinan had thought of this college in terms of a preparatory seminary for Mount St. Mary's. However, the college was never looked upon with any great degree of favor by Purcell. It lasted only one year.

In 1853 an event occurred which throws much light on Purcell's idea of a minor seminary. A young Irish priest offered Purcell a farm of 320 acres, worth about $35.00 an acre, for the construction of a "petit seminaire." The offer was not accepted because of Purcell's preference for the "mixed" college.[4] Purcell was a "Mountain" man, that is, he had come from Mount St. Mary's Seminary, Emmitsburg. The educational philosophy there was, and still is, that the preparatory seminary should contain both clerical and lay students.[5] This idea was responsible also for Purcell's failure to get the Sulpicians in 1851.

This is precisely the philosophy behind Purcell's establishment of Mount St. Mary's College in 1855. Both clerical and lay students were accepted here in the same fashion as at Mount St. Mary's Seminary, Emmitsburg.

Both were given thorough classical training for four years. The seminary-college combination did seem to have many advantages. Financially, it was a source of support to the seminary. Also, it was fertile recruiting ground for the secular clergy. Proximity made it possible for the secular clergy to exercise a very definite intellectual influence over the coming generation of possible clergymen.

In 1863, because of the war, Mount St. Mary's College ceased existence. However, the preparatory seminary at Mount St. Mary's Seminary continued operating until 1879. As was seen in Chapter Two, the students who went to the Mount in those days were called "Preparatorians."

It was not long after the "Preparatorians" were taken into Mount St. Mary's that this arrangement was found by some to be far from ideal. Toward the end of 1872, and around 1873, plans for a separate college and preparatory seminary were discussed. Hearing of the discussion of these plans, Engbers wrote to the archbishop on January 16, 1873, and explained his view that he diocese really ought to conduct a strictly preparatory seminary distinct in administration and location from the major seminary. He offered his own services for this project. Nothing came of it, however, most likely because Purcell still did not quite favor the idea of a "petit seminaire." No man from the "Mountain" would.[6]

In 1884 the Third Plenary Council of Baltimore in its decrees spoke about the need for strictly preparatory seminaries and gave a series of directives as to their government and the scope of their studies. As to "mixed" colleges, it states these might be tolerated as long as no other provisions could be made on account of pecuniary means.[7] This revived the old discussion of the decade before.

On September 12, 1887, when Mount St. Mary's opened, it was deemed advisable by the archbishop and his consultants to discontinue the preparatory department which had heretofore been annexed to the Theological School. It was then decided to erect as soon as possible a separate institution for preparatory studies.

In June of 1889 Elder urged the starting of a preparatory seminary where, as he put it, "young boys who show marks of vocation to the priesthood can foster their good dispositions while studying the preparatory Seminary."[8] A little after this, he gave Albrinck, along with Engbers, Richter and a few others who had been pushing the idea of a minor seminary completely separated from the major seminary for the last fifteen years or so, the permission to go ahead with their plans. Albrinck with Engbers now set themselves to the task with great earnestness. In less than a year the first classes were started, and a large tract of land was purchased for a permanent site.[9]

SITE AT CEDAR POINT (1890)

Late in the summer of 1890 a fine tract of land, comprising fifty-seven and one-half acres, was published at Cedar Point (now known as Mount Washington), and work on the man or center building was put into motion. It was thought that with luck the building might be occupied in the fall. A strike which occurred just at this time in the building trades union made it apparent that the fall occupancy date was out of the question. Construction was completed in August, 1891, and the seminarians moved in the following school year. It was estimated that he new building had cost $38,000.[10] Louis Picket was the architect and the one who supervised the actual work of construction.

The first building erected at Cedar Point was fifty-seven feet wide and one hundred eighteen feet long. It contained a basement, first and second floors, and an attic. In the basement were located the refectory, the students' recreation room, the kitchen, the provision cellars, the bakery, the laundry, and boiler rooms. On the first floor, to the left one entered a reception room, rector's suite, a parlor, and a classroom. On the right, as one entered, was the chapel, which later became the philosophers' hall. On the second floor there was a large study hall where the old library used to be, a classroom, and suites for the priests. In the attic was a large dormitory which continued to be used as such until very recent times. [11]

The original fifty-seven acres, upon which the first building was erected, were purchased with the money from the generous bequest of the late Reuben R. Springer. However, thirteen and one half additional acres adjoining the original property were bought in January of 1893. Another fourteen and one half acres were added to the property in 1927, and in the following year a tract of thirteen acres was bought. The grounds of St. Gregory's comprise today an area of ninety-eight-and-one-half acres in Mount Washington.

ALBRINCK, RECTOR (1890-1892)

The beginning of classes for the new preparatory seminary did not wait for the building to be erected. Classes for the new minor seminary began in the fall of 1890 in the old school hall of Holy Trinity parish in downtown Cincinnati. The *Telegraph* of September 11, 1890, had this prosaic comment to make on the occasion: "The classes for the Preparatory Seminary of St. Gregory were opened on last Monday, in the school building of Holy Trinity congregation. At nine o'clock, there was a solemn High Mass to the Holy Ghost, celebrated by the Very Rev. Vicar General, J. C. Albrinck." During the ensuing year Engbers, who had labored many years for a strictly clerical minor seminary in the diocese, was the only priest who taught the ten young students who were in attendance. Some of them were from out of town and had to board in the private homes of the parish.

Yet, though Engbers had labored for this cause over the years, John Albrinck, who had also labored manfully for the erection of a strictly clerical minor seminary, was appointed by Elder to be the first rector. Albrinck was born in Hunteburg, Hanover, German, on January 17, 1830. He had come with his parents to Cincinnati at the age of six. He attended the Holy Trinity Grade School, and then went on to graduate from St. Xavier College just at the time it had been taken over by the Jesuits. He wished to become a priest of the diocese of Cincinnati, and Purcell sent him as a seminarian to St. Sulpice in Paris. There he was ordained in the Cathedral of Notre Dame on May 21, 1853. For many years thereafter he labored for the church in Cincinnati, finally become the Vicar-General. It is interesting to note that he was a close friend of the famous Joseph Schroeder, the arch-foe of the Americanizers during the great debate in the last years of the eighteen-nineties. Another interesting note on Albrinck is that most of the fruit trees now growing in St. Gregory's were planted by him. It is estimated that during the two-year period that he was rector, he planted one thousand five hundred fruit trees on the property. [12]

SEMINARY OPENS AT CEDAR POINT (1891)

The new minor seminary in Mount Washington opened its doors for the first time on September 8, 1891. Twenty-three young students walked through its doors. Ten of these were the students that Engbers had been teaching downtown at Holy Trinity. The other thirteen were the new "freshman."[13] It is interesting to note that an article written concerning the opening of the new seminary referred to it as "Mount St. Gregory." [14]

In September of 1892 there were six full years of study, beginning wit the sixth class, or the first year of high school, and ending with the first class, or the second year of college. The curriculum was as follows. In the first year of high school (the sixth class) the student studied Christian Doctrine, Latin, English, German, arithmetic, history, geography, elocution, penmanship, zoology, singing, and the rubrics of Mass. In the second year of high school (the fifth class), the student studied the same subjects as before except that algebra was substituted for arithmetic and Greek was introduced. In the third year of high school (the fourth class), the students took Christian doctrine, Latin, Greek, English, German, algebra, history, geography, elocution, bookkeeping, geology, singing and rubrics. In the fourth year of high school (the third class), the student took Christian Doctrine, Latin, Greek, English, French, plane and solid geometry, natural philosophy, botany, history, bookkeeping, elocution, singing, and rubrics. In the first year of college (the second class), the course consisted of Christian Doctrine, Latin, Greek, English, French, trigonometry and measurement, natural philosophy, chemistry, history, astronomy, elocution, singing and rubrics. In the second year of college, (the first class), Christian Doctrine, Latin, Greek, English, French, mathematics, astronomy, chemistry, civics, history, elocution, singing, rubrics, and logic were taken.[15]

In regard to the Latin course, Schultz's *Latin Grammar* and Arnold's first and second Latin books were used in the first year of high school. Schultz and Arnold were studied further in the second year of high school with work in Lindsay's *Nepos* added to the work. Schultz was continued in the third year, with continuation of the work in *Nepos.* In the second section of the year, Lincoln's *Ovid* was entered. Casserly's prosody and Arnold's prose compositions were begun here. In the fourth year of high school, Schultz was still studied. The remainder of the year consisted of work in Casserly's prosody, Arnold's prose composition, (till Part II), Lincoln's *Ovid,* and Harkness' course in Caesar. Sallust and Cicero were continued, Frieze with Virgil's *Aeneid* and Arnold's prose composition, emphasizing original compositions, completed the course material.[16]

Greek was taken in every year except the first year of high school. English, mathematics, history, and some courses in science were taken every year. The shift away from the strictly classical course of the early Athenaeum had begun. Now greater emphasis was placed on the study of English and English Literature which had come in during the middle part of the century. Increasing emphasis was placed on scientific courses. Considering later developments, this was really quite progressive for the times.

The faculty for the first year at St. Gregory's was composed of the Very Reverend John C. Albrinck, Rector; the Reverend Bernard H. Engbers, Vice-Rector; the Reverend Joseph A. Shoe; the Reverend John Henry Holthuas, the Dean of Discipline. Joseph Shoe who became the rector of Mount St. Mary's, had been ordained in Rome in 1888, and came to the seminary fully qualified to teach. The other faculty member, John Henry Holthaus, was ordained in 1885 and now undertook to teach history and music in the seminary.[17]

Archbishop Elder came out to bless the new building on October 21, 1891.[18] The remainder of the year proceeded on a rather uneventful course. The seminary school year ended on June 27, 1892. As the students were going home, it was promised that on their return the following year teaching of the complete classical course outlined would begin.[19]

BRINKMEYER, RECTOR (1892-1907)
In July, 1892, John Albrinck decided that he had set the minor seminary on course, and that it would be well for him to return to his beloved parish of Holy Trinity. With the permission of the archbishop, he packed his bags and left at the end of the school year.[20]

The man chosen to succeed him as the second rector of the minor seminary was the Reverend Henry Brinkmeyer. At the time of his appointment he was forty-five years of age, and the pastor of St. James Church in Wyoming, Ohio. Born in Cincinnati on March 16, 1854, he attended St. Xavier College and then entered the Grand Seminary at Montreal. He was ordained in that city on December 22, 1877. After serving ten years as pastor in Xenia, Ohio and in Carthage, Ohio, he was appointed to the faculty of Mount St. Mary's when it reopened in 1877. In his first year back at Price Hill, Brinkmeyer taught the course in philosophy. In 1891, when the minor seminary opened at Cedar Point, he was appointed to the faculty there. [21]

During all the years that he was rector he was singularly loved and esteemed by the students and the faculty. He was respected as a man of learning, great gentleness, kindness, and goodness. The priests living today, who were students during these days at St. Gregory's tell of great virtues of the man. According to Monsignor Molloy, "to see him was a benediction." [22]

The late Father Stein, in after years recalled Father Brinkmeyer: "He was well fitted by his deep spirituality for the task of rector...(he was)...a staunch champion of the preparatory seminary as projected by the Council of Trent. In this he had the support of Bishop Henry J. Richter, first Bishop of Grand Rapids, who sent all his students to St. Gregory's."

While he was rector, Brinkmeyer composed a little devotional work entitled *The Lover of Souls.* In its day, it was received with sincere acclaim. Other works or his are not known. But along this same line, he was a member of the organization of the Priest's Eucharistic League, along with Bishop Maes of Covington and Father Bede Maler of St. Meinrad's Abbey. [23]

The faculty in the first year of the rectorship of Brinkmeyer consisted of Brinkmeyer, Engbers, Shee, Holthaus, and Drufner. Twenty-six more students than the previous year were now attending the seminary. Around January, to the rear of the main building at approximately the same site as the present day garages, there was a frame structure built to house the gymnasium and the bowling alleys. In January of 1893 examinations were held in the following subjects: German, religion, English, mathematics, Greek, natural science, history, geography, Latin, bookkeeping, and business letter writing. [24]

The faculty of St. Gregory's Seminary and the subjects they taught for scholastic year of 1893-94 were: Henry Brinkmeyer, rector, prefect of studies (Christian Doctrine, French, Ancient and U.S. History, geography, bookkeeping); Bernard H. Engbers (Latin, Greek, German, mathematics, ceremonies); Albert E. Drufner (Latin, Greek, zoology, elocution, German, arithmetic); H. Holthaus (Latin, English, German, church history, business letter writing, penmanship, music, elocution); Matthew O'Brien (Latin, English, algebra, geology, elocution). [25]

In the beginning of the school year of 1894, Bruegge, J. P. Downey, and J. Henry Schengber were added to the faculty. This faculty remained unchanged for the most part until the final days prior to the closing of the minor seminary.

On November 29, 1894, the south wing of St. Gregory's (which later burned down) was dedicated. Elder and Maes of Covington were present. The new addition consisted of "an annex or corridor, twenty-five by sixty feet, similar to the annex on the other side of the main building, and a large wing, fifty by one hundred and twenty five feet, adjoining the said annex." The annex was to be used for "Kitchens, etc., on the first floor and priests' rooms on the second with trunks in the attic." [26] The improvements on St. Gregory's had cost $40,337.25. [27] At the end of the year, Joseph Sieber became the first student from there to enter Mount St. Mary's. [28] The first class entered a year later.

The faculty of St. Gregory's Seminary for the scholastic year 1895-96 consisted of Henry Brinkmeyer, rector; Florence Bruegge; Albert Drufner; H. Holthaus; Matthew O'Brien; J. P. Downey; Augustine C. Adelmann; and J. Henry Schengber.

Augustine C. Adelman, the newcomer, was born in Germany on February 2, 1868. He came to this country in his youth and took his philosophy and theology at Mount St. Mary's Seminary. He was ordained by Archbishop Elder on June 21, 1893. After serving as assistant parish priest at St. Paul's, Cincinnati, then as pastor of Visitation parish in Eaton, he was appointed professor at St. Gregory's. Forced, because of ill health to retire from the seminary, he held various other posts in the diocese. On March 15, 1924, he was again appointed professor of dogmatic theology in the Mount St. Mary's seminary, a post he held for ten years. While a professor there, he obtained his degree of doctor of theology.[29]

On June 17, 1896, the first class of graduates left the institution. They were seven in number, with James W. Logarty the valedictorian of the class.[30]

At the beginning of the school year in 1896, St. Gregory's issued its first catalogue. The catalogue had this to say concerning the object of the minor seminary:

> The object of the Preparatory Seminary is to give to virtuous and talented young men an opportunity to develop their vocations to the priesthood, and to receive an education thoroughly fitting them for the prosecution of their philosophical and theological studies. Boys who evidently have no vocation to the priesthood are excluded. All pupils are supposed to have a vocation or to deliberate maturely whether they are called to God. For this reason, the priesthood is ceaselessly held up before them, and the greatest stress is laid upon the virile virtues its demands, and upon the importance of calmly and prayerfully reflecting on the priestly vocation for the purpose of self-examination. In other words, to take the boy at the most critical period of his life and form his character for the ardent and exclusive duties of the secular priest, is the exclusive aim of the Preparatory Seminary. The studies made in St. Gregory's are on the plan of our most successful institutions of higher learning, but they are all subsidiary to the special object of a preparatory seminary, viz., the training of a young man for the priesthood.[31]

Concerning the courses of studies for the minor seminary, the new catalogue stated that the Third Plenary Council of Baltimore had outlined with great clarity the plan of studies to be followed in the preparatory seminary. It had the following to say about the study of Christian Doctrine and languages:

These conciliar enactments, together in all classes and developed gradually. As pupils advance in their course a more thorough explanation of the principles of faith is given, and opposing errors are more fully confuted.

As English is the language of the country and every American priest is expected to speak and write it not only with accuracy and ease but with a certain degree of elegance, much attention is paid to this knowledge and culture. Frequent original compositions are exacted and carefully corrected; public reading is required to be given with exact pronunciation, clear utterance and due emphasis. Classes of elocution are graded for the six years.

Latin being the language of the Church deservedly receives marked attention. It is our aim to so teach it, that our pupils may not only write it correctly but also speak it with some fluency. In the two higher classes, the Catechism of the Council of Trent is explained in Latin and the students are required to answer in the same tongue. But, throughout the course translations must be rendered from English into Latin, for in this manner they will acquire a certain skill in applying the rules of Grammar and become acquainted with idiomatic properties of the Latin language.

As no scholarly study of the Sacred Scriptures can be made without knowledge of Greek, and as the study of that language is the door to the enjoyment of the world's greatest literature, we begin the Greek Grammar in the second year, and continue to allow it at least three hours a week.

Although English is the language of the Seminary we feel the need of insisting upon the study of the German language and making it obligatory upon all our students. We endeavor to enable all to at least understand it sufficiently to minister in that tongue in cases of necessity. French is taught to those who already speak German or who find it more useful to them in their respective dioceses.[32]

The faculty of St. Gregory's Seminary for the scholastic year 1896-97 were Brinkmeyer, Bruegge, Holthaus, O'Brien, Downey, Schengber, and two newcomers, F. M. Lamping and Francis Roth.

Father Roth was born in Reading, Ohio, July 21, 1872. His early studies were made at Sacred Heart and SS. Peter and Paul Schools in Reading, and he then entered St. Xavier College. Much of his training for the priesthood was received at Mount St. Mary's Emmitsburg, Maryland. He completed his studies at Mount St. Mary's in Cincinnati and was ordained on December 22, 1895. Father Roth's first appointment was as assistant at Holy Trinity where he remained for about nine months. He was then sent to St. Gregory's Seminary where he was professor, treasurer, and procurator for eleven years. Later he organized St. William's parish in Price Hill.[33]

In 1896 Archbishop Elder celebrated at St. Gregory's the Golden Jubilee of his consecration. The seminary arranged a "polyglot" program in his honor. The contribution of seminarian John G. Stein was an address in Latin, which began: "Utinam verbis laetitiam excequi possimus, quae corda nostra hodie tenet!" (Would that we might express by words the joy which today possesses our hearts!) Other contributions to the program included "A Garland of

Flowers," an English ode by Francis J. Beckman, destined to become Archbishop of Dubuque; "Te Pastor Optime," a Latin dissertation by Ed Hirschler, who returned to his native Alsace before his graduation and is still living there as a priest in retirement; a German acrostic poem by Herman Limbeck, who became a priest of the Cincinnati diocese and died in 1917 (the initial letters of this poem spelled out the name Wilhelm Heinrich Elder); and address in French, "Le Soir d'un Beau Jour" (The Evening of a Beautiful Day), by William Shuer who was ordained for his archdiocese in 1901, and who died in 1931; "Fifty Years in the Vineyard," an address in English by John Gallagher, who became a Cincinnati priest and who died in the 1918 influenza epidemic; and an address in Greek by Fred Polgsted, a student who died before his ordination.[34]

At the beginning of the scholastic year of 1897 the faculty of St. Gregory was composed of Brinkmeyer, Bruegge, O'Brien, Downey, Schengber, Lamping, Roth, and Hammersbach. Hammersbach, who had been the assistant at St. Joseph's Church in Cincinnati, was made the new professor of music. The faculty remained for four years, through 1901.

In 1897 there was an enrollment of ninety students. In September of 1900, however, St. Gregory's had an enrollment of only seventy-nine students, forty-one of whom were preparing for the diocese of Cincinnati. The remaining thirty-eight were for other dioceses.[35] In 1901, St. Gregory's seventy-two students, thirty-seven of whom were for the diocese of Cincinnati, and to the other thirty-seven were for other dioceses.[36] It was estimated that in this year the cost of educating one student for one year in the minor seminary was $330.00. In September of 1902 St. Gregory's had seventy-five students, thirty-six from Cincinnati and thirty-nine from outside the diocese. [37]

On March 12, 1902, the Feast of St. Gregory was observed at Cedar Point. Reverend J. J. Abell of Louisville read the Mass. Elder was in attendance. The Cecilian Choir rendered Witt's "Missa Exsultet." Those appearing in the literary and musical program which followed were J. Fehring, F. Varley, J. Roger, Oswald McGuinn, Bernard Robers, and Martin Molloy, (who recited a poem, "A Legend.") [38]

On June 22, 1902, the annual commencement exercises took place at St. Gregory's. Archbishop Elder was there and conferred the degrees. Diplomas were given to John Burke of Lebanon, Ohio, Oswald McGinn of Michigan, Martin Molloy of Washington, C. H. Bernard Robers, Frank Siefert, Henry Buse, George Meyer, William Spickelman (all of Cincinnati), and Frank Varley of Springfield. The essays delivered by the class were as follows: "True Greatness", Siefert; "Orestes A. Brownson", Spickelman; "Daniel O'Connel", Molloy; "Ludwig Windthorst", Meyer; "Garcia Moreno", Burke; "Most Rev. John Hughes", Varley; "Leo XIII", McGinn; "Cardinal Newman", Buse; "Pere Lacordaire," Robers; "Valedictory", Behan. [39]

At the beginning of the scholastic year 1902, Brinkmeyer was the rector and the faculty was composed of Bruegge, O'Brien, Lamping, Roth, Sieber and Hammersbach. Henry Schengber was not on the faculty this year. At the beginning of the scholastic year 1903, Brinkmeyer was the rector, and the faculty was composed of Bruegge, O'Brien, Lamping, Roth, Sieber, and Stein. [40]

DECISION TO MOVE THE MINOR SEMINARY (1904)

In the early part of March of 1904 F. X. Dutton, the Chancellor of the Archdiocese, sent a letter to the members of the clergy. The were asked to write their views on the matter of changing the sites of respective seminaries, and were asked to have their answers in the chancellor's office not later than Tuesday morning, March 29, 1904. The letter sent out by Dutton read as follows:

> The suppression of the Diocesan Preparatory Seminary should not for a moment be entertained. A Preparatory Seminary, in the opinion of Pope Leo XIII, Cardinal Satolli and other great educators, is even more necessary than a Theological Seminary to foster and test vocations. The only difficulty we have to face is the cost of maintaining two seminaries, each a boarding institution, and to bring the maintenance of both within the resources of the Diocese. In order to meet this difficulty, it has been suggested that the plan of that great educator, the Bishop of Rochester, be adopted, namely that a Preparatory Day School, to be called St. Gregory Preparatory Seminary, be established in the city of Cincinnati, near the Cathedral, to which only aspirants for the Priesthood should be admitted. The annual tuition fee is to be $50.00. The advantage of this plan, which has been successfully carried out in the Rochester Diocese, are many and various; among them being: One, the young student has that home training and influence which can never be supplied by the boarding school. Two, vocations are better tested in this manner than they could be in a boarding school. Three, economy to the parents and to the Diocese. Four, many a boy who has a vocation for the Priesthood, but whose parents find it impossible to raise the necessary $180 per annum, would find little or no difficulty in raising $50 annually for his tuition in a Preparatory Day School. Five, students from outside the city would find board with good Catholic families, preferably with the families of their fellow-students in the city. Six, the students would be visited by the rectory weekly. In order to reduce the expense for salary and board of the Professors of St. Gregory Preparatory Day School, these might act as Chaplains in the different institutions in the city with which no parochial work is connected.
>
> The priests of the Rochester Diocese, where this plan has been in operation for the last thirty-four years, have stamped it with their approval by voluntarily subscribing the sum of $10,000 to be used in the erection of a new St. Andrew Preparatory Seminary, a Day School.
>
> Rt. Rev. Camilus Maes, Bishop of Covington, in the Ecclesiastical Review, 1896—March, April, and May numbers—and Rt. Rev. Bernard McQuaid, Bishop of Rochester, in the same Review of 1897—May Number—more fully explained the method and advantages of a Day School for the candidates for the Priesthood. This plan has been adopted and successfully carried out in other Dioceses. New York opened such a school in 1903.
>
> All this is submitted for your consideration, and the Most Rev. Archbishop will be glad to hear your views on the subject, so as to submit them to his council for definite action.[41]

Answers to the letter indicated that while many of the clergy favored the plan, just as many opposed it. The faculty of St. Gregory's met and signed a statement to the effect that they opposed the suggested move. However, the move was deemed necessary and, at the end of school, the Preparatory Seminary vacated its site at Cedar Point, and moved into the old Perin Homestead on West Seventh Street in downtown Cincinnati. At the time the diocese had leased the building for $1,900.00 a year.[42]

THE SEMINARY ON SEVENTH STREET (1904-1907)

When St. Gregory's Seminary opened its doors on 220 West Seventh Street, it was first considered an ideal location. It was easily accessible and with a block of St. Peter's Cathedral. It was large, spacious house of twenty rooms, with a large barn in the rear. The students who live there during the three years of its occupancy seemed to have liked the location. However, it was very far cry from the pleasant country atmosphere at Cedar Point.

The course of study at this time was decreased to five years. The sixth year (or the second year of college) was now transferred to Mount St. Mary's. The tuition for one year at Seventh Street was $50.

Though they protested the move, Brinkmeyer, O'Brien, Roth, Stein, Sailor, Egan, Burke, and Manzetti went along to the new location and conducted their classes in the same fashion as before. The faculty did not change a very great deal for the next two years. In one important move, Florence Bruegge who had remained at Cedar Point when St. Mary's was transferred there, now returned to the faculty of St. Gregory's on Seventh Street.

Though things went smoothly enough for the seminary during the year 1904-1905, it became apparent in the middle of 1906 that some decision would have to be made about the future of the minor seminary. The Perin homestead had been leased for only three years, and at the end of the school year in 1907 that the lease would expire. At the time the archbishop stated: "It is a question whether the college will remain where it is, be moved to the country or be discontinued." [43]

As early as August 2, 1906, Archbishop Moeller was thinking of building the preparatory seminary at the new location in Norwood Heights. In February, 1907, Moeller stated that "we propose to build the Preparatory Seminary at Norwood Heights. In erecting the building, we will proceed along careful and conservative lines. There will be no useless or extravagant expenditure of money. Our aim shall be to put up a plain and substantial building."[44] Some time between this period and 1914, however, it was decided to put the major seminary in Norwood Heights. Probably the minor seminary would have gone back to Cedar Point. But the First World War was to come along and these plans were not to be put into effect until early in the twenties.

After an existence of seventeen years, the termination of the minor seminary and the closing of the Seventh Street location were announced on June 27, 1907. Brinkmeyer, the rector, accepted the post of chaplain at old Mount St. Mary's in Price Hill which was now the convent of the Good Shepherd Sisters.[45]

On August 27, 1907, the archbishop explained the reasons for the failure of the minor seminary. Expenses which were prohibitive seemed to be the main reason. It is interesting to note that some priests of the diocese suggested going back to the old system of combining the two seminaries at they had been in the late sixties and all through the seventies at old Mount St. Mary's on Price Hill. Moeller, however, decided against the idea and he now urged the students who desired to become diocesan priests to go to Xavier University in Cincinnati or St. Mary's Institute (now Dayton University) if they lived in Dayton.

To build a preparatory seminary was, as said before, one of the reasons why the Norwood Heights property was secured.

"I regret," he said, "that the preparatory day school, opened three years ago on Seventh Street, did not meet with full success. While the plan of a day school seminary, after three years experience, was not feasible, owing principally to the fact that parents, living outside of Cincinnati, were loath to send their boys to the city to the board with private families. And in consequence, the attendance was not what was expected, while the expenses were heavy. It was, therefore, considered best with the advice of the Consultors, to abandon the plan of the day school.

It was suggested in order to curtail expenses that it would be advisable to unite the theological and preparatory seminaries under one management. Such an arrangement it is true, as reported by the committee, would have lowered the expenses, but the amount saved did not seem satisfactory, to me nor to the Consultors. Moreover, I corresponded with the rectors of several seminaries and all of them are in favor of a separation of the preparatorians for the theologians. Hence, I resolved after advising with my Consultors to close St. Gregory's Seminary for a time, and in the meanwhile to accumulate the money needed to erect a preparatory seminary in Norwood. Provided the annual collections for the seminary continue to be as large as they have been in the past, I will be able to put aside, each year, about six thousand dollars. This amount together with donations and the interest due from the Good Shepard Convent on Price Hill, will enable me in a few years to begin the work.

I request that the preparatorians living in or near Cincinnati, until the new seminary is ready, attend St. Xavier College, and those living outside the city go to St. Mary's Institute, Dayton, either as boarders or as day scholars until the new preparatory seminary is ready. I desire this, because I deem it advisable, as far as it can be done, that the students of the Archdiocese be educated together.

I would be pleased if pastors, favoring in their congregation boys who wish to study for the priesthood, would confer with me about the place where they would like their boys to pursue their studies. In case the parents of the boys are unable to meet all expenses, I desire the pastors to inform me of this fact and I will then endeavor to make the necessary provisions. I do not wish any boy to say that he is unable to follow his vocation for want of means to pay for his education.

The diocesan students of St. Gregory's Seminary and the young men of the diocese who wish to begin the study for the priesthood, will please consult me in person or by letter in regard to the college in which they are to continue or begin with their classical culture.[46]

SUMMARY

This chapter has dealt with the chronological history of St. Gregory's Seminary in Mount Washington from 1890 until 1907. It has been pointed out that the task of preparing students for the priesthood began much earlier than 1890. Bishop Fenwick's seminary in the little frame structure of 1829 may truly be said to have housed a major and minor seminary. The Athenaeum, when it was built in 1831, was a "mixed" college, with some of the students taking classical courses in preparation for studies in theology. The preparatory seminarians lived with the major seminarians at Brown County, at the scholasticate, and at the Bishop's residence. All through his life Bishop Purcell continued to favor the idea of a "mixed" college attached to the major seminary. This was accomplished in the establishment of Mount St. Mary's College in 1856. The students who were preparing for the priesthood went to school with the lay students in the college, and the seminary professors and theological students could act as teachers and tutors.

In 1863 when the college ceased to exist because of the war, students who were preparing for the priesthood still studied at the same location and were called "preparatorians." This arrangement lasted all during the rectorship of Pabisch. There were certain difficulties in matters of discipline connected with this system. But in the overall picture, Purcell recruited an ample number of young men for his diocesan clergy under this educational arrangement.

In 1873 Father Engbers, Richter and Albrink worked for the creation of a minor seminary separated from the major seminary. Nothing happened, however, until 1887 when it was decided to erect a special institution for preparatory students. In 1889 Father Albrink received the sanction of Elder and began preparations for the minor seminary. In 1890 the first classes were held by Father Engbers in the school hall of Holy Trinity Church. Father Albrinck was the first rector. On September 8, 1891, the building at Mount Washington was ready for occupancy and the seminarians moved in. In 1892 Brinkmeyer was appointed rector, and served in that capacity until the closing of the seminary in 1907. He was a saintly man and was very highly revered by all of the students. The professors during this time were very competent. In 1904, as a result of the moving of Mount St. Mary's to Mount Washington, St. Gregory's became a day school on West Seventh Street. This plan was not successful, and in 1907 the Archdiocese of Cincinnati temporarily suspended the training of young men in preparation for the priesthood.

It can be said that in these years the seminary prospered. Throughout its twelve year existence as a boarding school the annual student enrollment numbered between eighty-five to one hundred seminarians. They were distributed over the six-year classical preparatory course, and represented the dioceses of Cincinnati, Columbus, Covington, Grand Rapids, Louisville, Nashville, and Detroit. Three hundred and ninety ecclesiastical students received their preparatory education, in a whole or in part, within its walls. The Holy See honored four of its former students by appointing them bishops. They were Most Reverend Francis J. Beckman, Archbishop of Dubuque; Most Reverend Samuel Stritch, Archbishop of Milwaukee, Right Reverend Alphonse Smith, Bishop of Nashville, and Right Reverend Urban J. Vehr, Bishop of Denver.

NOTES

1 Cf. Chapter Two.

2 Cf. Chapter Two.

3 Cf. Chapter Three.

4 Letter, Purcell to Blance, New Orleans, October 7, 1853, UNDA.

5 Meline and McSweeney, *op.cit.*, Vol. 2, pp. 128-137.

6 Lamott, *op. cit.*, p. 294.

7 *Catholic Telegraph*, June 9, 1892, p. 1.

8 *Ibid.*, June 6, 1889, p. 4.

9 Lamott, *op. cit.*, p. 294.

10 *Catholic Telegraph*, August 13, 1891, p. 4.

11 *Ibid.*, August 21, 1890, p. 1.

12 *Ibid.*, May 24, 1894, p. 1.

13 *Ibid.*, July 16, 1891, p. 5.

14 *Ibid.*, September 10, 1891, p. 4.

15 *Catalogue of St. Gregory Seminary*, pp. 13-17.

16 *Ibid.*, pp. 13-17.

17 *Catholic Telegraph*, July 16, 1891, p. 5.

18 *Ibid.*, July 16, 1891, p. 5.

19 *Ibid.*, June 30, 1892, p. 4.

20 *Ibid.*, July 17, 1892, p. 5.

21 *Catholic Telegraph*, July 7, 1892, p. 5.

22 Interview with Monsignor Martin Molloy, December 6, 1963.

23 Lamott, *op. cit.*, p. 299.

24 *Catholic Telegraph*, February 2, 1893, p. 5.

25 *Ibid.*, February 27, 1913, p. 4.

26 *Ibid.*, April 25, 1895, p. 4.

27 *Ibid.*, April 25, 1895, p. 1.

28 *Ibid.*, August 29, 1895, pp. 1-5.

29 *Ibid.*, June 11, 1943, pp. 1-4.

30 *Ibid.*, June 25, 1896, p. 5.

31 *Ibid.*, June 25, 1896, p. 5.

32 *Ibid.*, July 22, 1897, p. 4.

33 *Ibid.*, July 29, 1897. p. 5.

34 *Ibid.*, April 2, 1896, p. 5.

35 Records, (no date), MSMSA.

36 Records, (no date), MSMSA.

37 *Catholic Telegraph*, January 28, 1892, p. 5.

38 *Ibid.*, March 20, 1902, p. 5.

[39] *Ibid.*, June 26, 1902, p. 5.

[40] *Catalogue of St. Gregory's Seminary*, 1902-1903, p. 3.

[41] *Catholic Telegraph*, March 24, 1904, p. 4.

[42] *Ibid.*, August 25, 1904, p. 5.

[43] *Ibid.*, February 2, 1907, p. 4.

[44] *Ibid.*, February 21, 1907, p. 4.

[45] *Ibid.*, June 27, 1907, p. 5.

[46] *Ibid.*, August 29, 1907, p. 4.

CHAPTER FIVE

Mount Saint Mary's Seminary Moves to Mount Washington

INTRODUCTION

This chapter will treat events occurring in the history of Mount St. Mary's Seminary from the years 1904 to 1923. Having moved from its magnificent location on the brink of Price Hill, the seminary was now located at Mount Washington on the grounds vacated by St. Gregory's Seminary. This period can be best described as one of transition. The marvelous days of old Mount St. Mary's on Price Hill were over; the modern period of the seminary at Norwood was not to start for almost twenty years. This era can best be summarized by the statement "it maintained the status quo." Not a great deal was done. The administration began to improve a little toward the end of the period but, by and large, there were very few administrative directives. The faculty was quite learned and qualified but, in the main, was the product of an earlier generation. Only toward the end of the period is any effort made to improve the faculty by means of post-graduate studies. The curriculum remained completely static.

During this period the seminary had three rectors: Mackey, Shoe and Beckman. Mackey's administration had many shortcomings. Shoe accepted the position merely as a favor to his Episcopal superior until such a time as a competently trained man could fill the role. This was accomplished in the person of Monsignor Beckman, under whose administration the seminary once again began to move off "dead center." Most of the changes, however, were in the area of improving the faculty.

THE MOVE TO MOUNT WASHINGTON

In the meeting of the Board of Consultors held on April 7, 1904, Elder announced he had decided in favor of moving the major seminary to Cedar Point (Mount Washington). Letters indicated that there was as much opposition to the move as there was approval of it among the priests of Cincinnati.[1]

On August 17, 1904, it was announced that Mount. St. Mary's Seminary, Price Hill, had been moved to Cedar Point, a station on the Cincinnati, Georgetown, and Portsmouth Railroad. The same announcement also noted the following:

> The principal service of this road has changed from steam to electric and the cars leave hourly from Fourth and Sycamore Streets, Cincinnati. The new Cincinnati and eastern traction road with the depot on Sycamore Street between Fourth and Fifth passes the seminary gate. The seminary is thus removed from the noise and distractions of city life, and near enough for the enjoyment of its advantages. The seminary is situated on one of the high hills around Cincinnati, 800 feet above the Ohio River. The location is desirable for its pure air and general salubrity. An ample supply of pure water has been provided, the grounds embrace one hundred acres and are divided into lawns, gardens, orchards, natural forests, and a large campus for

outdoor exercise. The buildings at this place formerly occupied by St. Gregory's Preparatory Seminary have been remodeled and a new wing is being built.[2]

The buildings at St. Gregory's had been remodeled and now accommodated one-hundred and twenty-five students, allowing each student a single room. The new wing (the existing north wing) had been completed just in time for the opening of school in September. Work had begun on this section around April 29, shortly after the announcement of the Archbishop and the Board of Consultors.[3]

In the first year at Mount St. Mary's the student studied Latin, Greek, English, mathematics, logic, church history, German, chant, and introduction to Scripture. In the second year, which was the first year of the study of philosophy, the student studied philosophy, history of philosophy, introduction to Sacred Scripture, church history, Latin, German, and chant. The course in philosophy was being taught by one professor and thus, in the second year of philosophy, the student took the same subjects. They were merely divided into two cycles.

In the first year of theology, which was the beginning of the students fourth year at the seminary, he studied dogmatic and moral theology, introduction to Scripture, church history, exegesis, German and chant. The same course applied to the second and third years of the theological cycle, except that church history was dropped in favor of liturgy and homiletics.[4]

When the seminary moved to Mount Washington in 1904 the following textbooks were in use: in dogmatic theology, Tanqueray; in moral theology, Sabetti-Barrett, in philosophy, Zigliara, in canon law, Smith's Compendium; in church history, Brueck, in liturgy, Wapelhorst, in introduction to Sacred Scripture, Cornely, in homiletics, Potter; and in Hebrew, Gabriel.[5]

The student followed the same schedule as today, except that the school day was started earlier to permit more use of the daylight hours. The student arose at five-fifteen in the morning, attended Mass at six o'clock, and ate breakfast at seven o'clock. The first class in the morning was at eight o'clock. After noon meal, the classes began at two-thirty, and the evening meal was served at six o'clock. After the evening meal there was a study period, followed by evening prayers at quarter of nine. Lights went out at nine-thirty.[6]

MACKEY, RECTOR (1904-1908)

Sometime in the fall of 1904 (most likely not until August) Monsignor Mackey, who had been rector at the cathedral, was appointed rector of the seminary. He was sixty-eight years of age when he was appointed to this post by the archbishop. Mackey was born in Limerick, Ireland, on February 1, 1836. He was educated at Bardstown (Kentucky), Emmitsburg (Maryland), and at the Grand Seminare, D'Aix, Marseilles, France. He was ordained a priest on June 14, 1862, and was a pastor of many missions in Kentucky and Ohio before becoming rector or St. Patrick's Church on Third Street in 1870. In 1887 he accepted the post as rector of the cathedral. There is some evidence indicating that Mackey's appointment to the seminary was in the nature of a diplomatic move designed to relieve him of his post at the cathedral. During his tenure of office he taught only liturgy. Most of the burden of administration, especially discipline, fell on the younger professors.[7]

On January 23, 1908, when Mackey died, the *Catholic Telegraph* wrote the following about him:

> The distinguished rector may have had little opportunity to act as a professor disciplinarian, or administrator during his few years at Mount St. Mary's of the West; but his long, spotless life as a true priest of God must have been a daily inspiration to the young men; to them, his life could not be the best kind of reason for them to study. The young aspirants to the seminary were similarly privileged to come in contact with the dear "Soggarth Aroon."

When classes resumed in September 1904 the theology course lasted only three years. Philosophy lasted two years and followed the one year of classical studies called the "Propaedeuticon." In September of 1907 the fourth year of theology was added.[8]

The faculty for this first year at Mount Washington was composed of Mackey, Nau, Sele, Bruegge, Deasey, and Clarke. Mackey, the rector, taught the class in liturgy, Nau, the vice-rector, taught the classes in moral, canon law, church history, and patrology. Sele was professor of dogma as well as of Sacred Scripture and Hebrew. Deasey taught philosophy, the history of philosophy, and sacred eloquence. Clarke taught the introduction to Sacred Scripture and the courses in logic. Bruegge had charge of teaching the classics in the Prepaedeuticon.

On Sunday, December 11, 1904, the faculty and students assembled on the front lawn outside the main building for the solemn dedication of the statue of the Immaculate Conception. It had been donated by the Alumni Association of the seminary. When the new extension to St. Gregory's was built in 1963 this statue was moved to the courtyard on the north side of the building.[9] Monsignor Mackey's gift to the seminary was the famous two-thousand-pound bell which was installed in the tower of the center of the building on September 18, 1905. [10]

In September of 1905 Nau took a leave of absence to pursue graduate biblical studies. He was replaced by the Reverend Joseph Sieber who became the vice-rector and took over the classes in moral theology. The Reverend Anthony S. Siebaufacher came to the faculty as the spiritual director and speech director. The remained of the faculty was the same as the preceding year.[11]

In 1906 the only changes in the faculty were the departure of Father Bruegge and the addition of Harold Beckett Gibbs as professor of plain chant.[12] Father Bruegge had always been in ill health, and it now became physically impossible for him to continue his schedule of classes. He was an erudite classical scholar and the seminary was to miss his talent for teaching Latin and Greek. His classes were taken over by Clarke. Mackey did not exercise too firm a hand in the discipline of the seminary. After two years it became evident that this task could not be delegated to the faculty in general, but had to be assigned to one individual. Clarke exercised a very strong influence on the internal administration and discipline of the seminary.

At a faculty meeting held on September 21, 1906, logic, which had been taught in the sixth year (the second year of college), was now made a part of the philosophy course. Deasey was appointed to teach it. It was also decided that seven (of a possible ten) would be the passing grade for all major subjects, and six would be considered a passing grade for the minor subjects.[13] At a faculty meeting held two months later it was decided that history was to be taught three hours a week for the first three years.[14] At a meeting held at the end of that scholastic year the faculty voted against the introduction of English literature and science into the curriculum. On a question of the introduction of a class in English, the faculty was divided. The faculty was asked for their opinions concerning the introduction of a fourth year of theology. It was determined then that "If the Most Reverend Archbishop wishes to begin this course at this time, it can be done now without the aid of a new professor. A new professor will be required after the expiration of two years."[15] It seems that the faculty was not too much in favor of extending the course to four years.

The minutes of a faculty meeting held on July 24, 1907, indicate that a teaching schedule of ten hours per week was thought to be ideal for each professor. The faculty met at the end of each year, and classes were assigned. Starting with the rector and the senior members, class schedules were assigned in such a way that each professor would be teaching ten hours per week in the coming year.[16]

Two new members were added to the faculty in September of 1907. Matthew O'Brien arrived to teach the classes in church history and liturgy, and Luebberman took over the classes in Sacred Scripture from Doctor Sele. Siebenfaecher, in addition to his duties as spiritual director and speech director, undertook to uncrate some of the books sent over from Price Hill and began setting up the library. This work did not proceed very well and during the time Mount St. Mary's was at Mount Washington, for all practical purposes, there was no library.[17]

When the students returned in 1907 for the next year it was apparent that the rector, Monsignor Mackey, was a very ill man. During the autumn and winter his health did not improve. On January 23, 1908, he died. The archbishop asked the Reverend Joseph Shee to succeed him.[18]

SHEE, RECTOR (1908-1912)

Father Joseph Shee was a native of Cincinnati and was raised in St. Edward's parish. His classical and philosophical studies were made at St. Xavier College. From there he went to St. Mary's Seminary, Baltimore where he remained for three years. He was sent to Rome to continue his studies in the American College. He was ordained on February 25, 1888, in the Church of St. John Lateran by Cardinal Parocchi.[19]

His first appointment was an assistant pastor of St. Patrick's Church in Cincinnati where he remained for three years. He was transferred to a similar position at the Church of the Assumption. A short time later he was made professor of language at St. Gregory's Seminary. After two years in this position he was placed in charge of Hillsboro, Ohio, and its missions. In 1893 he was made pastor of St. Mary's Church, Cincinnati. It was with deep regret that the people of this parish parted with this when he was made rector of Mount St. Mary's Seminary, Ellenora, (Mount Washington), Ohio, on February 3, 1908.

During his five years at the seminary he proved to be a good rector. He was considered a capable teacher and a wise executive, "his dignified bearing, his uniform charity and saintly character furnished an inspiring exemplar, which could not have been but an edifying formative effect upon the students and others with whom he came into contact."[20]

At the beginning of the scholastic year in 1908 (the first full year for Shee), there were some significant changes and additions to the faculty. Matthew O'Brien became the vice-rector, Nau returned from his studies, and Francis Beckman took over the course in philosophy formerly taught by Deasey. In the light of subsequent events, September of 1908 will always be a memorable date in the history of the seminary. John J. Fehring, a layman, came to the seminary faculty at this time to teach Gregorian chant. Even in 1964, after fifty-five years, he was still teaching on the faculty. Though having been a student of Professor John Fehring, every student has come to appreciate sacred music and the power of its majestic cadences in bringing people closer to God in the ceremonies of divine worship. His devotion and dedication to the work of teaching seminarians in his chosen field have always been a source of great admiration.[21]

At the beginning of Shee's first full year as rector, 1908, the faculty, the officers, and the subjects they taught were as follows: Shoe was professor of homiletics and pastoral theology; Sele was professor of dogma and Hebrew; Matthew O'Brien was vice-rector and professor of church history, patrology, liturgy, Sacred Scripture, and English Literature; Nau was professor of Sacred Scripture, biblical archaeology and canon law, and filled the office of librarian; Sieber was the spiritual director and professor of moral; Clarke was professor of apologetics and Latin; Beckman was professor of philosophy, history of philosophy, and German; and John Fehring was professor of chant. [22]

The faculty in 1909 remained unchanged consisting of Shee, Sele, O'Brien, Nau, Sieber, Clarke, Beckman and Fehring. In 1910, however, there were some significant changes. John L. Seuffert came to the seminary faculty replacing Sieber in the teaching of moral theology. Father H. Rechtin became the new spiritual director, and Father Xavier Cotter was added to the staff.

John Lawrence Seuffert was born on August 10, 1869, in Althessingen near Wuersburg, Unterfranken, Germany. He often spoke of his hard life as child of poor parents, and remembered distinctly how rich he felt when a man of the neighborhood stuffed his pockets with dried prunes. To better their condition, his parents came to America when John was still a young boy. They settled in Columbus, Ohio, and it was not long until they the acquaintance of Father Jessing, who took a personal interest in John. After some time the boy was sent to St. Francis Gymnasium, then located on Brenon Street in Cincinnati, where he studied classics. Later he attended St. Vincent's in Latrobe, Pennsylvania. He studied philosophy at Mount St. Mary's Seminary of the West, Price Hill, Cincinnati, and in 1892 was sent to the Urban College of the Propaganda in Rome. The young seminarian was a very earnest student. His contemporaries recall how he studied with only one eye when the oculist had bandaged the other after an operation. He was ordained to the priesthood on May 30, 1896. After obtaining his doctorate in theology, maxima cum laude, he returned to the Josephinum. From 1896 until 1907 Father Seuffert taught in the Josephinum. His subjects included liturgy, canon law, moral theology, and Italian. In January 1911, he was appointed to teach moral and canon law at Mount St. Mary's Seminary of the West, an office he filled with the great fidelity and success until stricken by paralysis in the autumn of 1932.[23]

Father Seuffert was gifted with a quick and retentive memory. During his first year of teaching this let him to demand of his students memory tasks that were somewhat beyond their capacity. In later years he became more lenient. He prepared his classes thoroughly up to the very end of his life, and his ability to illustrate made it easy for his students to absorb his teachings. Always interested in elegant classic phrases and sentences, he loved the study of Latin and encouraged its teaching. In this, as in most questions concerning branches pursued by students in minor and major seminaries, his studied judgment was found correct by later students. Following the death of Father Sele, Father Stouffer's scholarship was put to use for many years in compiling the Order for Cincinnati and some other ecclesiastical provinces of the United States.[24]

Ill health forced his retirement from active teaching in 1932, but he continued to live at the seminary where he was often consulted for answers to various moral theological questions. During this year he also composed the yearly edition of the Ordo.

Speaking at his funeral (on Friday, September 24, 1942), Archbishop McNicholas extolled his virtues as a priest and his abilities as a theologian. "He possessed," said the archbishop, "a profound knowledge of moral theology; he had a penetrating perception of all details of theological problems." [25]

In September of 1910, the same year that Seuffert came to the seminary, H. H. Rechtin was the other newcomer. Father Rechtin was born in Cincinnati on July 2, 1871. He attended St. Joseph's Elementary School and St. Xavier's College (1887-1892). In 1892 Archbishop Elder sent him and the Reverent Engelbert Stehle, who was at that time pastor of St. Joseph's Church, to the North American College in Rome, where Father Rechtin pursued studies in philosophy and theology.

Father Rechtin offered his first Mass on July 26, 1898. When he returned to the United States in September of 1898, he was appointed assistant pastor of St. Mary's Church, Dayton, and later served in the same capacity at St. Michael's Church, Cincinnati. He received his first appointment as pastor in November, 1903, when he was placed in charge of Marysville and its four missions. After spending three years in Marysville, he served successively as pastor of St. Peter's Church, Hamilton; spiritual director of Mount St. Mary's Seminary; pastor of Guardian Angels Church, Cincinnati; pastor of St. Michael's Church, Cincinnati; and pastor of St. John's Church, Dry Ridge. After twenty years at St. John's parish he was forced to retire because of ill health.[26]

At the various faculty meetings held during 1910 some important issues were resolved. It was decided that he course in philosophy would be divided into two separate classes, with a professor for each. In this course, as well as in many others, a cycle method had been used with the idea of cutting down on the number of teachers necessary for any one course. In former days, this was sound reasoning. Now it was apparent that it was very important for the subject matter in philosophy to be approached in a certain sequence rather than in the cycle. The method of teaching in theology was slowly and gradually curtailed. Today, 1964, the remnant of the system continues in the second and third years of theology in both the courses in dogma and moral. Greek, patrology, and sociology were reintroduced into the course of theology. It was also decided that the course in theology should now be extended to the length recommended by the Third Plenary Council of Baltimore. The class entering the third year in September of 1910 were not ordained in the spring of 1911, and were asked to return for a forth year. Thus there was no ordination class in 1911. This year it was again set down that no student would be admitted to the first year of philosophy unless he had six years of Latin. Hickey's text in philosophy was substituted for Zigliara, and Sierieg was adopted as text in the Psalms.[27]

Clarke and Cotter left the faculty in the spring of 1911, and Father Francis A. Walsh took over the one class in philosophy and Beckman taught the other. A native of Cincinnati, Doctor Walsh was educated at the St. Charles Parish School, St. Xavier High School and College (from which he received his Bachelor of Arts degree in 1903), Mount St. Mary's Seminary in Cincinnati, and at the Gregorian University, of Rome where he studied philosophy in 1906-1907.

He was ordained to the priesthood by Archbishop Henry Moeller at St. Charles Church, Carthage, Ohio, on September 15, 1907. After parish work at St. Andrew in Cincinnati, and at Sacred Heart Church, Dayton, he became professor of philosophy and vice-rector at Mount St. Mary's Seminary in 1911. He remained there until 1918 at which time he entered the regular army as chaplain of 217th Engineers.

After the war he returned to his diocese for a short time and then went to the Catholic University of America in Washington to pursue graduate work. Almost immediately he was requested by the late Bishop Shahan, then rector of Catholic University, to carry on the work of the Most Reverend William Turner who had just been consecrated Bishop of Buffalo. His term of service in Washington was short, however, for his successor at Mount St. Mary's Seminary died suddenly. Father Walsh was recalled to Cincinnati to resume teaching and concurrently serve as pastor of St. Andrew Church.[28]

In 1923, in company with five other priests, he sailed from the United States to enter the English Congregation of the Benedictine Order at St. Benedict Abbey, Fort Augustine, Scotland. Father Walsh returned to this country in September, 1924, and was one of the original members of the Benedictine Foundation, now known as St. Anselm Friary, located at the Catholic University in Washington. Doctor Walsh became a member of the department of philosophy at the university and a regent of the seminary. Father Walsh had an active and varied career, and large numbers of priests in this country, particularly in the Middle West received instructions in his classes. In addition to his many pastoral and teaching duties he found time to lecture in many colleges and summer schools, and to serve as editor of the

Pacidian (the Benedictine review), and of the Benedictine historical monographs.[29]

BECKMAN, RECTOR (1912-1923)

In December of 1912 Francis J. Beckman, who was later to become Archbishop of Denver, was appointed rector of Mount St. Mary's Seminary. Beckman, like Archbishop Moeller, was born and baptized in St. Joseph's Parish in downtown Cincinnati. In those days the younger German families were moving to Price Hill, and Joseph Beckman received his early education at St. Lawrence School. He then entered St. Gregory's Preparatory Seminary and, after completing his course there, went to Mount St. Mary's while it was still on Price Hill. He was ordained by Elder on June 20, 1902. [30]

Father Beckman's first appointment was an assistant pastor of St. Paul Church, Cincinnati. Shortly after this he was sent abroad for advanced studied at Louvain, Belgium, and the Gregorian College in Rome, where he spent three years and received the degree of Doctor of Sacred Theology. [31]

On his return to Cincinnati, Monsignor Beckman was assigned professor of philosophy at Mount St. Mary's Seminary, at which post he remained until 1912. Upon the resignation of Reverend Joseph Shee, in 1912, he became rector. He was then thirty-seven years old. During his administration the seminary experienced a marked increase in enrollment. Attendance swelled from ninety men studying philosophy and theology in 1912 to a total of 260 in 1923. One hundred students were in attendance at "Mount St. Gregory's" and 160 at the new Mount St. Mary's Seminary in Norwood. [32] In recognition of his splendid services at the seminary Pope Benedict XV, on January 23, 1920, made him a member of the papal household with the title of monsignor. Monsignor Beckman had a great interest in sociology and spoke Greek, Latin, and Hebrew. [33]

At the beginning of Beckman's first year in 1913, the faculty comprised the following: Beckman taught philosophy, history of philosophy, sociology, and German; Sele taught dogma, exegesis, and Hebrew; Rectin was the spiritual director; Souffert taught moral theology, liturgy, and canon law; Walsh was the librarian and taught church history, patrology, introduction to Sacred Scripture, biblical archaeology, and English Literature, Markham taught apologetics, sacred eloquence, catechetics, and biblical Greek; Yanes was the procurator; Fehring taught chant; and William Langdon, M.D., was the physician in charge. During the following year, 1914, the faculty remained unchanged. [34]

The only change in the faculty of 1915 and 1916 was the replacement of Reverend Louis Yanes by the Very Reverent George A. Gorry.

Born in London on June 13, 1888, Monsignor Gorry studied for one year at the old St. Gregory's Seminary, Cincinnati, and then went to St. Charles College, Catonsville, Maryland, where he completed his classical course. He studied his philosophy and theology at the old Mount St. Mary's Seminary in Mount Washington. He was ordained to the priesthood by Archbishop Henry Moeller in St. Peter's Cathedral on June 19, 1914.[35] He was then sent to the Catholic University of America.

On September 9, 1915, he was appointed procurator and professor of fundamental theology at Mount St. Mary's. When the new seminary was completed in Norwood, he was sent to that location. He was connected with the seminary for twenty-four years during all of which time he served as procurator (or treasurer) of the institution. His marked ability to ascertain facts, his common sense, reasoned judgment, knowledge of human nature, exceptional business acumen, capacity for work, fidelity to every trust, thoughtfulness, and kindness enable him to render devoted service to the major seminary of the archdiocese.[36]

In 1933 he was relieved of his professorship in the seminary and was given other offices in the archdiocese. Monsignor Gorry was known as a kind and deeply religious priest by all his associates and acquaintances and held many positions of responsibility. One of the most beloved priests in the Archdiocese of Cincinnati, Monsignor Gorry died on March 18, 1939.[37] The faculty the year 1916 remained the same—Beckman, Walsh, Sele, Markham, Seuffert, Lamott, Gorry and Fehring.

On February 15, 1917, it was announced in the *Catholic Telegraph* that the post office address of Mount St. Mary's Seminary had been changed from "Ellenora, Ohio" to "Mount Washington Station, Cincinnati, Ohio." [38]

In the spring of 1917, extensive regulations concerning the administration and the curriculum of seminaries were brought forth in the new Code of Canon Law. In regard to administration, the code stated that the bishop had the right to pass whatever regulations he deemed necessary or opportune for the proper management and progress of the seminary.

The seminary enrollment in the year 1917 totaled 182 in the six-year course.[39] Three years previous to this there had been 141 students. The 1917 enrollment represented considerable increase over the previous years.

In the year 1918, as the First World Ward drew to a close, the administrative officers of the seminary were as follows: Beckman, rector; Walsh, vice-rector; Gorry, treasurer; and Markham, spiritual director. Beckman taught classes in dogma and pastoral theology; Seuffert was the professor of moral theology and also taught liturgy, canon law, and German; Stuber was the professor in Sacred Scripture and taught the class in biblical Greek; Lamott taught church history and German; Walsh was the professor of philosophy; Fehring continued to teach the course in chant; and O'Meara taught the course in public speaking. William Langdon was the staff physician.

In 1918 the Catholic Student's Mission Crusade was founded and the seminary students became its first members. [40] The Crusade was launched in the year 1918 as a result of a preliminary campaign carried by Clifford J. King, a student at the seminary of the Divine Word Fathers of Techny, Illinois. At the convention held at Techny in July, 1918, which marked the formal launching of the Crusade, three representatives from Mount St. Mary's in Cincinnati were elected to the executive positions in the organizations.[41]

There were no additions to the faculty in 1919. The only addition in 1920 was the Reverend Henry Grimmelman who replaced Father Stuber in the teaching of Sacred Scripture. Doctor Grimmelman was born in Cincinnati on December 22, 1890. After attending the Holy

Family parochial school, he entered the diocesan minor seminary, St. Gregory's in 1904. In 1907 he went to St. Joseph College, Rensseler, Indiana, where he spent two years. In 1909 he began his philosophy courts at Mount St. Mary's Seminary.[42]

On the completion of his philosophy course, Grimmelsman was selected one of the most promising students in the seminary and was sent to Innsbruck, Austria, where he spent four years in the study of theology. In 1915, due to the war, he was obliged to return to the United States. He was ordained to the priesthood at Cincinnati by Archbishop Moeller on August 15, 1915, and spent the following scholastic year at the Catholic University of America. When he returned to Cincinnati he served as assistant at St. Lawrence Church for a short time. His next appointment was to Mount St. Joseph's College, conducted by the Sisters of Charity in Cincinnati, where for more than three years he acted as chaplain and professor.[43]

In 1920 Archbishop Moeller appointed Father Grimmelsman professor of Sacred Scripture at the major seminary in which capacity he served until 1928. He then returned to Innsbruck to take his degree in sacred theology and to present his thesis. Both his examination and his thesis were regarded by the faculty as worthy of maxima cum laude. Father Grimmelsman now resumed his work of teaching at Mount St. Mary's Seminary. His works in Scripture, *The Book of Exodus* and *The Book of Ruth*, received very favorable comment in their day.[44]

In 1920 Father Lamott went back to Louvain for one year to finish and defend this thesis entitled *A History of the Archdiocese of Cincinnati*. He wrote various letters home to Cincinnati (published in the *Catholic Telegraph*) describing the work entailed in obtaining his degree. Father Lamott's thesis was published in book form in 1924 and continues to be an invaluable source of information for anyone doing historical research on matters pertaining to the history of the Archdiocese of Cincinnati.[45]

In the school year of 1921 the Reverend James Collins began his long career of service in the seminary when he took over the teaching of philosophy on the departure of Francis A. Walsh. Collins had studied theology at the old Mount St. Mary Seminary, and was ordained to the priesthood by Archbishop Moeller on March 15, 1919. After his ordination Father Collins was assigned as assistant at the cathedral. Two years later he was appointed professor of philosophy at the seminary. In 1926 he was sent to Rome to study theology at the Angelicum University from where he received his degree of Doctor of Theology in June, 1928. He returned to the diocese and again took up his duties as professor of philosophy at St. Gregory's. Five years later, in 1932, he became professor of moral theology at Mount St. Mary's Seminary, replacing Father Seuffert. During the latter part of his life he was a victim of arthritis, and for the last eight years of his life taught his class in moral theology from a wheel chair.[46]

When the seminary reopened in 1922, it was known that this was the last year it would be located in Mount Washington. In the spring of the year 1923 the four years of theology moved to a newly constructed seminary building in Norwood, Ohio. This represents the close of an era that interposed itself between the marvelous history and growth of the old Mount

St. Mary's on Price Hill and the modern period of growth and expansion of Norwood. Two hundred and twelve students attended the seminary this last year.[47]

THE LIBRARY

There is evidence that, when the seminary closed down at Price Hill, the books in the extensive library of old Mount St. Mary's were removed and placed in crates. The crates were placed in the basement of the seminary at Mount Washington and, with the exception of one or two valiant efforts, nothing was done with them during this time. Sad to say it seems that some of the crates were not reopened until almost twenty years later when the new library was constructed in Norwood. The reason for this was that at the new location no immediate provision could be made for a library. Conditions were just too crowded. As could be expected, many of the books were seriously damaged in storage.

SUMMARY

This chapter has dealt with the events in the history of Mount St. Mary's Seminary from the year 1904 to 1923. Moving from its historic location on Price Hill, where it had attained such eminence and prestige, the seminary's history now typified its remote country location. Quiet and serene, but undistinguished, were the years of this period.

In the area of administration a serious low point was reached during the rectorship of Mackey. The situation was corrected by the strictness of Shoe in the sense that the discipline was restored. But there seemed to be now new ideas, no progress, no development. By the end of the period, during the rectorship of Beckman, the administration slowly began to improve.

Two important changes made during this period had to do with the addition of a fourth years to the course in theology, and the breaking up of the philosophy course into two classes. The demands of the time made the addition of the fourth year imperative, and the cycle course as taught in philosophy, was proving to have serious drawbacks. Paradoxically, the faculty during this period of quite mediocrity was learned and well qualified. Men such as Nau, Sele, Bruegge, Seuffert, O'Brien, Grimmelsman, Walsh and Lamott were professors with excellent backgrounds of learning and scholarship. They are numbered among the men who produced some of the finest scholarly works in the history or the seminary.

During the two decades considered the curriculum and the teaching methods of the seminary remained completely unchanged. Development in these areas was simply nil. The Code of Canon Law in 1917 only confirmed by law what was already accomplished in fact; the curriculum and the methods of teaching had been determined and were rigidly maintained.

When Mount St. Mary's Seminary left Mount Washington in 1923, a rather disappointing and languid period in the history of the seminary came to a close. Lacking were the nerve and spirit of the old Mount St. Mary's, absent were the drive and energy that would characterize the new Mount St. Mary's in Norwood. An interlude between two great eras—it simply was a bridge over which the years crossed—not a great deal more.

NOTES

[1] *Catholic Telegraph*, April 7, 1904. p. 5.

[2] *Ibid.*, September 15, 1904. p. 5.

[3] *Ibid.*, April 14, 1904. p. 5.

[4] Catalogue, 1905, MSMSA.

[5] *Ibid.*, 1905, MSMSA.

[6] *Ibid.*, 1905, MSMSA.

[7] *Catholic Telegraph*, January 23, 1908, p. 5.

[8] Minutes of the Faculty Meeting, June 14, 1907. MSMSA.

[9] *Catholic Telegraph*, December 8, 1904, p. 5.

[10] *Ibid.*, August 31, 1905, p. 5.

[11] *Ibid.*, August 31, 1905, p. 5.

[12] Minutes of the Faculty Meeting, September 21, 1906. MSMSA.

[13] Minutes of the Faculty Meeting, September 21, 1906. MSMSA.

[14] Minutes of the Faculty Meeting, November 12, 1906. MSMSA.

[15] Minutes of the Faculty Meeting, June 14, 1907. MSMSA.

[16] Minutes of the Faculty Meeting, July 24, 1907. MSMSA.

[17] Minutes of the Faculty Meeting, July 24, 1907. MSMSA.

[18] *Catholic Telegraph*, January 23, 1908, p. 5.

[19] *Ibid.*, February 1, 1917. p. 4.

[20] *Ibid.*, February 1, 1917. p. 4.

[21] For an excellent account of Mr. Fehring's contributions to the development of music education at the seminary, consult Sister Mary Joeline Ebert's "A History of the Development of Music Education in the Archdiocese of Cincinnati." An Unpublished Doctor's Dissertation, University of Cincinnati, 1955. pp. vii., 259.

[22] *Catholic Telegraph*, August 27, 1908, p. 5.

[23] *Ibid.*, October 16, 1942, p. 4.

[24] *Ibid.*, October 16, 1942, p. 4.

[25] *Ibid.*, October 2, 1942, p. 1.

[26] *Ibid.*, June 13, 1947, p. 1.

[27] Faculty Minutes, February 1, 1910; September 1, 1910. MSMSA

[28] *Catholic Telegraph*, September 22, 1932, p. 2.

[29] *Ibid.*, September 22, 1932, p. 3.

[30] *Ibid.*, December 16, 1912, p. 5.

[31] *Ibid.*, December 27, 1923, p. 1.

[32] Cf. Chapter Eight.

[33] *Catholic Telegraph*, December 26, 1912, p. 5.; *Ibid.*, December 27, 1923, p. 1.

[34] "Annual Report of Subscriptions for the Theological Seminary, 1913-1914", p. 3.

[35] *Catholic Telegraph*, March 24, 1939, p. 1.

[36] *Ibid.*, March 24, 1939, p. 1.

[37] *Ibid.*, March 24, 1939, p. 1.

[38] *Ibid.*, February 15, 1917, p. 5.

[39] *Ibid.*, September 20, 1917, p. 5.

[40] *Catholic Telegraph*, October 22, 1948.

[41] The Shield, "Crusade Pioneers," p. 18.

[42] *Catholic Telegraph*, May 19, 1932, p. 1.

[43] *Ibid.*, May 19, 1932, p. 1.

[44] *Ibid.*, May 19, 1932, p. 1.

[45] *Ibid.*, March 3, 1950, p. 1.

[46] *Catholic Telegraph*, March 3, 1950, p. 1.

[47] *Ibid.*, September 21, 1922, p. 5.

CHAPTER SIX

The Moving of Mount St. Mary's Seminary to Norwood, Ohio

INTRODUCTION

This chapter considers the history of Mount St. Mary's Seminary from the time it was moved to the new site in Norwood in 1923 up until the year 1949. The plans for this move were initiated in 1906 and culminated in the newly built seminary in Norwood in 1923. The chapter begins with a description of events preceding the move. The rectorships of Beckman, Nau, Vehr, Rehring and O'Brien, along with various other faculty members of this time are also considered.

Several other important events shaped the course of the seminary development during this period. The Most Reverend Timothy McNicholas became the new Archbishop of Cincinnati on the death of Archbishop Henry Moeller in 1924. It will be seen that he sought to improve the standards of teaching in the seminary by an expanded program of graduate studies for priests. In 1928 he was the prime agent in having the seminary become a unit of the newly formed educations corporation known ask the Athenaeum of Ohio. The organization and purposes of this corporation, initiated by the new archbishop, will be discussed in Chapter Nine. In May of 1929, Mount St. Mary's Seminary, as a unit of the Athenaeum of Ohio, was authorized by the State of Ohio to grant Master of Arts degree.

In 1934 Mount St. Mary's Seminary became affiliated with the Catholic University of America. It now became possible to gain credit at Norwood toward theological degrees in the first three years of the course. This was an important step forward in the area of allowing gifted theological students to pursue graduate studies either in America or Europe without any loss of time.

EARLY PLANS FOR THE SEMINARY AT NORWOOD

In the month of June, 1906, a committee of priests met one morning in downtown Cincinnati and proceeded from there to look over some farm property in Norwood Heights. The committee included the Reverends Schoenhoeft, Feldman, A. Quatman, Scholl, Brinkmeyer, Varelman, Murray, Hickey and Conway. That afternoon they inspected the Ferguson farm on Montgomery Road. Their first report read as follows:

> We find the property well adapted for Diocesan use. It is advantageously located with a gradual ascent of about two hundred feet from Harris Avenue to its highest point and commands a splendid view of the surrounding country. There is an easy decline on all sides from an extensive plateau, which indicates that the property lends itself quite readily to good sanitary conditions. The property is located within the corporate boundaries of Norwood and is easy of access, being about ten minutes walk from Harris Avenue. The tract contains sixty-eight acres. The Sieber and Springer farms, adjacent to the Ferguson Farm, are for sale at $2250 and

$3000 per acre respectively. In comparison, the price quoted on the Ferguson Farm is considered remarkably low. A movement is now on foot to extend the route of the Cincinnati Traction Lines to Pleasant Ridge, and this will certainly enhance the value of the property. The B & O. S.W.R.R. and the Pennsylvania Lines are in close proximity to the property. With the exception of a frame house, some sheds, and perhaps a stable, the property is unimproved, i.e., in the way of buildings. The opinion of the committee is, (taking into consideration the relative prices asked for nearby farms) that, the Ferguson Farm, at the price quoted $5000 per acre is a safe investment and ought to be a valuable asset for the Diocese.[1]

About one month later, at the end of July, Archbishop Moeller stated that an option had been secured on these sixty-eight acres, plus ninety-two more from the Langdon and Thale farms. He explained the new venture in an official notice in the *Catholic Telegraph* as follows:

An opportunity presents itself of purchasing 160 acres at Norwood Heights. The property measures from Montgomery Road on the east, to Carthage Avenue on the west, about 3,000 feet from Feldman Avenue. And on the south to about 3,000 feet beyond Burgoyne Road on the north 2,600 feet approximately. The average cost per acre is $718.00 and the total cost of the property is $115, 000.00. The ground slopes from the center to all the sides. The small amount of leveling required is easy on account of the nature of the soil. There are four buildings on the grounds, one of which is centrally located and suited for pastoral residence.

At present, the Lebanon Rapid Railway skirts the Montgomery Road. The run from the Lebanon Railway depot (on Sycamore Street near fifth) to the property is made in thirty-five minutes. The fare is five cents. The Cincinnati Traction Company is considering the extension of the Gilbert Avenue and Vine and Norwood Lines over Montgomery Road and Carthage Avenue. The Pennsylvania Railroad (Cincinnati and Richmond Division) runs near the northern line of the property. The B & O railroad is within ten minutes of the southern lines. The Norwood Water Tower is about 1,500 feet east. There is sewer connection on the southeast corner at Feldman and Carthage Avenues. The natural gas mains traverse the center of the property from north to south.

As the elevation is at least one hundred feet about the Norwood plateau there is no danger of railroads or factories cutting near the property. All the ground west of Carthage Avenue and fronting on this site has been subdivided into lots 25x100 feet, some of which are now selling at $100.00 per lot. The nearest factory, the Globe Wernicke, with smoke consumers, is 2,000 feet from the southern end of the property. The other factories southeast of the property are at least 3,500 feet distant.

At present, there are in the immediate vicinity, sixty Catholic families from one and half to two miles distance from St. Elizabeth's Church, Norwood. The proposed church in southeast Norwood to Floral and Kenilworth Avenue, will have as its northern boundary the B & O Railroad, and all these sixty families are living north of this boundary.

It is proposed to reserve sixteen acres of the property for diocesan purposes—future Cathedral, Preparatory Seminary, etc., and to proceed immediately wit the establishment of a congregation and the erection of a combination church and school building. The remaining one hundred forty-four acres are to be in charge of a syndicate of priests and Catholic laymen holding one hundred fifty shares at $1,000.00 a share, each share and the accruing profits to be the personal property of the shareholder. A member of these persons have already signified their intention of identifying themselves with the syndicate. The archbishop is to be one of the members of the syndicate, which will be incorporated.

At the request of the archbishop, several of the consulters and members of the diocesan building committee, as well as a number of business and real estate men have carefully examined the site, and consider the investment excellent.

An option on the one hundred sixty acres has been secured. The property belongs to three different persons—one of the options expires August 8th and the other August 15th.[2]

At the end of July 1906 the archbishop decided to accept the site offered by the Norwood Heights Company for diocesan purpose. He came to this conclusion after careful personal examination of all eligible sites, numbering a dozen or more, in and around Cincinnati. As he had indicated in his letter published in the *Catholic Telegraph*, he consulted the members of his own Council of the Diocesan Building Committee and other prominent clergymen, as well as several reliable real estate agents, and quite a number of prominent business men including architects and contractors. [3]

There must have been further discussion about the move, for on August 25, 1907, he again wrote on the matter as follows:

There are a few matters of special interest to both clergy and laity about some of which I deem it necessary to enter into an explanation and about others to give direction. They are as follows:

The Norwood Heights project has been before the public for the last year, and realizing that many well meaning persons of the diocese desire to be informed in regard to its nature and success, I thought it would be well to give a clear and succinct statement of the enterprise.

In no way is this project a land speculation, nor has it been fostered by any real estate agent who desires to advance their property under the auspices of religion. Neither, I, nor the priests, nor the Catholic laymen, interested in the affair, were actuated by any other than religious motives, or the advancement of the Diocese. The following is the simply history of the project as it first arose and took from in the state in which it now exists. Some fourteen months ago at a meeting of the Diocesan Consulters, I called attention to the fact that the lease of the property on Seventh Street, occupied by St. Gregory's Preparatory Seminary, would expired in June 1907, and stated that I considered it advisable to secure another site for a Preparatory Seminary. I also suggested that it would be well to have the Seminary near the future Cathedral. A committee, appointed by me to select a suitable site, after careful investigation found no property in the heart of the present city of Cincinnati that answered the purpose. Various sites in Cincinnati and the suburbs were considered, but did not meet with approval; some became the price asked was too high, others because there was no prospect of a large congregation being formed in that locality.

The Ferguson, Langdon and Thale tracts in Norwood Heights, embracing 155-954-1000 acres, appeared, all things considered, the most suitable to the committee. The reason why it advised that this entire tract be secured was to command a prominent position for the cathedral on an elevation overlooking the valley. I informed the Committee that the diocese could not purchase that entire tract, an pay for the grading, the marking of the streets, etc., and beside, that I would and did not wish as Archbishop want to take part in any enterprise, in which the Archdiocese might in any way be involved. It was then proposed to organize a company to buy the property, do the grading, and make the streets, with expectance that the company after organization would offer to the Archdiocese sufficient ground for Cathedral, Seminary, Archbishop's house, and other diocesan buildings.

I then called a meeting of the consulters and asked their opinion as to the advisability of locating the Preparatory Seminary, the Archbishop's House, and eventually, if found feasible, the Cathedral at Norwood Heights. Before coming to any conclusion in regard to this important matter, the consulters first inspected the site. I then asked the Diocesan Building Committee, and also the Deans of the Archdiocese, and preeminent laymen to view the premises and give their judgment on the matter. With two or three exceptions all of them thought well fog the plan.

The Norwood Heights Company was then organized, and incorporated under the laws of Ohio. It purchased the one hundred fifty-six acres and of this amount it deeded to the Archbishop sixteen acres and a fraction for Diocesan purposes under the following conditions:

First: That I shall pay to the company $45,000.00 for grading, filling, making, and improving my macadam, the streets, bounding the sixteen acres, laying sewers, cementing the curbs and gutters. The company agreed to accept the $45,000.000 in three equal installments; the first to be paid August 15, 1907, the second July 1, 1908 and the third July 1, 1909; but no interest is to be paid on the deferred payments. Provision has been made to pay these installments without making an additional appeal to the diocese.

Second: That I shall build on the premises within twenty years a Seminary, Archbishop's house, and a Cathedral; the latter to be built only in the case "conditions warrant." By complying with these restriction the Archbishop of the Diocese will become the absolute owner of the property with all its improvements enumerated will cost the Diocese about $2,8000.00 per acre; which is cheaper than any other unimproved land in the vicinity of Norwood Heights. I am fully convinced that the company has been very generous towards the Archdiocese and ahs made a donation of a very valuable tract of land. [4]

It is interesting to note that in July 1907 tentative plans had been drawn up of the buildings to be put on the sixteen acre tract reserved for diocesan purposes. These plans showed the cathedral facing Moeller Avenue with the Archbishop's residence at the corner of Moeller and Quatman, and the parish house and parochial school at the corner of Moeller and Drex. The seminary, according to these plans, was to be built behind the cathedral and to face Montgomery Road. [5]

A little more than two years later, in September of 1908, the entire plan moved forward with the announcement that it had been decided to go ahead with the building of the archbishop's house. It seems that some time during that year the original plans calling for the cathedral to face Moeller Avenue and for the seminary to face Montgomery Road were changed for the parish house. [6] No information has been located to indicate what prompted this alteration of plans.

However, not until March 22, 1917, were the plans for the construction of the seminary put into operation. On that date the *Catholic Telegraph* announced that architect Anthony Kunz would receive separate and lump bids for the construction of the new Mounts St. Mary's Seminary in Norwood Heights. The plans were posted in the Builders and Traders Exchange, and the bids on them were to be submitted by April 16 of that year.[7] Yet, in the following April, the archbishop announced that "owing to the uncertainties, incident to the war, the building of the Archdiocesan Seminary has been temporarily postponed." [8]

BREAKING GROUND FOR THE NEW SEMINARY (1921)

Four years later, under a clear blue sky, Archbishop Moeller turned the first sod for the building of the new seminary at Norwood Heights. The date was June 1, 1921. Gathered around the archbishop on that historic occasion were many of the prominent clerics and Catholic laymen of the day. [9]

The ceremony of breaking ground was very impressive. After dinner at the archbishop's house, His Grace and his guests walked to the large, plain, unpainted wooden cross erected over the spot where the main altar of the seminary chapel will be built. Father Albers handed a spade to the archbishop and His Grace turned the sod. Several photographs were taken and the *Catholic Telegraph* had the Romell Motion Picture Company take a movie of the event. [10]

LAYING THE CORNERSTONE (1922)

Good weather prevailed the remainder of the summer and fall and by March of 1922, the entire extensive foundation and basement floors of the seminary were completed. Due to the rapid progress Archbishop Moeller, assisted by the clergy of the archdiocese, laid the cornerstone of the new seminary at Norwood Heights on March 16, 1922. The large amount of building material littering the site and the broken and muddy condition of the ground made it inadvisable, for reasons of health and comfort, to invite or permit a large crowd to attend. The invitations were thus restricted to the archdiocesan officials, professors of the seminary, the lay advisory committee, and the architects of the building. [11] Shortly after four o'clock the procession consisting of the archbishop, the other clerics, and Catholic laymen, moved from the archbishop's house out over the extensive foundations of the new structure to the cornerstone. [12] After the blessing of the cornerstone, it was put with its copper case and contents into the cavity of the large foundation stone. A mason then placed a slab over the cavity. [13]

THE OPENING OF THE NEW SEMINARY (1923)

When the new seminary at Norwood opened its doors in 1923, students arrived for class. This represented an increase of almost fifty students over the proceeding year. When the shift was made to Norwood it was decided that the two years of philosophy would remain at St. Gregory's in Mount Washington. In the long history of the diocesan seminary this was the first time that these two years were separated from the four years of theology. In 1948 the two years of philosophy were again transferred back to Norwood, and the traditional six year program has been maintained ever since.

The faculty for this first year at Norwood in 1923 was composed of the following men: Beckman was still the rector and taught dogma; Souffert taught moral; Grimmelman taught Sacred Scripture; Gorry taught fundamental theology; Rehring taught philosophy; Harbrecht was the librarian and taught sociology; and Francis S. Smith became the new procurator, succeeding Gorry. [14]

The new seminary had been opened for the inspection of the public on Saturday and Sunday, September 8 and September 9; and on Saturday and Sunday, September 15 and 16. It was announced at the time that those desiring to visit on these days could reach the seminary by taking the North Norwood or Kennedy Heights street cars or the buses leaving Fifth and Walnut Streets. [15]

THE NEW LIBRARY

In the first year immediate consideration was given to beginning the new library. A committee, consisting of the vicar-general and Fathers Nau and Roth was appointed by the archbishop to prepare the furniture requirements for the library. They met as early as August, 1923, and agreed to recommend that the contract for the library be awarded to the Snead & Company, Jersey City, New Jersey, who had submitted a bid of $4,170. Several other firms had submitted bids, but the committee decided in favor of Snead & Company.

Their report was submitted to the archbishop who approved it, and the contract was given to this firm. Snead was the largest company in that line in the United States at the time, and work commenced on the shelving immediately. The quality of their work was judged by the fact that they had installed the shelving in the Library of Congress at Washington, the New York City Library; the Ohio State University, Columbus; St. Charles Borromeo Seminary, Philadelphia; and the Sulpician Seminary, Montreal. Local specimens of their work may be seen in the Ohio Mechanics Institute and the Hebrew Union College.

The shelving was entirely of metal, standard construction, and consisted of fifteen double faced stacks, carrying six shelves of books, fifteen feet in length, placed in the middle of the room between the pillars. Besides these there were three single faced stacks, each eighteen feet in length, places against the north wall. It is estimated that this amount of shelving took care of twenty-five thousand, two hundred volumes. The shelving was so designed that its strength was sufficient to carry another series of stacks above if ever the need would arise. It was thought that in this way the capacity of the library could very easily be doubled at any time. [16]

With the appointment at the same time of a new librarian, John Harbrecht, the library began to assume a more important position in the life of the seminarians. John J. Harbrecht, the new librarian, was born in Cincinnati on April 12, 1892. Educated at St. Gregory's and at Mount St. Mary's, he later attended the Catholic University of America at Washington. He had filled various other parochial offices prior to his appointment to Mount St. Mary's Seminary. At the seminary he did exceptional work as the librarian in setting up, in part, the old section of the present library. In 1925 he took up higher studies at Fribourg, receiving his doctorate in theology in 1927. He then returned to the seminary to teach. While a professor he wrote a book, *The Lay Apostolate,* which was reputed to have been very advanced in its theological theories for the day.[17]

SOLEMN DEDICATION (1923)

The new, massive Mount St. Mary's Theological Seminary at Norwood Heights was solemnly dedicated on October 23, 1923, by the personal representative of Pope Pius XI, Most Reverent Peter Fumasoni-Biondi, Apostolic Delegate to the United States. Following the ceremony performed by the papal delegate, a solemn pontifical Mass was celebrated in the beautiful chapel of the seminary by Right Reverend James J. Hartley, Bishop of Columbus. The Reverend Raphael Markham, of the seminary faculty, was assistant priest; the Reverends Jacob Vogt and Leo Hildebrandt, seminarians, were deacon and sub-deacon respectively of the Mass.[18]

Right Reverent Bishop Gallagher of Detroit preached the dedicatory sermon. He congratulated Archbishop Moeller and the priests and people of the archdiocese upon the erection of such a handsome, commodious and suitable institution, and predicted for it a glorious and beneficent future. He spoke of the need of a trained and cultured clergy, capable of meeting the claims of so-called modern science, as well as of ministering to the spiritual needs of the unlearned and the lowly. He dwelt upon the paramount importance of religion, and decried the indifference of men toward the spiritual life:

> Money is freely given for the teaching of the physical sciences, universities are established and endowed for the spreading of secular knowledge; but for theology, the queen of the sciences, the work at large has no encouragement, no support, no regard...Here, however, in this splendid new seminary the nobler studies of the eternal verities will be pursued. From the halls of this university of the spiritual sciences, will be sent out men of the genuinely higher learning to teach and preach to a soul-starved world; the essential relations between the Creator and His creatures; the obligation and the sure sanction of the Divine Law; the vital necessity of justice of Christian charity; and the way to live through this temporary earthly existence, so as to win the everlasting life of ineffable happiness in Heaven.[19]

At the conclusion of the Mass, Monsignor Beckman, rector of the seminary, read the letter from the Pope to Archbishop Moeller congratulating him upon the happy occasion.[20]

A banquet was served in the refectory of the seminary shortly after the conclusion of the services in the chapel. At this banquet Right Reverent Monsignor Hickey, the toastmaster, made an address briefly reviewing interesting facts in the history of the diocese, and then introduced the sponsors of the toasts who were: His Excellency, the Apostolic Delegate; Right Reverent Bishop Kelly of Grand Rapids, and Right Reverent Bishop Schrems of Cleveland. The last speaker at the banquet was Archbishop Moeller who, in his short speech, expressed his thanks to all the prelates and the clergy who had taken part in the double celebration. He also expressed his gratitude to the priests and people who had contributed to the erection and furnishing of the seminary. He said that it had been his wish to have the seminary entirely paid for before its dedication, and that his wish had been gratified. Significant facts from his speech are as follows: (1) Two hundred and fifty thousand dollars had been spent in equipping and furnishing the seminary. (2) The total expenditure, up to October 29, was $1,049,339.37. (3) His Grace had paid that amount in full and a balance of $102,611.80 remained in the seminary fund. [21]

The newly dedicated seminary was the fulfillment of the hopes and plans of Archbishop Henry Moeller. No doubt his thoughts went back to Bishop Fenwick's dream of a seminary in which to train his candidates for the priesthood, "attempting to meet the needs of his day with a seminary conducted in a shack but little better than a stable. A hundred years has brought a great change."[22]

The seminary faces the west on Moeller Avenue with a frontage of 354 feet. As one approaches from the south on Moeller Avenue, he sees a massive, handsome three-story grey brick building in the Italian Renaissance style of architecture. The seminary was built in the form of the letter "E," the wings of which are approximately 253 feet long. The middle wing is occupied by the chapel on each side of which there is a court.

NAU, RECTOR (1924-1929)

During the middle of the first scholastic year at the new seminary in Norwood, word was received that the rector Monsignor Beckman, had made bishop of Lincoln, Nebraska. [23] Monsignor Nau established residency in the suite of rooms on the first floor of the main building, which today is referred to as the "archbishop's suite." At the end of the school year in 1924, Bishop Beckman left for his diocese and Nau became the rector of the seminary.

Louis Nau was a good choice. He was a man of vast learning and possessed a keen mind. He tended to be more liberal than his predecessor both in administration and in teaching. The seminary had functioned well during the time of Beckman, but one constantly gets the impression that it was functioning of an organism in the near state of suspended animation. As the post-war era swept the nation, changing its culture and demanding new approaches, the change in administration brought to the rectorship, in the person of Nau, a man who was ready and able to move in the direction of modern adaptation and improvement.

In this year, 1924, the faculty and the subjects they taught were as follows: man, the rector, taught sacramental theology and canon law; Souffort still taught the course in moral; Markham was the spiritual director, while teaching the class in speech and ascetical theology;

154

Rehring taught church history, history of dogma, and catechetics; Gorry taught fundamental theology; Grimmelsman taught Sacred Scriptures; Herbrecht the librarian, taught sociology and education; Smith taught liturgy; and Fehring taught church music. [24]

The three newcomers to the faculty that year were the Reverend Augustine Adelman, Mr. John Drury, and Doctor Carroll de Coursey. DeCoursey was the attending physician, and Drury was the new professor of dogma. He was born in Visbeck, Oldenberg, Germany, on February 2, 1968. He came to this country as a young man and entered old Mount St. Mary's in 1887, the first year it was reopened. After completing his philosophical and theological studies on Price Hill, he was ordained by Archbishop Elder on June 21, 1893. He was engaged in parochial work for a short time and in 1895 taught at St. Gregory's Seminary. The following year he returned to parochial work and remained thus engaged until 1924 at which he was appointed to the faculty of Mount St. Mary's Seminary. Here he served as professor until his retirement in 1934. [25]

In the first year of Nau's administration nine departments were organized in an attempt to modernize the curriculum. There were the departments of Sacred Scripture, Dogmatic Theology, Moral Theology, Canon Law, Church History, Ascetical-Pastoral Theology, Homiletics, Sacred Liturgy, and Sociology-Education. Each faculty member then proceeded to set up the curriculum for his department stating its purpose and settling on the texts to be used in each section. Two more departments—Speculative Theology and Catechetics—were added at a later date bringing the number of departments to eleven. [26]

During the entire period covered in this chapter, 1923 to 1949, it is interesting to note the amount of time devoted to classwork during a semester. Records kept of amount of class hours per semester gives some significant facts. Beginning with the administration of Nau, the number of class hours per semester rose from nineteen hours to twenty-two hours. The entire amount of class hours spent in theology increased from a low of seventy-six to a high of eighty-nine. The reason for the increase was evidently the seminary's desire to fit new courses into the curriculum as the times demanded.

Also in 1924, Nau introduced special courses in theology, liturgy, Sacred Scripture, sociology, and education in order to afford the brighter and more industrious students an opportunity of advanced study and work. [27]

Recognition was now being given to the more gifted seminarians. Also, for the first time, the word "elective" was mentioned in the theological curriculum.

At the twenty-second annual reunion of Mount St. Mary's Alumni on October 22, 1924, the familiar statue of the Immaculate Conception, which stands at the front of the building today, was presented to the seminary. The new statue stood sixteen feet high overall, the statue proper was eight feet high, and the pedestal eight feet. Both were of Bedford stone which harmonized well with the buff brick and Bedford stone trim of the building. The statue stood back from Moeller Avenue about one hundred feet, and about seventy-five feet to the front of the building. As the ground is slightly elevated at this point, the statue commanded an excellent view to the west and southwest. Mr. Clement Barnhorn, the noted sculptor of the day, designed and carved the Madonna. Mr. Barnhorn said that in fashioning the figure of the Immaculate Conception he thought of its precedent, Murillo's famous Blue Virgin, which hangs in thc Louvre. [28]

On January 5, 1925 death came suddenly to Archbishop Moeller. The present seminary building at Norwood was his idea, and stands today as a monument to him. He had dedicated many years of his life to its planning and building; it is his magnificent bequest to posterity.

After the Archbishop's death Monsignor Nau became administer *pro tem* of the archdiocese, in addition to his work as rector of the major seminary. Father Rese, the vice-president of the old Athenaeum on Sycamore Street, had acted in the same capacity just a little less than a hundred years before on the death of Bishop of Fenwick.

On July 8, 1925, Timothy McNicholas was appointed the new Archbishop of Cincinnati. He was then but forty-seven years of age. Highly educated in the Dominican traditions of learning, he was vitally interested in the advancement of Catholic education. [29] McNicholas' leadership for the next twenty-five years was to have a profound effect upon the two seminaries. He immediately launched an extensive program of advanced study for the priests of the diocese who would teach in the seminaries. During these years, 1925-1950, it is estimated that he sent more than 110 young priests to schools of higher education both in Europe and in the United States. It has been said that these schools were in the main Dominican. He also injected into the curriculum the course in speculative theology. He propounded the lecture and quiz method of study. All of these things had a lasting effect upon the curriculum and the educational methods of the two seminaries.

On the organizational level, Archbishop McNicholas desired to have a unifying and a coordinating agency for all the educational work in the diocese. This agency he formed into a corporation called the Athenaeum of Ohio. In Chapter Eight, the history, purposes, and the development of the Athenaeum of Ohio as envisioned by McNicholas will be treated at length. Suffice it to say at this point that the Athenaeum of Ohio was instrumental in making Mount St. Mary's and St. Gregory's Seminaries again conscious of the necessity of awarding degrees.

In 1925 there were no changes in the faculty. To encourage writing on the problems of the sacred sciences, a periodical called *Student Studies* was instituted at the urging of the archbishop. All the papers submitted were to be the individual work of the students and were to have direct reference to the subject matter treated in the classroom. In the following year the name of the periodical was changed to *Seminary Studies*. During the years that it was published it contained many fine articles, and gained a splendid reputation for scholarship in various fields of theological research. [30]

In 1926 McNicholas introduced a fifth year of theology for priests ordained for the Archdiocese of Cincinnati. During this added year it was the intention of the archbishop that these men be engaged in practical pastoral studies. The work comprised the writing and delivery of sermons, normal and advanced work in catechetics, bible history, pastoral accounting, special studies in apologetics, and the study of the moral theology of St. Thomas. On week-ends they were to assist at the various parishes in the diocese. The plan was ambitious but was soon found to be impractical and was abandoned.[31]

During the month of August 1927 the first of the layman's annual retreat was held at the seminary. The lay retreat movement started the previous summer. The first weekend retreat was held at Crusade Castle in January of 1927 and drew more than one-hundred men. In August, men from all over the archdiocese assembled at the seminary for spiritual exercises preached by the archbishop. In each succeeding year the retreat attendance grew, and in 1942 more than 250 men attended. World War II brought the retreats to an end and they were never resumed at Mount St. Mary's. During the period these exercises were held, such good was accomplished. Not only did the laymen benefit spiritually; he also became better acquainted and more familiar with the diocesan seminary itself. [32]

In September of 1928, with Mount St. Mary's Seminary now constituted as a unit of the Athenaeum of Ohio,[33] a program of post-graduate work leading to Master of Arts degrees in scholastic philosophy and in letters, along with proposals for the rewarding of a Doctor of Philosophy degree, were set into motion.

The program for these three degrees was well worked out, at least on paper. In retrospect, this plan was remarkably ambitious but the seminary did not have the faculty to initiate such a program. Apparently some time between September of 1928 and March of the following year, the doctoral program was abandoned. On May 28, 1929, the rector announced to the faculty that the State of Ohio had granted to the seminary faculty, through the Athenaeum of Ohio, the right to confer only the Master of Arts degree in scholastic philosophy. [34]

The history that led up to the ambitious program of 1929 began under Nau when he became rector in 1924. At the time advanced studies were offered in dogmatic and moral theology, Sacred Scripture, sociology, and education. These advanced courses were to be given only to the more gifted students. During 1924, 1925, 1926 and 1927, these courses were made electives. In the important four years of development, 1924 through 1927, the basic requirements of a curriculum suitable for the pursuit of degrees had been worked out. [35]

September, 1928, is extremely important in the history of the seminary because it was the first year the seminary functioned as a unit in the newly incorporated Athenaeum of Ohio. It is also significant that it was the first time for almost seventy year that the seminary had discussed or planned for the awarding of scholastic degrees. As has already been seen, the last Bachelor of Arts degree was awarded at old Mount St. Mary's College in 1853. Purcell had petitioned a short time before this for the Doctor of Philosophy degree and the Doctor of Theology degree but the petition was rejected.

The reasons for the sudden insurgence of interest in the awarding of academic degrees were twofold. First, it was quite evident in 1928 that the state of Ohio was definitely committed to raising the certificate requirements for those teaching at the secondary level. Secondly, in Catholic circles it was definitely seen that more Catholic Secondary schools were needed. It was also evident that if these new schools were to be staffed, much of the personnel was to come from the ranks of the diocesan clergy. It shall be seen later in Chapter IX that this was one of the important reasons for the information of the corporate educational entity known as the Athenaeum of Ohio.

A significant result of a faculty meeting held on January 18, 1930, was that a degree program was reintroduced into the seminary. A change of thought in regard to the conferring of degrees was much in evidence when the faculty decided to give all the fourth year men every opportunity to obtain the Master of Arts degree from Mount St. Mary's Seminary. The minutes indicate that the faculty wanted as many as possible to obtain their degree. [36]

Coming to the faculty in September of 1926 were the Reverends Raymond Stoll and Robert J. Sherry. Father Stoll had studied at Innsbruck and now took up his duties as a professor of Sacred Scripture along with Grimmelman. Stoll was later appointed vice-rector. [37] Father Sherry became the professor of moral theology and canon law. He taught for one year at Mount St. Mary's, and in 1927 transferred to St. Gregory's where he was appointed professor of philosophy. In 1928 he returned to the faculty of Mount St. Mary's.

At the faculty meeting held on Saturday, May 26, 1928, it was agreed that each professor in the coming year was to teach at least a minimum of eight hours a week (two hours less than twenty years before). It is interesting to note, in the light of a recent developments, that at this faculty meeting the issue of Latin arose. It was decided that the classes in dogma, moral, and canon law would hereafter be taught in Latin.

THE CENTENARY CELEBRATION (1929)

The celebration of the centenary of the founding of the Catholic Seminary in Cincinnati opened on Sunday, December 1, 1929. The celebration recalled the story of the great sacrifices made by the first bishops and clergy who laid the foundation for this venerable institution when Ohio was little more than a wilderness. Monsignor Joseph H. Albers, chancellor of the archdiocese, was chairman of the arrangements committee for the seminary celebration which extended from December 1 to December 5. "Out of Town Night" was observed Sunday, December 1, for the benefit of the alumni who lived outside of Cincinnati and who found it impossible to attend other days. Monday, December 2, was Alumni Day and was observed with a special program at Music Hall in the evening. Various Catholic societies of the archdiocese conducted appropriate ceremonies on Tuesday, December 3. The musical program which opened the celebration Sunday night was repeated on Tuesday. [38]

Alumni of Mount St. Mary's who were living numbered approximately six hundred. During the hundred years of the seminary's existence more than two thousand priests had been prepared for ordination. Of this number, twenty-six had been consecrated bishops.

His Holiness, Pope Pius XI, sent a personally autographed letter to Archbishop John T. McNicholas, O.P., congratulating him, the priests, and the laity of the archdiocese upon the occasion of the seminary's centenary. The letter from the Pope was transmitted to Archbishop McNicholas through the offices of Cardinal Gasparri, Papal Secretary of State. It read as follows:

To Our Venerable Brother, John Timothy, Archbishop of Cincinnati, and Assistant to the Papal Throne, Pius XI, Pope, Venerable Brother, Health and Blessings:

We have received these days, the very gratifying assurance that you, the clergy and the faithful of your diocese are preparing to celebrate in a fitting and worthy manner the centenary of the founding of your major seminary. We must be mindful of the great contribution which this institution of learning made during this time—truly a long span of years for Catholic America—toward the preservation and propagation of our holy faith. How many priests going forth from thence, year after year, allotted portion of the Lord's vineyard, to awaken that ardent Christian piety with which he was there imbued! Events have proved how happy were the fruits of their wise planning. For we learn there are so many young men who desire to follow an ecclesiastical vocation, that in addition to the major seminary, there will be dedicated soon with the solemn rites of the Church, a new minor seminary, which by reason of the size and equipment of its buildings, is able to meet the needs of the times and provide adequately for the increased number of students called to the service of the Lord...

Since the topic offers us an excellent occasion to write concerning the proper administration of seminaries, we desire to bring to your attention some things which are in perfect harmony with your wishes. In the first place, as all are fully aware, it is one of the most serious obligations of the Bishop to receive only select and proven young men into the seminary. For students must show from the very beginning that they are worthy of the most sacred office which they are to exercise. Although it is much to be desired, because the vast extent of the vineyard of the Lord, that as many priests as possible toil ceaselessly therein, still the Bishop should remember that it is not the number of students which is of prime consideration, but the quality of the education which they receive; for it is necessary that they excel above all else in apostolic zeal and that they become very proficient in learning, especially in the sacred sciences.

Given at Rome, at Saint Peter, on the fourth day of November, in the year 1929, the eighth of our pontificate. [39]

In February of 1930 Archbishop John T. McNicholas, O.P. went to Europe for his "Ad Limina" visit to the Holy See. Monsignor Urban J. Vehr accompanied him. [40] The Rome press announced that the Holy Father had presented the archbishop with the purse for Mount St. Mary's Seminary which provided funds for the education of a young man for the priesthood through the full seminary course. The gift was hailed as one of the most remarkable gifts from the Pope to an institution in the United States. The Pope made the gift in the nature of joining with the seminary in celebration of the centenary of its founding by Bishop Fenwick. It was known as the Pius XI burse.

About a year later an event occurred in Rome which had repercussion upon all Catholic seminaries throughout the world.

On May 24, 1931, in the apostolic constitution, *Deus Scienctiarum Dominus*.[41] Pope Pius XI provided for the organization of pontifical seminaries attached to pontifical universities which would offer courses in philosophy and theology. Although this apostolic constitution concerned many different aspects of university and seminary life, it did have a vital effect upon seminary curriculum. Through the apostolic constitution all major seminaries became fairly well standardized with respect to curriculum. The result was that the content of the core subjects in philosophy and theology would change very little in the coming years. With the curriculum standardized, it was apparent that any further progressing would necessarily be restricted to the area of improving the caliber of faculty personnel and their methods of instruction. As was already noted, Archbishop McNicholas had made a key move in the interest of improving the caliber of the seminary faculty by the instituting a long-range program of graduate studies. Certain improvements were made in administration at this time but were not far-reaching in nature.

VEHR, RECTOR (1929-1931)

On June 25, the Most Reverend Archbishop McNicholas called the faculty together. He expressed regret at the resignation of Monsignor Nan, and asked for suggestions on a new rector for Mount St. Mary's. The mention of Monsignor Vehr's name was received with general approval. At this meeting the archbiship also announced the appointment of Father Sherry to the post of rector of St. Gregory's Seminary.[537]

In the first year of Monsignor Vehr's administration, the faculty included Rehring (vice-rector), Markham, Gorry, Harbrecht, Stoll, and Grimmelman. The newcomer this year was William Gauche who now embarked on a long career of teaching at Mount St. Mary's, and who subsequently became rector of St. Gregory's in September of 1949.[538]

On June of 1931 it was announced that the rector of the seminary, Monsignor Vehr had been appointed Bishop of Denver. Succeeding Vehr was the Reverend George Rohring, a priest who had been on the faculty of Mount St. Mary's since 1923. He was a native of Cincinnati and was forty-one years old. Born on June 10, 1890, in Price Hill, he had attended St. Lawrence parish school. He entered Mount St. Mary's Seminary and was ordained there on March 28, 1914, by Archbishop Moeller. He came to the seminary to teach in 1923 as professor or moral theology. In 1926 he was granted a two-year leave to go to Rome where he earned a doctorate in theology. In 1928 he resumed his position on the seminary faculty. He was appointed to the rectorship in 1931, and two years later was elevated to monsignor. In 1937 he became the auxiliary bishop of Cincinnati, functioning concurrently as the rector of the seminary.[41]

Associated with Rehring in the administration of the seminary in 1931 were Grimmelman, vice-rector; Markham, spiritual director; Gorry, treasurer; and Stoll, secretary and dean of discipline. The faculty was composed of Rehring, Nau Adelman, Souffert, Markham, Gorry, Grimmelman, Stoll, Smith, Freking, Thill, Giuliani, Gauche, Heyker, and Fehring. In Rehring's first year of rectorship (1931) the seminary had a very large enrollment. Present were 240 students representing eighteen dioceses from all over the United States. The various dioceses represented were Amarillo, Boise, Charleston, (S.C.), Columbus, Covington, Detroit, Erie, Fort Wayne, Grand Rapids, Nashville, Sacramento, Salt Lake, San Juan (Puerto Rico),

Toledo, Dubuque, and Santa Fe. [43]

In 1932d Francis Smith became the new vice-rector and Father James O'Brien came to the faculty as the instructor in canon law. In 1933 there were no changes in administration or faculty. In September of 1934 the Reverend J. Dean McFarland became spiritual director of Mount St. Mary's Seminary replacing Markham. The Reverend James Hoban came to the faculty as instructor in moral theology, and James Collins became professor of dogma. [44]

In September of 1935 the speculative courses in moral and dogmatic theology, using the text of the *Summa Theologica* of St. Thomas Aquinas, were introduced into the seminary curriculum. Gauche taught the course in dogma, and O'Brien taught the course in moral.

In June of 1936 a Chair of Canon Law was established at Mount St. Mary's Seminary as a perpetual memorial to the late Monsignor Louis J. Nau, former rector of the seminary. Alumni of the seminary had agreed unanimously upon the plan at a business session incident to their annual reunion. Eighteen dioceses of the country were represented. The chair was established at the seminary in the year 1937 at the cost of $18,000. [45]

At this time Rehring, rector of the seminary, was elected President of the Alumni Association. Other officers were Reverend J. Doyle, Toledo, vice-president; Reverend James Sherman, professor at the seminary, secretary-treasurer; and Reverend John J. McCrystal, Covington, historian. Reverend W. P. O'Connor, pastor of the Church of the Assumption, was named poet laureate of the alumni group at a declamation contest.

Archbishop John T. McNicholas, O.P., who was a guest of honor at the annual dinner, discussed the seminary and its work, including the new formal courses in philosophy which had been introduced in 1928 for the Master of Acts degree program. Archbishop McNicholas said "The Seminary must prefer essentials to incidentals. Progress in the future, as in the past, must come through a progressive discontent, that it may go farther in preparing priests for their difficult tasks." [46]

Bishop Karl Alter, then of Toledo, officiated at the solemn Mass Tuesday morning and delivered the reunion sermon. "Individual salvation and social well-being must go hand in hand," Bishop Alter said. The civilization and culture of a nation depend upon its attitude toward certain fundamentals. Christianity has definite principles toward fundamentals. When Christianity prospers," Bishop Alter observed, "civilization also progresses, but where Christianity stagnates, there, too, civilization and culture wane and retreat. The Church today faces the problem of defending its moral principles against a new paganism." [47]

Cardinal Pacelli, then Papal Secretary of State and later Pope Pius XII, visited Cincinnati in November, 1936. He was driven from the airport with Archbishop McNicholas and Bishop Albers, accompanied by a motorize police escort. At the Archbishop's residence dinner was served to a small group of clergymen and laymen. Having spent the night at the archbishop's house, at an early hour on Saturday morning His Eminence said Mass at Mount St. Mary's Seminary. All of the 260 students had assembled. Following the Mass, Cardinal Pacelli was presented to the students by Archbishop McNicholas. He then spoke from the balcony to a crowd assembled on the front lawn.[48]

In September, 1936, Father Robert Krumholtz, later to become rector St. Gregory's Seminary, came to the faculty of Mount St. Mary's. He assumed the post of the librarian, and became the new instructor in fundamental dogma.

It is interesting to note that on May 22, 1937, seventeen men were ordained for the diocese of Cincinnati, the largest class in the history of the diocese up to that time. It is also worthy of note that all seventeen had completed their preparatory studies at St. Gregory's prior to coming to Mount St. Mary's Seminary. [49]

In August of 1937 Rehring, while still rector of the major seminary, was named auxiliary bishop of Cincinnati, succeeding Joseph Albers. The courteous head of the major seminary, now elevated to auxiliary bishop, continued in this post of rector.

The elevation of Rehring to auxiliary bishop occasioned a dinner in his honor given at the Hotel Alms on Thursday, October 7. It was at this dinner that Henry Grimmelman, a former professor at the seminary and now rector of the Pontifical College Josephinum at Worthington, Ohio, made the following noteworthy statements:

...Mt. St. Mary of the West seminary glories in 108 years of constantly renewing youth. In the two-score years of her pioneering she had little organization of staff or studies, yet she was meeting the need that day by sending apostles into the wilderness and among the scattered Catholics of the Middle West, or the complete seminary of St. Gregory—Mt. St. Mary, became a leader among institutions of higher learning in Cincinnati and one of the outstanding major seminaries in the United States.

Among its many capable professors of the classics, Doctor Engbers should be signalized, and of the sacred science Doctors Pabisch, Sele and Nau. Supporting the faculty and inspiring them to learned and holy endeavor, after the founder, Bishop Fenwick, were Archbishops Purcell, Elder, and Moeller, and His Excellency, Archbishop McNicholas. Our memory recalls the rectors of the restoration period: Bishop Byrne, Monsignor Mackey, Monsignor Murray, Father Shoe, Archbishop Beckman, Monsignor Nau, Bishop Vehr, and Bishop Rehring—a capable and colorful line of leaders...

...the majority can and do know full well what Mt. St. Mary was required and expected to do for its 2200 and more alumni, whom it prepared for ordination, in order to equip them properly for their great vocation.

It had to teach and train its students for a personal ministry; it was obliged to produce scholarly, zealous, and virtuous pastors. Answer, you who are most familiar with our seminary! Under the direction of its illustrious rectors, the latest of whom the Church has exalted today to Episcopal rank with its dignity and its cross, did not our alma mater do these things well and some of them eminently?

Mt. St. Mary stresses the pastoral ministry since the majority of her students were not to become professors but pastors. Some decades ago, when the debate began about the necessity of complete courses in the years in which these subjects had already been part of her curriculum. Before the question of detailing pastoral theology came up for discussion, our seminary had had distinct hours assigned to this discipline...

Our seminary was among the leaders in reform of liturgical music and liturgical services. For many years sociology and social ethics have their place in our seminary. Full well we realize that all these are applied sciences. It would be a mistake to let them use up the place and the time belonging to the systematic and thorough study of the essential theological subjects. Our seminary stressed the essentials. If she had would have had no seed to sow....

...Ascetical theology may be seen as one of the proper remedies for the impractical man of God. Long before suitable English texts in ascetical theology were available, our seminary trained its students in this eminently practical subject.

Mt. St. Mary's chief claim to recognition is the priests it has prepared for the care and cure of souls. To the seminary's ways of thinking it is of small importance that bishops have gone forth from St. Gregory's and Mt. St. Mary's but it is of great consequence that zealous, apostolic bishops and pastors, fired with holy zeal, are numbered among the alumni of our seminary.

...Because we who know Bishop George Rehring are convinced that he contributed in no small degree to the satisfactory scholarship and discipline of our seminary in his years of service as vice rector and rector, it was our pleasure to toast with him, his and our venerable alma mater. May both be blessed by God and may both go through long years of preparing priests who will be ready to bring an ageless Church and undying truth to the conquest of Communion, absolution, or whatever aberrations and ills modern paganism may employ to afflict the coming day. [50]

In September of 1937 there were several changes made in administration. Stoll now became the vice-rector; Francis Smith became the spiritual director; and Gauche became the dean of discipline. The new faculty members were John B. Stenz, Joseph Schneider, and Carl Steinbicker. Stenz was instructor in Sacred Scripture, Schneider was instructor in speculative moral, and Steinbicker became the instructor in homiletics. In 1983 there were no changes in administration or faculty. In 1939 Father Lawrence Montanus succeeded Gorry as treasurer, and the Reverend John Mussio became associate professor of canon law.

O'BRIEN, RECTOR (1940-1949)

The Very Reverend James W. O'Brien was named the new rector of Mount St. Mary's Seminary, Norwood, in the official column of the *Catholic Telegraph-Register* on June 21, 1940. He succeeded the Most Reverend Auxiliary Bishop George Rehring who was named pastor of St. Mary's parish in Hyde Park, Cincinnati. Father O'Brien was recalled to the archdiocese from the Catholic University of America, Washington, D.C., where he had been a member of the faculty for three years and had taught sacred theology. A son of Mr. and Mrs. Patrick O'Brien, the new major seminary rector was born in Springfield, Ohio, on October 29, 1902. He attended St. Raphael's grade school, and was graduated from high school in June, 1920. He spent the following two years at the present St. Gregory's Seminary, Mount Washington, Cincinnati. Archbishop Henry Moeller then sent him to the North American College in Rome, Italy, for his theological course. [51]

Father O'Brien was ordained to the priesthood by Archbishop Palica, Vice-Garent of Rome, on January 15, 1938, in the chapel of St. John Latern's Seminary. On June 1 of that year he was granted the degree of Doctor of Sacred Theology. He then returned to the United States. On September 26, 1928, Father O'Brien was appointed assistant at St. Lawrence parish, and instructor at Elder High School, Price Hill, Cincinnati. In August of 1929, he was appointed instructor at St. Gregory's Seminary, Mount Washington, where he remained for one year.

In August, 1930, Archbishop John T. McNicholas sent him to the University of Fribourg in Switzerland for graduate studies in canon law. After two years of study Father O'Brien obtained the degree of Licentiate in Canon Law and again returned to the archdiocese. He was appointed professor at Mount St. Mary's Seminary, Norwood, on September 1, 1932.

In 1940, the first year of the rectorship of O'Brien, Stoll was vice-rector; Smith was spiritual director; Montanus was treasurer; Gauche was dean of discipline; Krumholtz was librarian; and Kennedy was registrar. The faculty consisted of O'Brien Souffert, Collins, Stoll, Smith, Gauche, Krumholtz, Schneider, Steinbicker, Mussio, Freking, and Fehring. This new administration and faculty remained in 1941 and 1942.

In an article printed in the *Catholic Telegraph*, O'Brien, speaking of his faculty, is quoted as follows:

> Second to none in the country. The only theological faculty in the country which rivals is that of the Catholic University of America...Results of the training are evident in the success of post-graduate students from Mt. St. Mary's in other institutions...Without exception they have been a credit to the seminary...The students are industrious, loyal and devoted. They are not provincial in their outlook but have an unusually deep interest in the missions and the work of the church throughout the world.[52]

As an indication of the number of the students enrolled at Mount St. Mary's in the early 1940's, and the number of diocese represented, the following facts are significant: One hundred and eighty-six students, including sixty-one from the Archdiocese of Cincinnati, began the scholastic year of 1942-43 when classes resumed on September 4. Fifteen archdioceses and dioceses were represented in the student body that year. Detroit, forty students; Columbus, twenty-four; Toledo, thirteen; Covington, eleven: Lansing, nine; Dubuque, eight; Grand Rapids, six: Marquette, two: Oklahoma (Tulsa) two; Saginaw, two; Amarillo, one: Fort Wayne, one; Nashville, one; and San Juan, Puerto Rico, one. In addition, the Society of Home Missioners of America had sent four students.

In February of 1943 a quarterly publication to stimulate interest in liturgical music was established by the Archdiocesan Apostolate of the Liturgy of Mount St. Mary's Seminary, Norwood. [53]

In September of 1943 a quarterly publication to stimulate interest in liturgical music was established by the Archdiocese Apostolate of the Liturgy of Mount St. Mary's Seminary, Norwood. [54]

In September of 1943 Father Norbert Miller replaced Father Montanus as treasurer. Father Clarence Issenmann, later to become Bishop of Columbus, arrived on the faculty to teach fundamental moral. [55] There were no faculty changes in 1944.

On September 11, 1943, Mount St. Mary's Seminary was affiliated, on a probationary basis, to the Catholic University of America by the Sacred Congregation for Studies of Universities and Seminaries. On August 25, 1948, the affiliation was made permanent. The affiliation indicated that the theological courses of the Norwood seminary synchronized with those of the Catholic University. The work completed by students in three years of theology at St. Mary's would satisfy the requirement of the *Deus Scientiarum Dominus*. Students selected for theological degrees would then go to Catholic University for the fourth year of theology, after which they would receive the degree of Doctor of Theology. [56]

In September of 1945 Gauche replaced Stoll as vice-rector, and Father Edward Kotter replaced Frank Smith as spiritual director. The new additions to the faculty were James Hoban, Stanley Wolfer, Stanley Bertke, and Francis Flanagan.

In September of 1946 Father Thomas Devitt succeeded Norbert Miller as treasurer. The rest of the faculty remained the same as the preceding year.

At the board of trustees meeting on May 22, 1946, Monsignor Ryan and Monsignor Gauche submitted a report containing a general outline of a plan for conferring the Degree of Master of Arts in Religious Education by Mount St. Mary's Seminary. They were used to submit the plan in more detail but for reasons not ascertained, nothing more came of it. In the light of current educational practices, the report contained some progressive views. It read in part as follows:

> The committee appointed at the meeting of the Athenaeum in 1945, to investigate the possibilities of offering the Master's Degree at Mt. St. Mary Seminary in other subjects then Thomistic Philosophy, begs to submit the following report...
>
> There remains, however, one field (other than philosophy) in which we may consider the possibility of offering a Master's degree, namely, in that of teaching Religion. There are several reasons why such a program would be feasible; 1. It is work in which many priests are engaged. 2. It is a field where we have, or could provide, the facilities for giving this type of work. 3. Since it pertains to the field of teaching religion, we could more likely secure recognition for this degree by standardizing agencies where we could not hope so in some of the secular subjects.
>
> While this report does not propose a detailed plan, it suggests the outline of a program which, if approved by the Athenaeum, could be worked out in detail.
>
> There are two aspects to such a program—on involving knowledge of Religion and allied subjects, which we call the content portion of the program; the other knowledge of pedagogy, which we might call the methods part of the program. Before beginning work for a Master's degree, the student would have to complete the equivalent of an undergraduate program in this field, which of course, would involve both phases of the program previously mentioned...
>
> On the successful completion of such a program, the student would be awarded the mas-

ter's degree in religious education.

Since an increasing number of priests are called upon to teach some religion, especially in high schools, it is quite possible that some of the bishops would want some of their men to qualify for this degree. 57

Coming to the faculty in September of 1947 was the Reverend Joseph T. Rosenbauer. He was an eminent Scripture scholar, formerly of the faculty of St. Charles Seminary, Carthagena. A native of Germany, he was born on December 13, 1902, and had studied at Marienstitt (Germany) and Mehreran (Austria) prior to his ordination at Marienstitt on July 7, 1929. He was ordained as a member of the Cistercian Order. After his ordination he studied in Rome, and obtained a doctorate in Sacred Theology and a Licentiate in Sacred Scripture. When his superiors advised against his returning to Germany, which was then in the hands of his Nazi regime, he came to America. After spending some time in the Diocese of Portland, he joined the faculty of St. Charles Seminary of the Precious Blood Fathers in Carthagena. He came to Mount St. Mary's in the fall of 1947 and became the professor of Sacred Scripture. In addition to his work at Mount St. Mary's he taught at the Archdiocesan Teachers' College. In September, 1949, he was named administer of St. Aloysius' Church, Shandon. 58

His Eminence, Cardinal Mooney, Archbishop of Detroit, announced early in 1947 that a new major seminary (St. John's), would be established near Detroit. Many students from the diocese of Michigan who were training for the priesthood at Norwood would now be removed. As a result of this announcement a major change in the operation of the two archdiocesan seminaries was announced in August of 1948. Fifty students in the first and second years of philosophy would now reside and take their philosophy studies at the major seminary in Norwood, leaving the minor seminary devoted exclusively to the high school and two years of college. 59

The transfer of the philosophy department to Norwood was simply a move made to relieve the crowded conditions at Mount Washington, and thereby fill the void created by the removal from Norwood of the Michigan students.

The priests who served as professors to the thirty-five first-year philosophy students and the twenty-three second-year philosophy students at Norwood were Father Robert H. Tensing (who held the degrees of Doctor of Theology and Doctor of Philosophy), and Father Charles H. Hollencamp (who had just returned to this country from Rome where he had received his doctorate in theology.) He had previously received the degree of Doctor of Philosophy from Laval University, Quebec, Canada.

The transfer of the department of philosophy to Mount St. Mary's in 1948 returned the seminary to the traditional six-six program under which it had opened prior to 1923. It had been thought best to operate Mount St. Mary's as a strictly theological school. The plan did have a great deal of merit, but practicality and expediency prompted its abandonment in 1948. 60

By September of 1948 enrollment had grown to 230 students at the major seminary. Seventeen dioceses and two mission societies were represented in the student body. The

Cincinnati archdiocese had fifty-eight students studying at Mount St. Mary's Seminary. The total number of students in the last year of theology was forty-two; the third year numbered fifty-four; the second year numbered forty-seven; and the first year numbered twenty-eight. The philosophy department, which had been transferred from St. Gregory's to Norwood this year, had twenty-three students in the second year, and thirty-five students in the first.[61]

After the second World War and a six-week summer vacation school program was initiated. Each seminarian, from those who had completed the second year of college to and including those who were just one year away from ordination, was required to attend six hours a day, five days a week for six weeks at the Teachers' College. This meant that nine hundred hours of class credits had been merited by the time the seminarian reached his third year of theology. This extra training was aimed at familiarizing the philosopher and the theologian with the practical techniques of classroom education, and making him better equipped for handling parochial school problems. During the summer school sessions he learned the latest methods of teaching and pupil motivation. The seminarians attending the Teachers' College enjoyed the advantage of taking summer courses in four major fields—education, English, history, and mathematics.[61]

In the summer of 1949 a total of 390 students were enrolled in the summer session of the archdiocesan Teachers' College. This enrollment was one of the largest in the history of the college. Some forty subjects were being taught during the session, which opened June 20 and closed July 29.

Monsignor O'Brien, the rector of the seminary, died in his room at the seminary at 12:30 p.m. on September 1, 1949. [62] It was the eve of the return of the students to the seminary for another school year. The Right Reverend Monsignor Clarence G. Issenmann, Vicar General, delivered the funeral sermon to a congregation which included four bishops, more than twenty-five monsignors, some two-hundred priests, many seminarians, representing the sisterhoods in the archdiocese, and lay friends of the late Monsignor O'Brien. In the memories of the vast majority of priests who were in attendance, never before had they seen such a spontaneous outpouring of love and devotion. Due homage was rendered the man who had guided the destinies of the seminary since 1940.[63]

An editorial in the *Catholic Telegraph* stated the following:

Monsignor O'Brien was truly a priest in every fiber of being...he was beloved by his Ordinary, admired by many of the Hierarchy, loved by his classmates, and held in high esteem by the hundreds of young priests and seminarians taught by him...

...Intellectually, Monsignor O'Brien was the outstanding theologian of the Archdiocese, and one of the great theologians of our country. He was an eminent scholar of the Sacred Sciences. He loved theology and had never ceased his habits of study. He strove to engender this love of study and especially of theology by his students...His love and accomplishments are a credit to the seminary training given him by the Archdiocese of Cincinnati and by the North American College in Rome where he received his degree of Doctor of Theology from the Propaganda University; to the University of Fribourg in Switzerland, where he was awarded a Licentiate in canon law, and where, as he always used to say, "I learned actually to love theology; and later taught as a professor of speculative moral theology...As a secretary professor for seventeen years and as a rector of Mount St. Mary's Seminary for ten years, Monsignor came to be loved by thousands of his Students. He was a qualified trainer of priests. He was always understanding, patient, and merciful in his dealings with his seminarians. Of all the questions of St. Thomas' Summa Theologica taught by Monsignor O'Brien, the one that seemed best to characterize his life as rector might be: "Deus Maxime est in sua misericordia." He strove ever to be merciful in his decisions and to emulate in a finite way, this perfection of God. His prudent judgment gave him a sure balance in enforcing discipline...Human wisdom balks at accepting the untimely death of such an eminently qualified priest, prelate, and professor. But Divine Providence saw fit to permit the death of Monsignor O'Brien in his forty-seventh year. In harmony with the expressions of the saints, we can assume that although his death is a great loss to the Archdiocese of Cincinnati, still he will, through his death, be the means of even greater blessings for his family, his fellow priests, his Ordinary, and the Archdiocese. [64]

SUMMARY

In this chapter the history of Mount St. Mary's Seminary from 1923 to 1949 has been considered.

An important even was the erection in Norwood of a new building has for many years provided excellent educational facilities for both the faculty and students. In all truth it is an educational monument to Archbishop Moeller who labored over the planning, building, and financing of the structure.

It has been seen in this chapter that while the curriculum of the major seminary became increasingly standardized, there were now significant advances in the availability of post-graduate work for the seminary faculty, and an ever increasing awareness of the necessity of obtaining academic degrees.

To facilitate the obtaining of academic degrees, it was noted that Mount St. Mary's Seminary in 1928 became a unit of the newly incorporated Athenaeum of Ohio. The incorporation, and subsequent approval by the State of Ohio made possible at Mount St. Mary's the issuance of the first academic degree in over seventy-five years. This was the Master of Arts degree in scholastic philosophy. During this entire era, from 1928 to 1949, there were not as many degrees awarded (fifteen in all) as had been anticipated. But the step had been taken, and the goal of academic degrees for seminarians was again an educational reality.

A noteworthy development took place in 1943 when the seminary was affiliated, on a probationary basis, with the Catholic University of America. This probationary period end in 1948, at which time the seminary entered upon a permanent affiliation with the Catholic University of America. By reason of this affiliation the course work give at the seminary in the first three years of theology was recognized as equivalent to three years of work done at the Catholic University. This greatly facilitated the opportunity for students to obtain their theological education at Mount St. Mary's Seminary and not lose time in doing graduate work toward obtaining degrees in philosophy and theology.

It has also been seen that the faculty at the seminary was improved through an extensive program of post-graduate work in the universities of Europe and America. The administration of the seminary was markedly improved. All of the rectors who saw service from 1923-1949 were men of great ability and administrative talent.

All of these things bring us to the conclusion that this era was an era of new beginnings. The anvil was readied and the furnace primed for the educational advances which were to occur in the 1950's and 1960's.

After the death of Monsignor O'Brien, there were many significant changes in the administration of the seminaries and in the administration of the dioceses. Considering these necessary and significant changes, one would be very well justified in speaking of Monsignor O'Brien's death as the end of an era. On September 9, 1949, Monsignor Joseph Schneider was appointed rector of Mount St. Mary's and Monsignor Gauche was appointed rector of St. Gregory's Seminary in Mount Washington. Nine months later Archbishop McNicholas died after having been bishop of the diocese of Cincinnati for over two and one-half decades. These events ushered in a new era, and their subsequent effect upon the organization and administration of both seminaries will be the subject matter of Chapter X.

NOTES

[1] Letter to Moeller, July 2, 1906, MSMSA.

[2] *Catholic Telegraph*, July 23, 1906, p. 1.

[3] *Ibid.*, July 23, 1906, p. 4.

[4] *Ibid.*, August 25, 1907, p. 1.

[5] "Plans, Thomas B. Punchon, July, 1907," MSMSA.

[6] *Catholic Telegraph*, September 24, 1908, p. 5.

[7] *Ibid.*, March 22, 1917, p. 5.

[8] *Ibid.*, April 26, 1917, p. 5.

[9] *Ibid.*, June 2, 1921, p. 1.

[10] At the time of writing this thesis, the film could not be located.

[11] Appendix F.

[12] Appendix G.

[13] *Catholic Telegraph*, March 23, 1922, pp. 1, 4.

[14] *Ibid.*, October 4, 1923, p. 5.

[15] *Ibid.*, September 6, 1923, p. 5.

[16] *Ibid.*, August 23 1923, p. 5.

[17] *Ibid.*, May 22, 1942, p. 4., *Ibid.*, January 14, 1929, pp. 1, 4.

[18] *Ibid.*, October 25, 1923, pp. 1, 4.

[19] *Ibid.*

[20] *Ibid.*, p. 11.

[21] *Ibid.*, October 25, 1923, 1, 11.

[22] Cf. Chapter II.

[23] *Catholic Telegraph*, December 27, 1923.

[24] Catalogue, 1924-25, MSMSA.

[25] *Catholic Telegraph*, May 15, 1953, p. 1 (After going back to Germany in 1934, he returned to America with the outbreak of the Second World War. This time, resided on Glenside Avenue in Norwood. Until his final illness in May of 1953, he walked up to the seminary for his daily mass.)

[26] *Catalogue*, 1924-1925, MSMSA.

[27] *Ibid.*.

[28] *Catholic Telegraph*, October 23, 1924, p. 5.

[29] *Ibid.*, July 16, 1925, p. 6.

[30] Catalogue, 1925-1926, MSMSA.

[31] *Catholic Telegraph*, August 21, 1942, p. 1.

[32] Cf. Chapter IX.

[33] *Catholic Telegraph*, June 27, 1929, p. 1

[34] *Catalogue*, 1927-1928, MSMSA.

[35] "Minutes of the Faculty Meeting, January 18, 1930." MSMSA.

[36] *Catholic Telegraph*, March 10, 1943, p. 1.

[37] *Ibid.*, November 14, 1929, p. 4.

[38] *Ibid.*, December 5, 1929, p. 10.

[39] *Ibid.*, February 6, 1930, p. 1.

[40] *Acta Apostolica Sedis*, Volume 23, No. 7, 1 July, 1931, pp. 241-284.

[41] *Catholic Telegraph*, June 27, 1929, p. 1.

[42] *Ibid.*, August 19, 1949, p. 1.

[43] *Ibid.*, June 18, 1931, p. 1.

[44] *Ibid.*, September 27, 1934, p. 1.

[45] *Ibid.*, September 27, 1934, p. 4.

[46] *Ibid.*, June 18, 1931, p. 2.

[47] *Ibid.*, June 18, 1936, p. 2.

[48] *Ibid.*, June 18, 1936, p. 2.

[49] *Ibid.*, November 5, 1936, p. 1.

[50] *Ibid.*, May 20, 1937, p. 1.

[51] *Ibid.*, October 15, 1937, p. 7.

[52] *Ibid.*, June 21, 1940, p. 1.

[53] *Ibid.*, June 21, 1940, p. 1.

[54] *Ibid.*, April 30, 1943, p. 1.

[55] *Ibid.*, July 3, 1943, p. 1.

[57] *Ibid.*, March 17, 1944, p. 1.

[56] "Meeting of the Board of Trustees of Athenaeum of Ohio, May 22, 1946." MSMSA.

[57] *Catholic Telegraph*, January 5, 1951, p. 1.

[58] *Ibid.*, March 21, 1947, p. 1.

[59] *Ibid.*, August 13, 1948, p. 1.

[60] *Ibid.*, September 17, 1948, p. 1.

[61] *Catholic Telegraph*, July 1, 1949, p. 1.

[62] *Ibid.*, December 30, 1959, p. 2.

[63] *Ibid.*, September 9, 1949, p. 1.

[64] *Ibid.*, September 9, 1949, p. 1.

CHAPTER SEVEN

St. Gregory's Seminary (1923-1949)

INTRODUCTION

This chapter will deal with the history of St. Gregory's Seminary from the time of its re-establishment in 1923 until the year 1949. Sixteen years before, in the spring of 1907, the failure of the day school on Seventh Street in downtown Cincinnati brought down the curtain on the first attempt to establish a strictly preparatory seminary in the Archdiocese of Cincinnati. It wasn't until 1923 that the theological seminary of Mount St. Mary's of the West moved to its new location in Mount Washington. In this move, it has already been seen that the two years of philosophy were separated from the four years of theology and now remained at St. Gregory's. It was planned to begin with the first year of high school and add one class each succeeding year until there would be the four years of high school and the four years of college.

The educational arrangement thus effected was a radical departure from the traditional six-six arrangement which had been the practice of the seminary in its entire previous history. This new arrangement was an adaptation of the modern American division of four years of high school, four years of college, and four years of post-graduate or professional studies. As was seen in the previous chapter, this new plan lasted until the end of the present era under consideration. In 1948, mainly to equalize facilities with enrollment, the last two years of college (the two years of philosophy) were moved back to Norwood with the four years of theology.

This chapter will discuss the administrations of Sieber, Vehr, Sherry and Roddy, the rectors of St. Gregory's Seminary during the period under consideration. Sieber's task was to re-establish the high school and college departments. He began with only the two years of philosophy, but he laid well the foundations for the seminary's future expansion. Vehr's short administration continued the program begun by Sieber. Vehr, however, was the rector who brought to his office new ideas, methods, and educational philosophy of the new ordinary. During the rectorship of Sherry, the minor seminary in the early 30's reached a maturity of development that was maintained and, in many instances, perfected to a high degree during the succeeding administration of Roddy. In the 30's and 40's the administration was excellent and the faculty, in almost every field, was exceedingly competent.

One thing that contributed a great deal to this excellence during the 30's and 40's was the establishment of St. Gregory's in 1928 as a unit of the newly incorporated Athenaeum of Ohio. As in the case of Mount St. Mary's, becoming a unit of the Athenaeum of Ohio was an important development in many ways. The seminary, in addition to preparing students for the priesthood, became geared to preparing students to teach in the secondary schools of the archdiocese. As a consequence, standards set up by the State of Ohio concerning the matter of certification and the conferring of degrees, injected a new stimulus into the areas of faculty competence, student requirements, and physical facilities.

In regard to physical facilities, as the high school department grew from 1923 to 1928, it became readily apparent the housing in the old dormitories in the center and south wings was unsafe. This factor, plus the previously mentioned matter of state's approval, resulted in the early planning and construction in 1928 of a new high school building. This chapter will consider also the development and completion of this building program.

SIEBER, RECTOR (1923-1926)

When it was determined to build the seminary in Norwood, it was decided by Archbishop Moeller that only the theological students would be located there. It was to be the theological school only. At the same time, it was determined that the students in the two years of philosophy would remain at Mount Washington. They would constitute the nucleus around which would be built an entire program covering the four years of high school and the four years of college. Time would be needed to build up the faculty and to provide the necessary facilities.

In September of 1923 the students in the two years of philosophy returned to Mount Washington to be joined there with the first group of high school seminarians since 1907. This group was all in the first year of high school, and the plan was that one class would be added each year for the following six years. By 1928 the entire program had been completed.

During the years under consideration in this chapter, it is important to point out that, although the high school and college departments were on one campus and had one rector, the studies and activities of the two groups were quite distinct and separate. In 1928, after the erection of the new building for the high school students, the autonomous functioning of the two sections was quite evident.

There is some evidence that when the theological department moved to Norwood, a discussion took place concerning the name to use for the school in Mount Washington. It is interesting in the light of subsequent discussion that almost thirty years later some of the priests of the diocese favored reverting to the old system of calling both the seminaries by the one name "Mount St. Mary's of the West," even though there were two campuses. This did not gain acceptance for many practical reasons and "St. Gregory's" was the name it was given in 1923. There were some references made to it at the time as "Mount St. Gregory's Seminary."

In December 1922, the Reverend Joseph S. Sieber left Emmanuel Church in Dayton to assume his duties as rector of the new St. Gregory's Seminary which would begin to function in the following autumn. Sieber was known in his day as a learned classical scholar, speaking and writing Latin and Greek fluently. Some who attended his lectures while he was a professor at Mount St. Mary's, in the previous decade, attest to his fluency in conducting classes in Latin. He was a kindly man and while not a strict disciplinarian, he worked hard and succeeded admirably in getting the institution started again. It might well be said that he attained a surprising amount of success in his short tenure of two and one-half years as rector.[1]

174

Associated with Joseph Sieber in his first year as rector in 1923 were James L. Collins, the vice rector and professor of philosophy;[2] Alphonse Schumacher, professor of Scripture, church history, and Hebrew; Urban Koehl, professor of history and Latin; and Lawrence Montanus, the professor of mathematics. They were all able men and provided a firm foundation for the expansion of the faculty in the next few years.[3]

St. Gregory's Seminary, Mount Washington, reopened its doors on Monday, September 17, 1923, at six o'clock in the evening. The first students comprised the two years of philosophy and the first year of high school. The philosophers occupied the single rooms in the north wing, and the high school students occupied the dormitory on the top floor of the central wing.[4]

In the year 1924 there were two additions to the faculty in the personages of Leo Walsh (who taught second year Latin), and William A. Shine, who began teaching the course in Hebrew. Father Shine did not live at the seminary this first year, but came to live there in September of 1925. Father Shine spent many years on the faculty of St. Gregory's and later became the vice-rector.

With the addition of still another class in 1925, the newcomers to the faculty were the Reverend Giles Allais, who taught music, and the Reverend Joseph D. McFarland, who succeeded Koehl in the teaching of the first year Latin students. Father McFarland had completed his theological coarse at the North American College in Rome where he was ordained in the Lateran. In 1934, he became the spiritual director of St. Gregory's succeeding Father O'Regan, and several months after that was appointed to the same post at the major seminary at Norwood.

The appointment of Timothy McNicholas as Archbishop of Cincinnati in 1925 resulted in sending away for further post-graduate studies men who were to teach on the theological and philosophical faculties. This resulted in a marked increase in the professional competency of the respective professors. The same thing occurred among the ranks of those teaching languages and the classics in the minor seminary. [5] Many were sent away for post-graduate work in their respective fields.

VEHR, RECTOR (1926-1929)

Succeeding Joseph Sieber as rector of the minor seminary in January of 1926 was the Reverend Urban Vehr, who had been superintendent of the parochial schools of the archdiocese. A Cincinnatian by birth, the new rector was only forty years of age when he assumed the new post. Ordained in 1915, he was the chaplain and professor of Mount St. Joseph before becoming superintendent of the parochial schools of the archdiocese. As previously indicated, he became the rector of Mount St. Mary's in Norwood three years later, in June of 1929, succeeding Monsignor Louis Nau.[6]

In September of 1926, the first complete year of the rectorship of Vehr, the faculty consisted of twelve men, an increase of seven in only four years. This was mainly because the minor seminary now embraced the four complete years of high school and the two years of philosophy. Those on the faculty in this year were Giles Allais, Jerome O'Regan, Alphonse Schumacher, Charles E. Spence, Carly Ryan, Constantine Pettigrew, Alexander Koenig, William Shine, Lawrence Montanus, Joseph D. McFarland, and Cornelius Jansen. It should be noted that included in this group of new professors were two men who were destined to dedicate practically the remainder of their lives to the work of the minor seminary. These two were the Fathers Pettigrew and Spence.

Father Pettigrew, known to hundreds of seminarians as "the Dean," became the dean of discipline in the high school and the treasure of the seminary. He did not do a great deal of teaching. His particular ability was making accurate assessment of each student over whom acted as dean. He had an uncanny knack of picking out those whom he thought should go on to study for the priesthood, and those who should act. It sometimes happened that his opinion was not shared by others on the faculty. But long range results showed that he indeed had a great gift of discernment on such matters.[7]

Father Spence, the seminary's great Latin scholar, is another who has endeared himself to over three generations of students. Ordained in 1919, Father Spence's special talents and abilities in the classics were immediately recognized. In 1922 he was sent to the Catholic University and from there to Oxford in England for a Master's degree. Upon obtaining the degree in 1926, he was appointed to the faculty of St. Gregory's and is still teaching Latin and Greek there today. Unique in character and personality, Monsignor Spence graciously bore the terrible loss of his valuable library in the seminar fire in the fifties. Still presiding over the young minds of a new generation, it is certainly true to say that all his present and former students would agree that here indeed has presided a gentleman and a scholar.[8]

In September of 1928, St. Gregory's began to function as a unit of the newly incorporated Athenaeum of Ohio. It was now empowered to grant the Bachelor's degree in liberal arts. This was the first time since 1863 that the seminary had granted the degree. The awarding of degrees was necessary because the diocese was entering upon an era of expansion in secondary education which demanded the employment of diocesan priests. Also, the State of Ohio, was more insistent upon certain certification requirements and educational standards.

As a direct result of functioning as a unit of the Athenaeum of Ohio, a larger percentage of each class of second philosophers (fourth year college) received the degree Bachelor of Arts. The large percentage of each class did receive them was indicative of the newly found appreciation and value attached to academic degrees. For years, a little less than three quarters of a century, the consensus had been that no more than professional religious training was necessary for seminarians. The only requirement was to have the amount of training and knowledge necessary to perform the work of a parish and ministry. One could even detect the feeling that degrees were quite superfluous, and at that time this attitude may have been well justified. But the picture was radically changing, and the church now was entering on a broad front into the area of secondary education. With this came the necessity of employing the cleric, at least for a time, as professional educators.[9]

To assess the total effect that being a unit of the Athenaeum of Ohio had upon the faculty, students, and the curriculum of St. Gregory's Seminary would be difficult. But there seems no doubt that becoming a unit of the Athenaeum had a major influence in a very positive way, and was responsible in part for the large number of priests who were sent away for post-graduate studies in their respective fields. The introduction of certain required courses demanded by the state broadened the curriculum, and the research required for the writing of theses added immeasurably to the stature of students.[10]

THE NEW BUILDING AT ST. GREGORY'S

In the spring of 1927, under the leadership of the archbishop, plans were discussed for the erection of a new seminary building on the campus in Mount Washington. For this reason, twenty-seven acres adjoining the seminary grounds to the south wing were purchased, and building operations were started on November 20, 1927. It had been decided that the existing facilities for the high school were entirely inadequate. The dormitories located on the top floor of the central wing and the south wing were now completely outmoded and dangerous firetraps. The new building was to be constructed in sections and the first section would house the high school department. The completed building would ultimately house both the high school and college sections. The initial building was scheduled to begin on the new property to the south.[11]

The new seminary building was to be of the Lombard style of architecture, and was to be three stories high with two wings, north and south, with a chapel built in the center. The south wing was to be for the high school and the north wing for the college. When completed, both sections were to provide accommodations for over two-hundred students. In making plans for the building, the archbishop and Vehr visited and inspected facilities of more than twenty Catholic seminaries in the United States.[12]

When completed the new building stood six-hundred feet back from Beechmont Avenue. For the day, it embodied all of the latest tried and proved features of school construction. It was built entirely of fireproof material, concrete floors, steel beams and girders, granite exterior, limestone trim, and variegated tile roof, and gave every evidence of lasting durability.[13]

Some of the outstanding features of the new building were the large handball court; the gymnasium; the recessed radiators; the soundproof music rooms; the orchestra room; and the student's large recreation area. Extremely important additions to the seminary were the spacious chemistry and physics laboratories, and the new lecture hall.

While the planning and construction of the new building was going on, the Archbishop intended to use the old building only until such time as the entire new building could be constructed. For many reasons, the new building was not completely finished until 1962. In the meantime the old building was later reconditioned, and two of the original wings are still in use.[14]

Thousands of the clergy and laymen from all parts of the Archdiocese of Cincinnati gathered at Mount Washington in October of 1929 for the dedication program of the new unit of St. Gregory's. It had been completed at the cost of over one-million dollars. At the ceremony,

Archbishop McNicholas blessed and dedicated the new section.

In his address of that day, he stated the following:

The new St. Gregory's Seminary, which we have this day formally dedicated to God assumes importance not so much because it unites bishops, priests, and people in a work in which by reason of their lives and profession they are intensely interested, but because in the mind of Christ and in the mind of his Living, authoritative Church, the seminary is in very truth the continuation of the school of Apostles which Christ Himself conducted for three years.

The history of the Preparatory Seminary of the Archdiocese of Cincinnati is an inspiring record of great vision on the part of bishops and priests; of the courageous struggle of pioneers in establishing 40 years ago a strictly diocesan institution to which only boys aspiring to the priesthood could be admitted; of reverses, of disappointments, but all of great achievements in giving to the Church of the Middle West priests who have been great-minded and great-hearted in their complete consecration of the work of saving souls. Today three bishops, alumni of St. Gregory's Seminary, are members of our Hierarchy. Learned and zealous priests, formed in this very seminary, are today serving the Church in this archdiocese and in many of the neighboring dioceses.

When sent to you by the Vicar of Christ for four years, dearly beloved brethren, our first thought was given to the Preparatory Seminary. After most careful study it became apparent that without a building program we must either close at once the doors of St. Gregory's Seminary or allow it to function partially on the level of mediocrity.

When the Minor Seminary was reopened but six years ago, it was provided that one class should be added each year until the complete high school and college course should be established. But even this necessitated development. Prayer, study, consultation, and the conviction that both priests and people were deeply interested in the seminary made us decide on a building program that would give to our future priests the assurance of the Preparatory Seminary as a most stable element in the life of the Church of Cincinnati, a seminary that would set up and maintain the very highest standards.

A portion of the new seminary—the high school section—is completed and had received today the solemn blessing of the Church. The building that your eyes gaze upon is characterized by a strength, a simplicity, and austerity, and yet withal, a beauty which fittingly symbolizes the priesthood. Its great architects are to be congratulated upon having achieved a notable triumph....

One hundred years ago, at this very time, the first saintly and zealous Bishop of Cincinnati, with great foresight and courage love for souls, was struggling with what to us today seems insurmountable difficulties opening a seminary. A son of a distinguished pioneer family of Maryland, and ardent lover of his new-born country, with the advantages of a long and excellent ecclesiastical training in Belgium, with missionary experience in England, he came with the zeal of a true apostle from his arduous labors in Kentucky and Ohio to set up weight of the great responsibility he assumed in founding a seminary for the training of priests. His task was a truly heroic one. Since then a century has passed. This is neither the time nor the place to recount the reverse, the disappointments, the anxieties; the hopes, the fears, the triumphs that bishops, professors, priests and people have had during this long span of time.

It is gratifying to mark the completion of a hundred years of seminary life with the erection of at least a part of the new St. Gregory's. While we this day give thanks to Almighty God for all that eh seminary had accomplished in a hundred years, we are more concerned to be able to equip the priests who succeed for us for their work, that they may face their problems with greater confidence than we have faced ours, and with greater assurance, in a human way, of success...[15]

It wasn't until November of 1955 that, at the direction of Archbishop Karl Alter, ground was broken in the first step toward completing the entire building program planned by Archbishop McNicholas. This was twenty-six years after the "new" unit of St. Gregory's had been occupied.

SHERRY, RECTOR (1929-1937)

In June of 1929, when the archbishop announced the appointment of Vehr as rector of Mount St. Mary's in Norwood, he also announced that Vehr's successor as rector of St. Gregory's would be the Reverend Robert Sherry. The new rector of St. Gregory's was a native of Dayton, and received his college education at the University of Dayton. After four years of post-graduate work at the Catholic University, in Washington and the Angelicum in Rome, he was appointed professor of moral theology and canon law at the major seminary. This post he held until June of 1929, when he succeeded Vehr as rector of the minor seminary.[16]

It was now that the minor seminary began to bear fruit. Through the 30's and 40's the minor seminary had a very high degree of administrative efficiency. It had a capable faculty which was comparatively young and well-qualified in their respective fields of endeavor, and an excellent spirit prevailed among the student body.

In September of 1929 the seminary faculty was composed of Sherry, Shine, Allais, O'Regan, Spence, Pettigrew, McFarland, Jansen, Koenig, and Ryan. The newcomers were Lawrence Kroum, Edward Roelker, Walter Roddy, Ferdinand Vonder Haar, James O'Brien and William Shultz. Roddy and Collins, who had just returned from studies abroad, took over the classes in philosophy. The same faculty from studies abroad, too over the classes in philosophy. The same faculty returned in 1930.

On May 11, 1031, Mr. J. L. Clifton, Director of Education of the State of Ohio, certified that St. Gregory's high school department was "recognized as the equivalent of a Public High School of the First Grade and as such merits similar recognition on the part of the higher educational institutions and of the public."[17]

In 1931 the officers of administration at the minor seminary were listed as follows: Sherry was rector; Shine, the vice-rector; Pettigrew, the registrar, treasurer, and dean of discipline; O'Regan, spiritual director; McFarland, principal of the high school; Koenig, college librarian; and Vonder Haar, the high school librarian. On the faculty, the following men were teaching: Shine taught Sacred Scripture; Roddy and Collins, philosophy; Ryan, biology and chemistry; Allais, music and Italian; Spence and Jansen, Latin and Greek; Kroum, English and History; Koenig, German; Vonder Haar, mathematics and science; Gregory Miller, English and mathematics; Schultz, history; and Thill, public speaking.[18]

The curriculum in the 30's and 40's was the classical liberal arts course until such time as a student reached philosophy. In the high school and two years of college, Latin was still considered the main subject. The importance attached to it at this time can be seen from the following words:

> The thorough and accurate knowledge of Latin is next in importance (to the study of religion), as the canons of the Church law prescribe. Latin will be the tool with the which the seminarian will study throughout his seminary days, and so he must learn it well. But for an even greater reason, he must be well versed in Latin. His daily Mass and the official prayers of the priest are to be Latin. His daily Mass and the official prayers of the priest are to be in Latin, and so it is important that he be able to pray well in that language. The difficulties inherent in the learning of Latin are considerably reduced by the expert and careful efforts of the priests who teach it and the very earnest spirit of study which the boys soon acquire. With the goal ahead demanding that they learn the language....many grow very fond of the noble tongue, "forever old, forever new." [19]

English held the next place of importance in the curriculum of the minor seminary. The following was stated concerning its importance:

> ...the priest is to be a teacher and must be able to use his mother tongue to bring the light of truth to the minds and hearts of men. Not only the mechanics of grammar and composition, but the very best products of classical English are taught and recommended to the future priests. The arts in public reading and speaking are (also) stressed and practiced so that very best presentation of the Gospel may be made by the students once they become priests. [20]

Late in the 30's, with the arrival of the Fathers Madden and Berwanger, the English Department became very active. In grammar, literature, and speech, its program was excellent. Starting in 1941, a series of Shakespearean plays was put on each year until 1960. At first the performances were held in the little stage in the philosophers' hall. Many students who were present at these plays were never to forget scenes from *Julius Caesar*, *The Tempest*, *Hamlet*, and *Richard III*. Later, in the rear of the college, an amphitheater was built in which the great historical dramas of the "Bard" were performed with rare gusto. It was indeed an ambitious chapter in the history of the minor seminary.

At this time in addition to the modern languages of French and German, the study of Greek was emphasized. The following item appeared in the *Catholic Telegraph*:

> "...that their knowledge of Latin assists them considerably in learning this language. It is recognized as most useful not only for its cultural value and its ability to train young minds and memories, but also as a foundation for the study of Sacred Scriptures. Hebrew, too, is studied by the older students in philosophy as they begin their introduction to Sacred Scripture...."[21]

Another aspect of the curriculum which developed during these years was the time allotted to the two sciences—chemistry and biology—in the first two years of college. Attendance both at lectures as well as laboratory periods were required of the students. In regard to the social sciences, there was definitely an increased awareness of their importance. Attempts were made to fit them into the curriculum in a more important way, but they were not emphasized.[22]

As an indication of the growth in enrollment during these years, two hundred sixty students attended the minor seminary on September 8, 1931. At that date, it was the largest enrollment in its history. Of this number, 148 were registered in the college department, and 112 were registered in the high school. Students from Cincinnati number 181 of the total; the other students came from the diocese of Toledo, Covington, Fort Wayne, Nashville, Grand Rapids, Charleston, Wheeling, and Sacramento. The enrollment remained about the same through the 30's and into the late 40's. Then there was a noticeable increase which necessitated moving the last two years of college (the first and second years of philosophy), back to Mount St. Mary's in 1948.[23]

In 1931 the students returning to the seminary found that the old chapel in the south wing had been redecorated during the summer vacation. Through the generosity of Miss Anna Maloney and Mr. and Mrs. George Harrigan of Cincinnati, the sanctuary was carpeted, and the wall behind the main altar was covered with new drapes.[24]

In 1932 and 1933 there were no significant changes in administration or faculty. In 1934 this was not so. Father Raphael Sourd replaced McFarland as spiritual director and Father James Sherman replaced Collins in teaching the second philosophers. Father Alfred Stritch began his long career as a professor of history at the seminary. Father Paul Ratterman arrived to take the class in theology. Joseph Urbain, after studying at the Sorbonne and the University of Poitiers, became the professor of French.

On January 9, 1935, at a meeting of the Board of Trustees of the Athenaeum of Ohio, Father Ryan called attention to an important oversight. The high school department of St. Gregory's Seminary was not listed among the high schools affiliated with the Athenaeum. Nau said that when the Athenaeum was formed and St. Gregory's was made a part of the original Athenaeum group, it was the intention to include the college and high school departments. In order to obviate any difficulty, Father Sherry made formal application for the affiliation of St. Gregory's Seminary high school department with the Athenaeum of Ohio. From that time until early in the 50's, when the affiliations of the Athenaeum were dropped, the seminarians graduating form the high school received their diplomas from the Athenaeum and attended the joint June commencement exercises of the Athenaeum.[25]

RODDY, RECTOR (1937-1949)

In June of 1937 Sherry was appointed pastor of St. Andrew Church in Avondale, and he was succeeded by Father Walter A. Roddy. Father Roddy was a native of South Charleston, Ohio. He studied at Mount St. Mary's and was ordained in 1915. He engaged in parochial work until 1926, at which time he was sent to Rome for post graduate study. Upon his return from

Rome, he became professor of philosophy, along with Father Collins, and taught on the faculty for many years.[26]

The faculty present for the first year Roddy served as rector had not changed a great deal from the faculty of 1934. Included were Shine, Pettigrew, Allais, Spence, Sourd, Koenig, Kroum, Powers, G. Miller, Vonder Haar, Ratterman, Stritch, Stenz, Urbain, Sherman, Freking, Merfield, and Roedel. For the next several years there were no significant changes.

In October, 1937, Henry Grimmelsman, former professor of Sacred Scripture at the major seminary and rector of the Pontifical College Josephinum at Worthington, Ohio, made the following remarks about the seminary at Mount Washington:

> St. Gregory's was busy with the classics. They who taught in the major seminary in the period following upon the closing of the preparatory seminary will bear me out that the knowledge of Latin on the part of our students was never at so low an ebb. All will admit that since the reopening of St. Gregory's, Latin is again begin learned. We expect the day to come when St. Gregory's will teach all our students to read, write and speak Latin fluently.
>
> Our age and its culture have taken a scientific trend. Science invades and pervades through, conversation, and all living. Scientific culture, like the old classical culture, must be made the handmaid of religion. Our priests dare not be out of touch with their day and its interests. They must be able to bring revealed truth, unchanging as it is, to the modern thinker and the man of modern culture and make it clear to them that Christian truth is timeless. Our seminary is pioneering in this work.[27]

On October 28, 1941, the alumni, faculty members, students, and friends of St. Gregory's celebrated the fiftieth anniversary of the founding of the minor seminary. Actually, it was the fifty-first anniversary of its founding, and the fiftieth anniversary of the coming of the seminary to Mount Washington. Bishop Rehring had the Mass and the archbishop of Chicago, a former student of the minor seminary, preached the sermon.

The following was the letter of congratulation received by the seminary from the Most Reverend Amleto G. Cicognani, Apostolic Delegate to the United States, who transmitted the message of the Holy Father:

> It gives me the greatest pleasure to inform you that His Holiness Pope Pius XII, has most graciously imparted his paternal Apostolic blessing to the members of the faculty, the alumni, the students, and the benefactors of St. Gregory's Seminary for the golden jubilee of its founding, a mark of sovereign appreciation for the golden jubilee of its founding, a mark of sovereign appreciation for the fifty years of devoted service rendered the cause of Christ by this institution, and a pledge of abundant Divine graces for the continuation of this fruitful work. I am confident that nothing could bring greater happiness for the anniversary than the participation of the Vicar Christ in the joy of the present occasion. For my part, I desire to share in the gracious kindness manifested by the Sovereign Pontiff, voicing heartfelt congratulations on the splendid achievements of the past and cordial good wishes for the years ahead. I pray that the blessing of the Holy Father may be earnest of Divine favor and a lasting assurance of copious heavenly benedictions. [28]

At the close of the 30's and beginning of the 40's, the enrollment at St. Gregory's hovered at around slightly less than two-hundred students. Starting in 1943, the continued lagging enrollment in the college reflected the fact that the country was at war. The enrollment for the war was lower, and remained down until the opening of the school year in 1946. The veterans returning crowded conditions made it necessary to transfer to Mount St. Mary's in Norwood (in 1948), the last two years of philosophy.[29]

During these years Roddy and Sherman taught the course in philosophy. Father Shine taught the courses in history of philosophy, the introduction to Sacred Scripture, and Hebrew. The first year philosophy classes were held in a room in the basement of the north wing. College Latin (both years) was taught by Monsignor Spence. Fathers Madden and Berwanger taught the classes in English; Father Steinbicker taught the classes in church history; Father Ratterman conducted the class in biology; and Father Vonder Haar taught the class in chemistry. As the students in each class were few in number each received a great deal of individual attention.[30]

As St. Gregory's emerged from the war years and entered into a new era, there were only three students graduated from the college. Monsignor Roddy pointed out that St. Gregory's graduating class of three students from the archdiocese that year was comparable to classes on the same level in other American Catholic seminaries. He took the opportunity to praise the faculty, and said that he was proud of the quality of the students who had been educated at St. Gregory's over the years. He told the story of a younger brother of one of the seminarians who explored the school on visiting day. The boy examined class pictures of earlier graduates, and finally came to a large framed collection of small portraits of all the Popes. "Say," he exclaimed, "that was a big class, wasn't it?"[31]

A major change in the operation of St. Gregory's was announced in the *Catholic Telegraph* in August of 1948. It was decided to ease the crowded conditions at St. Gregory's by taking advantage of the space made available by the departure of the Michigan seminarians from Mount St. Mary's. The philosophy department was transferred to Norwood at the beginning of the scholastic year in September of 1948. The change meant that fifty students in the first and second years of philosophy departed St. Gregory's. The minor seminar was then left with the four years of high school and the first two years of college.[32]

In November, 1949 (a little more than two months after the death of Monsignor O'Brien, and the appointment of Monsignor Schneider as rector of Mount St. Mary's), it was announced that Monsignor Walter Roddy had been named rector of St. Catherine's parish in Cincinnati. Roddy had been rector of St. Gregory's for twelve years and a professor there since 1928. He was succeeded in the rectorship for twelve years and a professor there since 1928. He was succeeded in the rectorship of St. Gregory's by Monsignor William J. Gauche, the former vice-rector of Mount St. Mary's Seminary. Archbishop McNicholas died six months later and was succeeded by Bishop Karl J. Alter of Toledo. These three significant changes marked the end of one era and the beginning of another. The new era in the history of the seminaries will be considered in Chapter Nine.

SUMMARY

The chronological history of the minor seminary has been treated from the years 1923-1949. It was seen that the twenties were devoted to re-establishing the minor seminary which had failed in 1907. Slowly, under the rectorships of Sieber and Vehr, the seminary continued the work of educating minor seminarians. During the 30's and 40's, under Sherry and Roddy, the seminary grew in competence of faculty, excellence of curriculum, and quality of students, and reached a high educational standard.

In 1928, as a result of being constituted a unit in the Athenaeum of Ohio, the minor seminary began the issuance of the Bachelor of Arts degree. This considerably influenced and improved the standards of academic excellence.

The decision in 1923 to locate the four years of high school and the four years of college at St. Gregory's undoubtedly also had a great deal to do with the high standards reached in the 30's and 40's. It was a break with the traditional six-six system in which the first six years of study were taken at the minor seminary, and the last six years of study were taken at the major seminary. Over-crowding at the minor seminary caused the plan to be abandoned in 1948.

The building program initiated in the year 1927 also helped the cause of educating the seminarians; the fine new building which housed the high school was certainly conducive to study. All in all, it was an era of commendable accomplishment in the history of the seminary.

NOTES
[1] *Catholic Telegraph*, December 14, 1922, p. 5.

[2] Cf. Chapter VI.

[3] *Catholic Telegraph*, March 10, 1944, p. 3.

[4] *Ibid.*, September 6, 1923, p. 5.

[5] Cf. Chapter VII.

[6] Cf. Chapter VII.

[7] *Catholic Telegraph*, January 15, 1943, p. 1.

[8] *Ibid.*, May 5, 1944, p. 4.

[9] *Ibid.*, May 5, 1944, p. 5.

[10] *Ibid.*, May 5, 1944, p. 4.

[11] *Ibid.*, April 26, 1928, p.1.

[12] *Ibid.*, April 26, 1928, p. 4.

[13] *Ibid.*, April 26, 1928, p. 5.

[14] Cf. Chapter XI.

[15] *Catholic Telegraph*, October 10, 1929, p. 8.

[16] *Ibid.*, October 23, 1942, p. 1.

[17] "Minutes of the Board of Trustees, Mt. St. Mary's Seminary," Registrar's Office, Book No. 1.

[18] *Catholic Telegraph*, September 17, 1931, p. 1.

[19] *Ibid.*, June 22, 1945, p. 3.

[20] *Ibid.*, June 22, 1945, p. 3.

[21] *Ibid.*, June 22, 1945, p. 1.

[22] *Ibid.*, June 22, 1945, p. 4.

[23] *Ibid.*, September 13, 1934, p. 4.

[24] *Ibid.*, September 8, 1931, p. 4.

[25] "Minutes of the Board of Trustees, January 9, 1935," Office of the Registrar, Mount St. Mary's Seminary.

[26] *Catholic Telegraph*, November 11, 1949, p. 1.

[27] *Ibid.*, October 15, 1937, p. 7.

[28] *Ibid.*, October 24, 1941, p. 1.

[29] *Ibid.*, September 9, 1947, p. 1. In September of 1947, a record of 320 students presented themselves at St. Gregory's. Acute problems of space were created in the chapel and in the dining hall. In this year, the faculty moved to their own private dining room.

[30] Personal recollection of the author.

[31] *Catholic Telegraph*, September 17, 1948, p.1.

[32] *Ibid.*, August 13, 1948, p.1.

CHAPTER EIGHT

The Organization of the Athenaeum of Ohio

INTRODUCTION

Archbishop McNicholas came to the Archdiocese of Cincinnati in July 1925. One of the main objectives of his early administration was the creation of several central archdiocesan high schools. With increased pressure from the state of Ohio for better teacher-training, the archdiocese set out to accomplish many things that were necessary in such an undertaking by forming, in 1928, an educational corporation that was called the "Athenaeum of Ohio."

This chapter will discuss the formation of the Athenaeum of Ohio, its purposes, and its organization as conceived and planned by the archbishop.

At this chapter will go back to the year 1928 to pick up the development of the Athenaeum, it is necessary to keep in mind that Mount St. Mary's Seminary and St. Gregory's Seminary were the first units of this new educational corporation. At the time of incorporation, two additional units were admitted, the Archdiocesan Teachers' college and the Institutum Divi Thomae. In addition to these units, there were affiliations entered into by the Athenaeum with several other colleges and high schools. Since the history of the first two units has already been considered in Chapters VII and VIII and, since ultimately they will be shown to have been the only lasting and permanent segment of the Athenaeum, this chapter will but briefly describe units and affiliations.

FORMATION OF THE ATHENAEUM OF OHIO

When Archbishop McNicholas came to Cincinnati in 1925, he wisely saw that future demands in the area of secondary education would be drastically expanded. He also saw that as the church moved into this area on a diocesan level, many purposes would better be served if there were coordination of effort. Training teachers who would be recognized as qualified by the state would require the issuance of degrees. To obtain the power to issue degrees meant meeting certain state requirements. The educational entity formed finally in 1928, and called the "Athenaeum of Ohio," was instituted by Archbishop McNicholas to direct and supervise the fulfilling of these needs.

There is some evidence that the archbishop toyed with the idea of taking an even further step. It seems that he did think at least of forming a Catholic University of Southern Ohio. This would have solved his problems but, at the time, there were far too many practical difficulties for such a project to become a reality.

Perhaps Archbishop McNicholas chose the name "Athenaeum of Ohio" because it had been selected as the name for the very earliest of educational institutions in the history of the archdiocese. The fact that he was a member of the Dominican Order, and that this name had been applied by an earlier Dominican bishop of the diocese, without doubt had a major influence upon the decision.

The policy of expansion in the field of education inaugurated in 1927 by Archbishop McNicholas made it advisable to place all educational work at the higher levels on a coordinated basis, and under immediate archdiocesan auspices. The Athenaeum of Ohio was incorporated under the law of the State of Ohio on March 24, 1928.

The purpose of the Athenaeum of Ohio, as originally conceived, was for the promotion of education by means of control, direction, and supervision of all schools of secondary and higher learning by the archdiocese.[1] This purpose is clearly sets forth in the third article of incorporation of the charter which reads as follows:

> The purpose or purposes for which said corporation is formed are:
>
> To place and vest in said corporation, in order the more satisfactorily to promote education, religion, morality, and the fine arts, the sole final control, direction and supervision of the administration and manner and method of conduct of all colleges, seminaries, academies, high schools, and other institutions of the higher learning, that man, now or hereafter be operated in the state of Ohio, under the auspices of the Roman Catholic Church and that either may be founded by said corporation, or by agreement, become affiliated herewith, and to possess and exercise all powers conferred on educational corporations by the laws of the State of Ohio; and to do any and all things reasonable and necessary to be done to carry out the purposes aforesaid.[2]

It was also said at the time, in the *Catholic Telegraph*, that the "Athenaeum was incorporated by Archbishop McNicholas...to administer and supervise the Catholic Institutions of the archdiocese in harmony with the prevailing standards and distinctly Catholic philosophy of education."[3]

According to the official statement made by the Reverend Francis J.Bredistaege, around the time of the early organization of the Athenaeum, the corporation had the following purposes:

> 1. The foundation, maintenance and supervision of such institutions of college level, as may be found advisable, and the prescriptions of standards and regulations for such other institutions as may desire to affiliate themselves with it.
>
> 2. The adoption of courses and standards for its institutions and for the secondary schools of the archdiocese.
>
> 3. The accreditation and supervision of the instruction in high schools of the archdiocese and of the affiliated schools of the secondary level.[4]

In May of 1936, when Our Lady of Cincinnati College was affiliated with the Athenaeum, the following was stated in the terms of the agreement:

> The Athenaeum was formed for the purpose of exercising control, direction, and supervision over all the colleges and institutions of higher learning, now or hereafter, operated in the State of Ohio, under the auspices of the Roman Catholic Church, and which might be founded in

said corporation...[5]

The following statement concerning the purposes of the Athenaeum of this period was made in the *Catholic Telegraph*:

> "The Athenaeum, which was organized in 1928, is the unifying bond of educational institutions in the archdiocese. Established by the Archbishop it ought to coordinate the programs of studies in its various affiliates, which are divided into graduate, college, and high school department.[6]

As to its organization, the Athenaeum of Ohio had a board of trustees consisting of five persons, one of whom was the archbishop. The original trustees in 1928, in addition to the archbishop, were Daniel A. Buckley, Bernard Moeller, Louis J. Nau, and R. Marcellus Wagner. The code of regulations of the newly formed corporation said the following regarding the trustees:

> The number of trustees shall be five, one of whom shall always be, by virtue of his office and without further election or designation, the Archbishop of Cincinnati, for the time being incumbent. Candidates for the other four trustees shall be proposed by the Archbishop and their names on at the annual meeting of the members.
>
> The elected trustees shall hold office for one year or until successors are elected and qualified. If for any reason, the elected trustee shall forfeit memberships in the Athenaeum, he shall therefore forfeit any and all offices by him held in aforesaid Athenaeum.[7]

The Archbishop of Cincinnati, by virtue of his office, was the president of the Athenaeum. The other officers (vice-president, secretary, and treasurer), were to be chosen by ballot of the trustees. [8]

Membership in the corporation of the Athenaeum of Ohio originally was limited to those whom the archbishop selected. This was set forth in the sixth article of incorporation, text of which follows:

> Memberships in said corporation are subject to the following qualifications:

> The membership of the said corporation shall consist only of the Most Reverend Archbishop of the Roman Catholic Archdiocese of Cincinnati, Ohio, for the time being incumbent, and such other persons, as said Archbishop of Cincinnati may from time to time, select and designate as members by the issuance to them of certificates of membership in such form as may be prescribed in the Code of Regulations of the Corporation.
>
> All membership in said corporation shall terminate at the will of said Archbishop of Cincinnati, to be evidenced in such manner as may be prescribed in said Code of Regulations of the Corporation. [9]

The Athenaeum was composed of "units" and "affiliates." The two archdiocesan seminaries were the sole units of the Athenaeum prior to its incorporation. When the Athenaeum was incorporated in 1928, a third unit (the Teachers' College), was added. In 1935 the Institutum

Divi Thomae became the fourth unit. These four units became the constituents of the Athenaeum, and operated directly under its charter.

Under the articles of incorporation, the Athenaeum could, by agreement, affiliate to itself other institutions of learning. On the college level, Our Lady of Cincinnati College was affiliated with the Athenaeum, and the Schuster-Martin School of Drama was affiliated with the Teachers' College. On the high school level, all the Catholic high schools directly under diocesan control were affiliated with the Athenaeum. The conditions contingent upon high school affiliation were that the high school be approved and accredited by the Department of Education of the State of Ohio, and the application be filed with the Athenaeum.

Academic degrees, certificates, and high school diplomas were issued by the Athenaeum in virtue of its charter and authorization by the Secretary of State and the Department of Education of the State of Ohio. Letters from J.L. Clifton, Director of Education of the State of Ohio, indicated that the filing with the State of the curriculum certificate from the Department of Education had been made. Thus, in accordance with the provisions of Sections 9922 and 9923, Ohio General Code, these certificates having been filed, the power to issue degrees was vested in the Athenaeum as of May 28, 1929. [10]

During the era under consideration, the following degrees were issued by the Athenaeum: The Master of Arts through Mount St. Mary's Seminary; the Master of Science and Doctor of Philosophy through the Institutum Dive Thomae; the Bachelor of Arts through St. Gregory's Seminary and Our Lady of Cincinnati College; the Bachelor of Science through Our Lady of Cincinnati College; the Bachelor of Music, the Bachelor of Science in School Music, the Bachelor of Science in Education, and the Bachelor of Science in Speech Arts through the Teacher's College.

TEACHERS' COLLEGE (1928)
The Teachers' College, [11] the first unit to be created after the Athenaeum was established, was incorporated in March of 1928.

While McNicholas was busy with the reorganization and expansion of the high school system of the archdiocese, he was at the same time interested in furthering the education and preparation of teachers with which to staff his schools. The situation in regard to teacher training came under scrutiny.

An effort to form a normal school had been made early in 1863 by Archbishop Purcell. In his concern for the establishment of Catholic schools he wrote as follows:

> To accomplish this great object, we must have well educated teachers. And for this purpose, we must have normal or training schools. To establish, endow, sustain these schools is, therefore, our imperative duty. We must not be deterred by the difficulties that lie in the way. Faith can remove mountains. "Impossible" is a word which, in connection with such a project, should not be found in a Catholic vocabulary. [12]

The written account of the proceedings of the Catholic teachers' convention in August of

1863 laments the fact that nothing could be done about the Purcell plan. Its sentiments were expressed in the words, "Thus terminated, the initiation is one of the most important movements yet projected in the high cause of Catholic education in this country."[13]

The training of teachers for service in the Catholic schools was that time undertaken in normal schools maintained by the various religious communities, usually in connection with their novitiate program. In the archdiocese at this time there were four community normal schools, one each conducted by the Sisters of Charity, the Sisters of Notre Dame, the Sisters of Mercy, and the Sisters of the Precious Blood. Although teacher preparations in these communities date back to the very beginning of their activity in the diocese, the establishment of normal schools as such occurred years later. The sisters of Charity formed a community normal school in various houses of the diocese, the work being centralized in a provincial house. Notre Dame Normal School, Grandin Road, Cincinnati, was established in September, 1922,, and approved by the State of Ohio as an accredited normal school for the preparation of elementary teachers. The establishment of the normal school for the Sisters of Mercy dates back to the year 1883. In the year 1926 the school was accredited by the Ohio State Department of Education. The Sisters of the Precious Blood established their normal school in the year 1916, although teacher training for them dates back to the year 1848. [14]

In 1924 a survey was made of teacher training and preparation in the State of Ohio. The survey, published under the title of *A Teacher Training Program for Ohio.*[15] The state department of education made an agreement with the four dioceses that if the dioceses would close all the normal schools and set up one central training agency for teachers, the state department would recognize that agency.

In as much as Xavier University was already engaged to some extent in teacher education, the archbishop looked first in that direction for central training center. On September 14, 1927 the Reverend H. F. Brockman, president of Xavier University, announced that a teacher training school would be opened the following week at the college. The college was to begin with the freshman and sophomore classes. Father Bredistaege, superintendent of parochial schools, became the supervisor of the program; Father Daniel O'Connor became the dean of the college.[16]

Though the college at Xavier University did help to raise the educational standards, the archbishop deemed it advisable to found (in 1928), the Athenaeum of Ohio. The Athenaeum was the unifying center and the coordinating agency of educational institutions in the archdiocese, therefore, it seemed only natural to bring the teacher training program within the scope of this newly formed corporation. It was readily seen that such central teacher training institution, working under archdiocesan auspices, would be of calculable worth to the expanded diocesan educational program.[17]

The Teachers' College was immediately organized as a unit of the Athenaeum of Ohio. A board of regents consisting of the archbishop as chairman, and Matthew O'Brien, Henry Schengber, and Francis Bredistaege, was set up. Bredistaege, the superintendent of parochial schools, was appointed the dean of the college. A faculty of twenty-eight professors was assembled, consisting of eight priests, eight sisters, and twelve lay people.[18]

The officers of the Teachers' College in 1928 were Francis Bredistaege; and Miss Alma L'Hommediu, the librarian. The faculty consisted of Sister M. Adelaide, head of the department of art education, Sister Agnes, professor of organ; Reverend William Schmitt, professor of secondary education; John J. Fehring, head of the department of music and professor of Gregorian Chant, Reverend Peter Goren, professor of modern languages, J. Alfred Schehl, professor of organ; Reverend William Schmitt, professor of secondary education, Reverend Edward Roekler, professor of liturgy and religion; Leo Thuis, professor of voice and theory; Elmer Von Pichler, professor of piano and organ; Reverend Cornelius Jansen, professor of mathematics; Reverend Charles E. Spence, professor of English and literature; Edward Sethers, professor of the hygiene course and physical education; Frey Meyer, professor of the organ; Sister Serepta, professor of public school music; Garner Rowell, professor of violin; and Miss Luella Saurer, professor of sociology.

In addition to the department for the professional training of teachers, arrangements were made for the Teachers' College to have a department of music. McNicholas recognized the desirability of a more specialized training for the organists and choir directors of the parishes. In the year 1926 he formed an archdiocesan department of music to provide for training in church music.[19]

In 1928 the faculties of the new Teachers' College were extended to include this department of music, and a complete section of courses in the study of church and school music was thereby added to the curriculum of the Teachers' College.[20]

To house the Teachers' College, the authorities secured the use of the building formerly occupied by St. George Parochial High School, Calhoun Street Cincinnati. The building contained eight large lecture halls and classrooms, space for a library, the registrar's office and some laboratories. The Teachers' College opened its doors for registration on September 17, 1928. Thirty-three full-time students and 116 part-time students were enrolled.

The Teachers' College now became a working unit of the Athenaeum of Ohio. Its purpose was to provide a complete normal school training for teachers, both religious and lay, preparing them for service in the Catholic Schools. In addition to providing a general education and professional training, the college also met the requirements of the State Departments of Education of Ohio, Kentucky, and Indiana.

In order to achieve the purpose for which it was intended, the Teachers' College offered the following programs:

1. A four-year course for elementary teachers, leading to the degree of Bachelor of Science in Education.

2. A four-year course for high school teachers, leading to the Bachelor of Science in Education.

3. A four-year course for teachers in the special fields of school music, leading to the degree of bachelor of Science in School Music, or to the Bachelor of Science in Speech Arts.

4. A four-year course in music for Church organists and choir directors, leading to the degree of Bachelor of Music.[21]

The affiliation between the Teachers' College and the Schuster-Martin School of Drama, Cincinnati, was effected on June 1, 1930. The affiliation enabled qualified students preparing to be teachers of the dramatic arts in parochial or public schools (both elementary and secondary), to receive dramatic arts training at the Schuster-Martin School, and educational training at the Teachers' College. Those who satisfied the requirements of the program received the degree of Bachelor of Science in Speech Arts from the Teachers' College.

In January of 1932, Father Ryan became the new superintendent of schools in the archdiocese and at the same time was appointed the dean of the Teachers' College, succeeding Father Bredistaege. Monsignor Ryan was born in Dayton and attended old St. Mary's Institute (later the University of Dayton). In 1928 he went to the Catholic University of America, where he remained for three years, and obtained the Doctor of Philosophy degree in education. Father Ryan then returned to Cincinnati and taught at both Elder High School and St. Gregory's Seminary prior to his appointment as superintendent and dean of the Teachers' College.[22]

In 1947 the Teachers' College vacated the old quarters on Calhoun Street and moved into the archbishop's former residence on Moeller Avenue in Norwood, adjacent to the major Seminary. The building had been completely remodeled to accommodate the offices and the library. Classroom space was provided at Regina High School (across the street), and at the seminary next door. The Teachers' College functioned here until the early fifties at which time the college was discontinued. The building now contains the offices of the superintendent of schools of the archdiocese.

INSTITUTUM DIVI THOMAE (1935)

At a special meeting of the Board of Trustees of the Athenaeum of Ohio held on January 9, 1935, the principal business was the consideration of ways and means to erect a new scientific institute of learning to be known as the "Institutum Divi Thomae," and of formerly incorporating this new unit into the Athenaeum of Ohio. The archbishop explained that the purpose of this proposed new unit of the Athenaeum was to offer graduate work in the field of scientific research, and to study the basic laws of physical science in connection with the other correlated branches of human knowledge with a view toward unifying the results.[23]

It was at this meeting also that the Institutum Divi Thomae was formally incorporated into the Athenaeum as a new and distinct unit offering graduate work in the field of science. It was decided that the institute should be governed by a board of regents under the direction of the trustees of the Athenaeum.

Archbishop McNicholas dedicated the new school to St. Thomas, under the name Institutum Divi Thomae. He secured Doctor George Sperti as director of the institute. Doctor Sperti came from the University of Cincinnati, where he had been a professor and director of the basic science research laboratory.[24] Several of his associates in the field of science at the University of Cincinnati accompanied him. The Reverend Cletus A. Miller was appointed by the archbishop to be dean of the institute. The Institutum Divi Thomae formally opened on June 1, 1935. At that time it was housed in part of the new building of St. Gregory's Seminary.

The purpose of the Institutum was twofold: theoretical and practical scientific research, and graduate scientific instruction. It was to instruct in science and at, the same time, foster fundamental research in the natural sciences. The Institutum attempted, by this method, to ally modern scientific research more closely with the speculative investigations of the philosopher so that each branch of knowledge could benefit more directly from the other.

In addition to the staff members, the Institutum had a very limited number of select students. Formal classes were held, but greater emphasis was given to actual research and laboratory study. Small groups of students worked with their professors in the investigation of problems in the field of their major subject. Successful completion of the student's program (covering three school years of eleven months each), led to the degree of Master of Science; additional graduate work led to the Doctor of Philosophy Degree. The program was not geared to train teachers of science. It was directed toward developing, as workers in research, a limited number of persons who demonstrated creative ability in the field of science.

When its laboratories as St. Gregory's proved to be much too small, headquarters were moved to Madison Road, Cincinnati. In the next chapter, dissolution of the bond between the Athenaeum and the Institutum will be discussed.

THE AFFILIATION OF OUR LADY OF CINCINNATI COLLEGE

Our Lady of Cincinnati College opened in September, 1935. [25] On May 29, of the following year, it was affiliated with the Athenaeum of Ohio. [26] The affiliation was officially recoginzed by the Department of Education of the State of Ohio on October 7, 1936. [27] The main terms or conditions of the agreement were as follows:

1. The affiliation extends only to educational affairs, policies, and standards, which shall be within the final control and direction of the Athenaeum. All otherwise remain vested in the Board of Trustees of the College.

2. The members of the faculty of the College are appointed by its Board of Trustees, acting alone or in conjunction with the proper authorities of the Community of the Religious Sisters of Mercy, as the case may be. The Athenaeum then investigates and approves the academic qualifications of the members of the faculty. If, on account of academic unfitness, the Athenaeum disapproves of a person, that person may not be appointed to the faculty of the College, or be continued thereon. In a similar manner, the courses of study of the college are subject to the vise and approval of the Athenaeum.

3. The College's degrees and certificates are granted and issued by the Athenaeum, upon recommmendation of the faculty of the College. (The degrees are the Bachelor of Arts degree and the Bachelor of Science.)

4. The Athenaeum has the right to inspect and investigate the college, from time to time, to ascertain whether or not its academic work and the educational background of its faculty are

being maintained at the standards set by the Athenaeum. If the College fails to meet the requirements of the Athenaeum over a period of one year, the affiliation agreement terminates.

5. The Athenaeum makes available to the College, as it needs may require, for direction and teaching, such faculty members of the other units of the Athenaeum, as may be conveniently spared for that additional work.28(Thus the science classes of the College are under direction and supervision of Professors of the Seminaries and of the Teachers' College are on the faculty of Our Lady of Cincinnati College.)

LATER YEARS

The Board of Trustees of the Athenaeum of Ohio met annually from 1928 to 1949, the period covered by this chapter. At these meetings the decisions on policy and planning were made; degrees were granted; and affiliations were approved and disapproved.

At a meeting of the board of trustees and members of the corporation of the Athenaeum held in the rector's office in Mount St. Mary's Seminary on May 10, 1950, three resolutions of sympathy were drawn up and voted upon. They were more than resolutions of sympathy; they were the epitaph for an era in the history of the Athenaeum. The resolutions of sympathy read as follows:

WHEREAS: The Archdiocese of Cincinnati and the Church in the United States have sustained a great loss by the death of His Grace, the Most Reverend John T. McNicholas, Archbishop of Cincinnati, and WHEREAS: has repeated elections as President of the National Catholic Educational Association and as Episcopal Chairman of the Department of Education of the National Catholic Welfare Conference were a fitting recognition of his leadership in the field of education, and WHEREAS: his interest in the cause of Catholic education in the Archdiocese of Cincinnati is reflected in founding of the Athenaeum of Ohio and in the building, developing and strengthening of its several affiliations of units, THEREFORE: Be it resolved that we, the Trustees and Members of the Corporation of the Athenaeum of Ohio, on the occasion of our annual meeting, acknowledge our loss in the death of the Archbishop, President of the Athenaeum of Ohio, and express our deepest sympathy to the members of his bereaved family.

WHEREAS: The Archdiocese of Cincinnati and especially the cause of Catholic education in the archdiocese have, during the past year, sustained a great loss in the death of the Right Reverend James W. O'Brien, Rector of Mount Saint Mary's Seminary, member of the Corporation of the Athenaeum of Ohio, and brilliant professor of the Sacred Sciences, THEREFORE: Be it resolved that we, the Trustees and members of the Corporation of the Athenaeum of Ohio, on the occasion of our annual meeting, acknowledge our serious loss and express our deepest sympathy to the members of his bereaved family.

Much has been written and more said reviewing the life and accomplishments of the late beloved Judge Dempsey. We all held him in high regard and deep esteem for his fine character and beloved qualities...

The death of Judge Dempsey is a great loss to the archdiocese and to the community of Cincinnati, as well as to all of us as members of the various associations which he so ably served...

We honor him and cherish his memory.

THEREFORE: Be it resolved that we, the Trustees and Members of the corporation of the Athenaeum of Ohio acknowledge our loss in the death of Judge Dempsey and express our deepest sympathy to the members of his bereaved family.

SUMMARY

The Athenaeum of Ohio was formed in 1928 for the purpose of taking care of expanding educational needs of the archdiocese. The Athenaeum directed, supervised, and controlled all the schools of secondary and higher learning in the archdiocese on a coordinated basis for the betterment of education.

The Athenaeum as originally incorporated consisted of four units—the two seminaries of the archdiocese (Mount St. Mary's Seminary of the West and St. Gregory's Seminary), the Teachers' College, and the Institutum Divi Thomae. Later many other affiliations at the college and high school levels were added.

This chapter has considered the organization of the Teachers' College, its purposes, and the history of its twenty-five year existence. The college functioned well and adequately served the purpose for which it was intended.

The organization of the Institutum Divi Thomae was considered. As a unit of the Athenaeum, its purpose was to ally more closely the findings of science with the works of philosophy.

It was shown in this chapter that two units of the Athenaeum (Mount St. Mary's Seminary and St. Gregory's Seminary), were in existence long before the Athenaeum was formally incorporated. After the reorganization in the next decade, these two seminaries alone comprised the Athenaeum. The reorganization of the Athenaeum will be treated in the next chapter.

NOTES

[1]Sister Mary Vincent de Paul Leinweber, "History of Catholic Secondary Education in Cincinnati." Unpublished Master's thesis, Butler University, 1944, p. 115.

[2]*Articles of Incorporation of the Athenaeum of Ohio*, Incorporation Records of Office of Secretary of State of Ohio, Vol. 360, p. 576. A copy is in the minutes of the Board of Trustees Book No.1. Office of the Registrar, Mount St. Mary's Seminary, Cf. Appendix. H.

[3]*Catholic Telegraph*, August 2, 1928, p. 1.

[4]*Ibid.*, August 2, 1928, p. 1.

[5] "Minutes of the Board of Trustees, May, 1936." MSMSA.

[6]*Catholic Telegraph*, February 10, 1950, p. 1.

[7] "Minutes of the Board of Trustees." Code of Regulations of the Athenaeum of Ohio. Book No. 1. Office of the Registrar. Mount St. Mary's Seminary.

[8] "Minutes of the Board of Trustees." Book No. 1. Office of the Registrar. Mount St. Mary's Seminary.

[9] "Minutes of the Board of Trustees." Book No. 1. Office of the Registrar. Mount St. Mary's Seminary.

[10] "Minutes of the Board of Trustees." Book No. 1. Office of the Registrar. Mount St. Mary's Seminary.

[11] Sister Mary Mildred Schnapp, "The History of Diocesan Teachers College in Ohio, with Particular Reference to the Athenaeum of Ohio." Unpublished Master's Thesis, University of Cincinnati, 1942. Pp. iv., 85.

[12] *Catholic Telegraph*, May 27, p. 1.

[13] Edward A. Connaughton, *A History of Educational Legislation and Administration in the Archdiocese of Cincinnati*, p. 85. Washington: The Catholic University of America Press, 1946.

[14] Connaughton, *op. cit.*, p. 153.

[15] Alonzo, Franklin Myers, *Education in Democracy*. Third Edition. New York: Prentice Hall, 1948. Pp. 361.

[16] Connaughton, *op. cit.*, p. 155.

[17] *Ibid.*, p. 156.

[18] *Ibid.*, p. 157.

[19] Sister Mary Joeline Ebertz, "A History of the Development of Music Education in the Archdiocese of Cincinnati." An Unpublished Doctor's Dissertation, University of Cincinnati, 1955. pp. vii., 259.

[20] Connaughton, *op. cit.*, p. 156.

[21] Connaughton, *op. cit.*, p. 157.

[22] *Catholic Telegraph*, May 2, 1947, p. 3.

[23] "Minutes of the Board of Trustees." Book 1. Office of the Registrar, Mount St. Mary's Seminary.

[24] Reginald C. McGrane, The University of Cincinnati, pp. 271, 286. New York: Harper and Row, 1963.

[25] Sister Mary Grace, "History of the Educational Work of the Sisters of Mercy in the Archdiocese of Cincinnati." Unpublished Master's thesis. University of Cincinnati, 1941.

[26] Minutes of the Board of Trustees, May 29, 1935. Office of the Registrar, Mount St. Mary's Seminary.

[27] Letter, E. L. Bowsher, Director of Education, Department of Education, State of Ohio, to Father C. J. Ryan, October 7, 1936.

[28] Affiliation Agreement, May 29, 1936, MSMSA.

CHAPTER NINE

The Athenaeum Until 1960

INTRODUCTION

This chapter will deal with the important events in the history of the Athenaeum of Ohio in the 1950's. Under the direction of the Most Reverend Karl J. Alter (then archbishop of Cincinnati), Monsignor Joseph Scheider, and the facilities of the two seminaries, the work of reorganizing the Athenaeum was started. This work proceeded in three phases. First, the teachers' college and the Institutum Divi Thomae were dropped as "units" of the Athenaeum, along with all former "affiliations." The two seminaries alone now comprised the Athenaeum. Secondly the Athenaeum, thus constituted, sought and obtained membership in the Ohio College Association, and accreditation by the North Central Association. Lastly, the administrative structure of the Athenaeum was brought into accord with the best procedures of prevalent educational practices.

This chapter deals with several other items of importance which occurred during these ten years. The modern curriculum of the college of liberal arts and the school of theology is discussed. The faculty of this period, along with the subjects taught is considered. In the final section consideration is given to the building projects of the times, both at St. Gregory's and Mount St. Mary's Seminary in Norwood.

THE THREE PHASES OF REORGANIZATION

In April of 1950 Archbishop John T. McNicholas died. Had he lived just about three months longer, he would have celebrated the twenty-fifty anniversary of his appointment as Bishop of the archdiocese of Cincinnati.[1]

Two months later, in June of 1950, the Most Reverend Karl J. Alter Bishop of Toledo, was named archbishop of Cincinnati. Archbishop Alter born in Toledo on August 18, 1885, was educated at St. Mary's Seminary in Cleveland. He received the Master of Arts degree in 1902. He was ordained a priest on June 4, 1910. Early in his priesthood Father Alter displayed a marked executive and administrative ability which led to his appointment, in 1914, as the first director of Catholic Charities for the Diocese of Toledo. In 1929, he was called to serve as director of the National Catholic School of Social Services in Washington.

Alter served as director only until he was consecrated bishop of the diocese of Toledo on June 17, 1931. During his tenure in the diocese of Toledo, Bishop Alter received national recognition as one of the foremost members of American hierarchy. In 1935 he was named assistant chairman of the social action department of the National Catholic Welfare Conference. Holding successively higher posts, in 1952 he became the chairman of the administrative board of the National Catholic Welfare Conference. The Holy See underlined the status of the archbishop among his peers in the American Hierarchy when Pope John name him, along with the three United States Cardinals, to the coordinating commission for the Second Ecumenical Council of the Vatican.

In 1950, when Archbishop Alter came to the See of Cincinnati, one of the major areas of his attention was focused on the organizational structure, purposes, and aims of the Athenaeum of Ohio. Under his impetus, the Athenaeum of Ohio, in less than a decade, was organized and given a direction and purpose which has placed the two seminaries, Mount St. Mary's and St. Gregory's, not only in the forefront as excellent Catholic schools for clerical students, but in a highly respected position among American Institutions of higher learning as well.

The reorganization initiated by Archbishop Alter proceeded in three phases. First, early in his administration the former "units" and "affililiations" of the Athenaeum of Ohio (with the exception of the two seminaries), were dissolved. Next, membership in the Ohio College Association and accreditation by the North Central Association were sought and obtained. Lastly the Athenaeum, whose component parts were now the two seminaries, was reorganized in its administration. These three phases often proceeded concurrently, but fundamentally they were accomplished in the sequence given.

Reorganization of the Athenaeum fell, in large measure, upon the shoulders of the two seminary faculties. The man most responsible for the work of implementation was Monsignor Joseph J. Schneider, who at the age of forty-two, had succeeded Monsignor O'Brien as rector of Mount St. Mary's Seminary in 1949. Monsignor Scheider had been a professor at the major seminary since 1937, having taught the courses in speculative, moral and dogmatic theology. Born in Springfield, Ohio, he was ordained in 1932 and took his post-graduate studies in Fribourg, Switzerland, where he received a Doctorate in sacred theology.[2]

Aiding Monsignor Scheider in the initial phase was Monsignor William Gauche, who had been appointed rector of St. Gregory's Seminary in November, 1949, succeeding Walter Roddy. William Gauche was a native of Cincinnati. He attended St. Meinrad's Seminary in Indiana; St. Gregory's and Mount St. Mary's; and completed his theology course in Rome. After his ordination in 1928 he received various posts in the diocese. In September of 1929 he was appointed a professor at Mount St. Mary's. In the early thirties he took post-graduate courses at the Catholic University and at Fribourg, Switzerland. In 1935 he resumed his professorship at the major seminary. While at the seminary he also had directed the history department of Our Lady of Cincinnati College. [3]

First Phase—The first phase of the reorganization began at the meeting of the board of trustees on May 28, 1951. It was suggested then that the several items in the organization of the Athenaeum be reconsidered. It was agreed that the responsibilities of the board of trustees of the Athenaeum of Ohio, under its charter and by-laws, be more sufficiently defined; that the structure, function, policies, and duties of the officers of the respective divisions of the Athenaeum be set forth specifically in writing; and that an educational survey be promptly initiated in order to bring about the clarification of rights, duties, and the responsibilities of the various divisions to each other.

At this meeting it was determined that the educational survey then under discussion should be made by a qualified agency such as the Catholic University of America, the Ohio

Department of Education, or the North Central Association of Colleges and Universities. It was also determined that this survey should include an evaluation of the curriculum of the Teachers' College and the curriculum of the Institutum Divi Thomae.[4]

In regard to the Institutum Divi Thomae, it was decided that certain circumstances had altered the situation of the institute in relation to the Athenaeum. It was noted that the number of fellowship students at the Institutum had decreased; that the diocese could no longer provide the number of faculty members necessary; that certain religious communities had withdrawn their students; and that the financial support necessary for a stabilized budget of operation was now uncertain and indefinite. Due to these conditions it was further determined to discontinue the registration of students for graduate work in the Institutum and also suspend indefinitely the maintenance and operation of the Institutum Divi Thomae as a teacher training department of scientific responsibility for scholastic work, research, or scientific projects assumed by the Institutum under the charter and responsibility of the Athenaeum of Ohio. It was further decided that the Institutum could proceed under its own responsibility.[5]

In the fall of 1951 the Athenaeum of Ohio was inspected by a committee from the Catholic University in Washington under the direction of Doctor Deferrari. A year later, May 29, 1952, at the meeting of the board of trustees, a report was made on the suggestions and results of the survey. The report stated that the Athenaeum of Ohio would discontinue the granting of degrees to the Teachers' College, the Institutum Divi Thomae, and Our Lady of Cincinnati College beginning with the year 1953; that the Athenaeum would suspend operation of the Institutum Divi Thomae as a department of the Athenaeum; and that the Athenaeum would discontinue the operation of the Teachers' College beginning with the year 1953.[6]

Second Phase—The second phase[7] was now already underway. At the meeting of the board on May 28, 1951, the archbishop had directed the rector of Mount St. Mary's Seminary to initiate proceedings for the securing of membership of the seminaries in the Ohio College Association and accreditation by the North Central Association.[8]

It was now becoming increasingly clear to those in authority that Catholic Seminaries should be accredited by the State and by regional accrediting agencies. Some questioned the advisability of following this principle, but it could no longer be denied that the policy of accrediting had to be the practical standard of evaluation for any educational program. Impartial accreditors can turn up more than a few defects in seminary education which administrative personnel and faculties can pass over year after year. In the light of Pius XII's statement in recent years that the literary and scientific education of future priests should be at least not inferior to that of laymen who take similar courses of study, it would seem that the existence of a non-accredited seminary would be difficult to justify this day and age. Accreditation also helps a large number of students who are preparing for the priesthood but who do not continue on to the priesthood. Their work at the seminary is recognized, and each knows that his education is at least on a par with other colleges and universities.[9]

On the subject of accreditation Archbishop Alter pointed out that it was now sought because forty percent of the students in the seminary entering the third year of college did not persevere. When they applied to other colleges for admission for other courses they did not, under this program, receive due recognition for their work. In addition, the archbishop pointed out that the majority of newly ordained priests would be well equipped for high school teaching or administration.[10]

On January 22, 1953, the Athenaeum applied for admission to the Ohio College Association. The inspection team of the Ohio College Association came to the seminaries later that month, visiting both Mount St. Mary's and St. Gregory's. The Athenaeum, now comprising only the two seminaries, was accepted as an associate member of the Ohio College Association at the spring meeting of 1953. At the time only two of the seven applicants were accepted.[11]

This being accomplished, Monsignor Schneider wrote to Mr. Norman Burns, the Executive Secretary of the North Central Association on June 17, 1953, to the effect that the Athenaeum of Ohio would like to initiate proceedings for accreditation with that organization. In his letter, Monsignor Schneider explained as follows:[12]

> The Athenaeum of Ohio (as now constituted) is a senior institution comprised of a College of Liberal Arts and a School of Theology. The School of Theology and the upper division of the College of Liberal Arts (third and fourth year) constitute Mount St. Mary's Seminary of the West Norwood, Ohio. The lower division of the College of Liberal Arts (first and second year college) is at St. Gregory's Seminary, Mount Washington, Cincinnati, Ohio.[13]

During the school year 1953-1954 the first self-evaluation report was prepared by the faculty committees of the two seminaries. A revision of this was made in 1956, and a second revision was published in June of 1958. The actual work on the original surveys in 1953 began after the president of the Athenaeum requested and received from the North Central Association directives for proceeding with these surveys.[14]

In preparation for entrance into the Ohio College Association, by May of 1954 the following matters had been taken care of: the catalogue had been published; faculty files had been set up; faculty grade lists had been arranged; a dean of studies had been appointed; separate offices had been arranged for the dean and the registrar; the scholastic files had been separated from the sacramental files; further determination had been made for the Bachelor's and Master's degrees; changes in bookkeeping procedures had been introduced into the treasurer's office; and a librarian with a Master's degree in library science had been appointed as a full-time librarian.[15]

Of the matters still pending the following were the most important. A self-survey participated in by all the officers of the seminary and all the members of the faculty, according to the criteria of the Revised Manual of Accrediting, still remained to be finished. The system of recording scholastic grades and of issuing transcripts of credits had to be revised, and the academic counseling file on students had to be set up.[16]

At the annual meeting of the board on June 13, 1955, Monsignor Schneider announced, among other points of business, the organization of committees in preparation for accreditation by the North Central Association. These committees were to be named at a later date.[17]

The value of academic degrees as pertaining to the priesthood was the subject of the twenty-fifth annual commencement address of Bishop Issenman of Columbus in December of 1955. The bishop stated the following:

> The more acquisition of academic degrees is not going to change the priestly essence. But such degrees do give a certain standing to the priest in many secular professional circles in which he must move and work; indeed, in this day in our country, when a college education is within the reach of so many, the priest will often find in his parish many men and women possessing these marks of their college and university training. It is not going to hinder the effectiveness of his ministry, but rather should enhance it, that the priest should be graced with no less knowledge and culture than is usual among well-bred and well-educated people.

On May 28, 1956, Monsignor Schneider gave a report to the board of trustees on the work which had been done by the various committees of faculty members from Mount St. Mary's and St. Gregory's in regard to the future accreditation by the North Central Association of Colleges and Secondary Schools. It was reported that the particular committees had met in twenty-five or thirty meetings throughout the year, and that the joint committees had met seven or eight times. Two volumes were presented to the board: a self-survey made by the faculty committees of both seminaries, consisting of 193 pages, and a survey of student activities made by the student committees of both seminaries.[18]

On March 23, 1956, Mr. B.L. Stradley of Ohio State University and Doctor McFall of Bowling Green University, members of the Committee on Inspection and Membership of the Ohio College Association, paid a visit to both seminaries. As a result of this visit, Mr. Stradley pointed out what he considered to be four weaknesses in the Athenaeum (1) a split administration; (2) method of grading; (3) the testing program; and (4) the system of records.[19]

In April of 1956 it was announced that in order to get expert help and advice in strengthening the Athenaeum of Ohio with a view to Colleges and Secondary Schools, Father Julian Maline, S.J., a member of the executive of the North Central Association, had been invited to make a thorough inspection of both seminaries. Certain points relative to organization were recommended by Father Maline and those were resolved at the meeting on May 28, 1956.[20]

The Athenaeum of Ohio was admitted to full membership in the Ohio College Association in April, 1957. Admission of the two diocesan seminaries was voted on April 6, 1957, at the eighty-sixth annual meeting of the association. Mount St. Mary's and St. Gregory's thus became the first seminaries to be admitted to full membership in the Ohio College Association.[21]

Doctor Vincent Smith visited the Athenaeum at this time and recommended that accreditation of the Master's degree in Thomistic Philosophy be sought from the North Central Association. He added that Notre Dame would allow the Doctor's degree in philosophy be granted to graduates of the Athenaeum's course in Thomistic Philosophy after just two years of further work instead of the customary three years. They would accept the Master of Arts course in Thomistic Philosophy as equivalent to theirs. Doctor DeKonick of Lavalle University had written that Dean Parent of Lavalle University, Quebec, would accept the Master of Arts degree as the equivalent of theirs.[22]

Bishop Paul Leibold, the auxiliary bishop of Cincinnati, discussed the current program of seeking academic accreditation for the two seminaries at the annual commencement of the Athenaeum in December of 1958. The bishop stated that it was quite proper for the church to urge her educational institutions to conform to standards set by accrediting agencies. "To isolate Catholic institutions from such agencies is not in strict conformity with the Church's claims in the field of education; and it is eminently not realistic." Noting, however, that most of the Athenaeum's graduates would become "teaching assistants," the bishop urged them not to forget that "you were trained primarily to be priests." [23]

The Athenaeum of Ohio was accredited on the Master's level on October 12, 1959. In a letter from John Forbes, the assistant secretary of the North Central Association, Monsignor Schneider was informed that the executive board, at its meeting on September 29, had voted to accredit the Athenaeum of Ohio retroactive to April 24, 1959.[24]

Third Phase—The last phase of the reorganization of the Athenaeum concerned itself with the administrative structure of the institution. By August of 1953 the two seminaries were the only two remaining units. The Athenaeum of Ohio consisted of the college of liberal arts (with a graduate program in philosophy), and the school of theology. The college of liberal arts was divided into the lower and upper divisions. Classes in the lower division of the college were conducted at St. Gregory's Seminary, and classes in the upper division were conducted at Mount St. Mary's Seminary in Norwood. Classes in the graduate program in Thomistic philosophy and classes in the school of theology were also conducted at Mount St. Mary's Seminary of the West.

According to the sixth article of the Articles of Incorporation, the membership of the corporation of the Athenaeum of Ohio consists of the archbishop of Cincinnati and the other persons whom he selects and designates as members of the board of trustees. Such membership terminates at the will of the archbishop of Cincinnati. The Code of Regulations of the Athenaeum of Ohio, as amended at the meeting of the trustees on June 13, 1955, demands that "The number of trustees shall be not less than five nor more than fifteen. The elected trustees shall hold office for three years or until their successors are elected and qualified." In 1958 the members of the board of trustees of the Athenaeum of Ohio were: the Most Reverend Karl J. Alter, chairman; the Most Reverent Paul F. Leibold, vice-chairman; Monsignor Robert Sherry, secretary; Monsignor Ralph Asplan, treasurer; Monsignor R. Marcellus Wagner, Carl J. Ryan, Joseph McFarland, Joseph J. Schneider, Edward Freking, Basil Haneberg, and Father Urban Stang.[25]

Ordinarily the board of trustees of the Athenaeum meets once each year. The matters discussed and the problems settled at the meetings are those which are the ordinary concern of the board of trustees of any college. The minutes of these meetings, dating back to the 1928, are in the files at the office of the registrar at Mount St. Mary's Seminary.

The archbishop of Cincinnati is not only the chairman of the board of trustees of the Athenaeum, but also the chancellor of the Athenaeum. As chancellor, the archbishop fulfills the obligations imposed upon him by the canon law of the church. The president is also the rector of Mount St. Mary's Seminary. As president he is subject directly to the archbishop who acts as chancellor of the Athenaeum and chairman of the board of trustees. The president is academic nature both at Mount St. Mary's Seminary and in the lower division of the college of liberal arts at St. Gregory's Seminary. As vice-president of the Athenaeum he is subordinate to the president in matters of a scholastic and academic nature; as rector of St. Gregory's he is charge of discipline.

The plan of administration of the Athenaeum of Ohio is of the unit type of control. Unity of administration and control is achieved through the board of trustees; with the archbishop of Cincinnati acting as chairman of the board and the chancellor of the Athenaeum, and through the president acting as the chief administrative officer.

CURRICULUM IN THE COLLEGE OF LIBERAL ARTS

The ultimate aim of the college of liberal arts is the production of a finished man of character, "the true Christian who thinks, judges, and acts constantly in accordance with right reason illumined by the example and teachings of Christ." [26]

The curriculum of the college of liberal arts seeks to form students who will be well rounded in all the cultural and intellectual heritage of our age, and who will enter theology with a background in Latin and philosophy, since these are indispensable to the future of priests. The courses in philosophy are given in the upper division of the college of liberal arts and are the integrating and ultimate offering of the curriculum. [27]

Most other courses offered are in some way related to them. Language, history, and science are the three areas stressed throughout the college as having special relation to the study of philosophy.[28]

Language is considered a primary tool for the study of philosophy and theology, and an indispensable means of communication for the future priests. English is studied in the lower division of the college with emphasis on composition and cultivating an appreciation of the literature of America and English authors. The courses in speech given in the upper division of the college continue the stressing of English as a vital vehicle of communication. [29]

Latin is given great stress in the lower division for two reasons: (1) it is the official language of the church; and (2) so many of the basic writings of Christian philosophers and theologians are in this language. For those who are especially proficient in Latin, courses in advanced classical Latin are offered in the upper division. Modern languages are also offered throughout the college curriculum to enable those of special ability to ground themselves in the culture of other people. [30]

The course offerings in history in the lower division include both American and modern

European History, enabling students to understand the many influences which have helped to form the modern world. In the upper division a survey of history places before the student the entire panorama of western civilization. [31]

These course in history form a basis for the social studies of the Athenaeum curriculum. The course in moral philosophy given in the upper division grounds the student in ethical principles and also in the principles of sociology and political science. In addition there is a special course in modern sociological theory. [32]

Because modern science has made and is making such rapid strides, and because findings of science have definite relation to many of the problems of philosophy, the Athenaeum offers a variety of science courses. Every student in the lower division of the college is required to take a semester each of physics and chemistry. Those who show ability and interest in science may follow a course in general biology, or may further their knowledge of mathematics by taking courses in trigonometry and analytic geometry. Special seminars in science are also offered in the lower division. In the upper division special courses are offered in genetics, the history of mathematics, particles of physics, and the atomic theory of chemistry. [33]

The lower division student is offered two courses in religion designed to give him a comprehensive grasp of the life of Jesus Christ, and to help him attain a more detailed appreciation of Christian doctrine. Throughout the Athenaeum curriculum the student is trained in Gregorian chant, the traditional liturgical music of the church. [34]

Since many young priests are being called upon today to teach various high school subjects, the upper division students are offered the opportunity of following the basic courses in professional education which are offered as part of a teacher training program.[35]

The philosophy courses which integrate and complete the college curriculum include a variety of disciplines. These begin by training the student in accurate thinking through the science of logic which considers grammar and language in their root operations. In philosophy of nature the student is introduced to the fundamental problems of the nature of matter and motion, problems about which modern chemistry and physics have much to say. Psychology offers the study of living things from plants to human beings, considers the theory of evolution, and penetrates certain problems of modern biology. Athenaeum students are also able to take special work in the findings of modern experimental psychology and in anthropology. Moral philosophy, as has been mentioned, directs human moral activity and lays the foundation for sociological and economic considerations. Metaphysics (first philosophy) comes to grips with the problem of human knowledge itself, and recognizing its validity, goes on to analyze the most basic concepts known to man and finally establishes through reason and existence of a Supreme Being, the first cause of the world. In all these courses, and in a special course in history, the culture of ancient Greece as well as the roots and trends of modern thinkers from Descartes and Kant to our own day are described.[36]

CURRICULUM IN THE SCHOOL OF THEOLOGY

In the school of theology greatest emphasis is placed upon the content of the moral and dogmatic teachings of the Catholic church as well as upon the code of law by which the church is governed. Close attention is paid to the liturgy and to the sacred music of the church. A careful study is made of the individual books of the Bible. The seminarian studies dogmatic, moral, and pastoral theology along with the Sacred Scripture, Israelite history, New Testament history, church history, liturgy, Gregorian chant, and canon law not only in order to be able to perform the ministry of the priesthood for the benefit of others, but also for his own personal development and perfection. The Sacred Scripture and theology are subjects most deserving of study by the human intellect because they deal with the object most demanding of man's reverence and attention. The study of the theological sciences may seem to be a specialization along professional lines. It is that and more. In the very process of this specialized professional preparation there is a liberalizing influence exerted on the student because of the dignity of the content-matter studied.[37]

Awareness of the need for competency in oral communication is felt throughout the liberal arts course, but more especially as the student approaches the actual exercise of the priestly ministry. For this reason training in public reading and speaking carries through from the lower division in the college of liberal arts to the end of the four years in the school of theology.[38]

FACULTY OF THE ATHENAEUM

On the faculty of the Athenaeum of Ohio in September of 1953 were the following professors: Stanley Bertke (dogmatic theology and sociology); George Berwanger (English); John Fehring (sacred music); William J. Gauche (religion); Robert Krumholtz (sacred scripture); John de Deo Oldesgeering (sacred music); Carl Peipenbreier (German); Frank Roedel (Latin and Greek); Carl J. Ryan (education); Joseph Schneider (pastoral theology); Louis Smith (French); Charles E. Spence (Latin and Greek); Carl Steinbicker (church history and sacred eloquence); John Stenz (Hebrew and Greek); and Alfred Stritch (history).[39]

The associate professors were: Robert Buschmiller (speculative dogmatic theology, ascetical theology, and French); Robert Hagedorn (moral theology); Charles H. Hollencamp (philosophy); Vincent Lewis (biology, chemistry, and religion); Eugene H. Maly (Sacred Scripture and Spanish); Thomas G. Pater (fundamental dogmatic theology); Robert Tensing (philosophy); and Raymond Haun (Latin). [40]

The instructors were: Conrad H. Boffa (Italian); William Franer (education); Edward Gratsch (dogmatic theology and liturgy); Raymond Hahn (Latin); John Jacquerin (religion); Herman Kenning (education); Edward Kotter (ascetical and pastoral theology); Lawrence Mick (sacred music); and James Shappelle (moral theology and education).[41]

In February of 1955 Robert Sherry was reappointed rector of St. Gregory's Seminary. Monsignor Gauche had died in the previous December and the post was now given to the man who had been the rector from 1929-1937. From 1937 Sherry had served five years as pastor of St. Andrew's parish in Cincinnati. In 1941 he entered the military service as chaplain, serving in France during the second World War. He returned to the United States in 1946 and was made assistant commandant of an army chaplain's school. He went to the Far East in 1950, and received the Legion of Merit Award for service in Japan and Korea. When he left the army to become rector of St. Gregory's, he had attained the rank of lieutenant colonel. His appointment became effective on February 25, and he was formally installed by the arch-bishop in a ceremony at the seminary on February 27, 1955.[42]

The new additions to the faculty of the Athenaeum in 1955 were: Robert Sherry (the new rector and professor of religion); Thomas Bokenkotter (church history); John Cunningham (speech); John Jennings (moral theology); Arthur Leen (Sacred Scripture); John Sauter (church history); and Robert Stricker (librarian). There were no significant changes during the succeeding four years, 1956-1959, and the faculty and administrators worked diligently on the plans to accredit the seminary with the Ohio College Association and the North Central Association.

As the decade came to a close the administration and faculty were completely organized. The Board of Trustees of the Athenaeum was composed of the following members: The Most Reverend Karl J. Alter (Chairman of the Board and Chancellor); the Most Reverend Paul F. Leibold (Vice-chairman of the Board and Vice Chancellor); Monsignor Robert H. Krumholtz (Secretary), Ralph A. Asplan (Treasurer); and the Right Reverend Monsignors Edward A. Freking, Basil H. Haneberg, Joseph D. McFarland, Carl J. Ryan, Joseph J. Schneider, Robert J. Sherry, Henry Vogelpohl, and Urban Stang.[43]

The officers of administration in 1960 were: Joseph J. Schneider (President; Rector of Mount St. Mary's Seminary); Robert H. Tensing (Vice-Rector, Mount St. Mary's Seminary); Joseph C. Meinderding (Vice Rector, St. Gregory's Seminary; Associate Registrar); Charles H. Hollencamp (Dean, College of Liberal Arts); Robert J. Buschmiller (Director of the Graduate Program of Summer School Studies); Angelo C. Caserta (Associate Dean, College of Liberal Arts); Robert A. Stricker (Librarian); John D. Sauter (Associate librarian); Francis J. Miller (Treasurer); John M. Jacquemin (Associate Treasurer) and John J. Jennings (Registrar). [44]

The faculty of the college of Liberal Arts consisted of professors, assistant professors, associate professors, and instructors. The professors were: George J. Berwanger (English); Robert J. Buschmiller (graduate philosophy and French); Angelo C. Caserta (religion; Raymond J. Haun (Latin); Charles H. Hollencamp (philosophy, summer courses in graduate program, and science); Carl a. Peipenbreier (German); Francis F. Roedel (Latin and Greek); Joseph J. Schneider (graduate seminar); and Charles E. Spence (Latin and Greek).[45]

The associate professors were: John J. Cunningham (speech); Vincent J. Lewis (science and religion); Lawrence J. Mick (sacred music); Louis F. Smith (French); and Robert A. Stricker (Latin). The assistant professors were William Huseman (mathematics and science); John D. Sauter (Latin and religion); and the instructors were Thomas Bokenkotter (History) and Donald McCarthy (philosophy). [46]

The Faculty of the school of theology also consisted of professors, associate professors, assistant professors and instructors. The professors were: Robert Hagedorn (moral theology);

Timothy J. McNicholas (sacramental theology and canon law); Eugene Maly (Sacred Scripture); and Robert Tensing (dogmatic theology and sacred eloquence). The associate professors were Edward Gratsch (dogmatic theology and liturgy), and John J. Jennings (moral theology). The lone assistant professor was Arthur Leen (Sacred Scripture). The instructors were Ralph Lawrence (sacramental theology), and Francis J. Miller (dogmatic theology).[47]

THE LIBRARY

The library facilities of the Athenaeum at the end of the decade were in keeping with the scholastic aims of the two seminaries. Since St. Gregory's Seminary bases its curriculum on the classics and on the foundation of the physical sciences, its library is extensive in English, Latin, and Greek classics, as well as scientific books and periodicals. The college library at St. Gregory's contains around eighteen thousand bound volumes, and is located on the ground floor in a new wing completed in 1956. The reading room contains periodicals and general reference materials. It also serves as the "stack room" and is open to the students at all times.

The library at Mount St. Mary's Seminary contains forty-five thousand volumes, and emphasizes the fields of philosophy, education, theology, Sacred Scripture, church history, canon law, and liturgy. The main section which embraces twenty-five volumes, is located on the ground floor in the main the building. The library subscribes to a large number of periodicals on ecclesiastical, educational and general cultural subjects. The shelves in the main library are open to the students at all times. There is a trained librarian on duty throughout the day to facilitate the research work of the seminarians.

The Athenaeum library possesses a notable collection of manuscripts and incunabula. Among the manuscripts is a thirteenth-century vellum copy of the *Liber Sententiarum* of Peter Lombard, which for a long time was the standard text in the schools of theology. The incunabula include a rare Low-German Bible printed in 1478, and one in High German printed in 1483.

THE BUILDING PROJECTS OF THE ERA

In July of 1952 Archbishop Alter announced plans for the erection of the second section of St. Gregory's Seminary at the expense of about $2,000,000. Plans called for additions to the central building which was erected in 1929. A campaign to raise $5,000,000 for the seminary project and to renovate the old cathedral building, had been inaugurated throughout the archdiocese in September. Concerning the seminary, Archbishop Alter made the following statement:

> There is another project which we wish to include in the campaign for funds. Twenty-five years ago, the rebuilding of St. Gregory's Seminary was begun. One-third of it, viz., the high school section, was completed at that time. We cannot wait any longer to continue our program. In justice to our need for more priests and in justice to the students themselves we must provide more ample facilities for their care and ecclesiastical training. Our late Archbishop, shortly before his death, drafted a letter in which he asked the priests and the faithful to commemo-

rate the centenary of the archdiocese by resuming the building operation at the Seminary. To avoid the necessity of an extra campaign, we are combining both of these cherished projects in the one appeal which we shall make during the month of September.[48]

The proposed construction and renovation project at St. Gregory's Seminary was the fifth such undertaking in the institution's sixty-one year history. The central section of the first building was opened in 1891, and was soon augmented by the erection of one wing in 1894 and another a few years later. The erection of the new central building was completed in 1929. The current project (1952) saw extensive repairs on the old buildings, and the erection of another unit to the new building. Most urgently needed was the repair work which required more than a year to complete. With sharp increases in enrollment in the minor seminary in recent years, the inadequacies of the old building became more and more acute. The principal problems were overcrowding and outwork facilities.

There was no hall which would accommodate all the students at one time except the refectory and the chapel. The refectory had become so crowded that faculty members had to occupy a separate dining room.

The chapel scarcely accommodated all the students. It had been formed from several classrooms many years ago when the original chapel could no longer contain all the students. It was a makeshift affair having such unchurchly features as a low ceiling, clear glass windows of no distinctive size or shape, and canvas partitions separating the sanctuary from the sacristy. Although the chapel was and is hallowed in the memories of the hundreds of priests who have attended St. Gregory's, their recollections pay tribute to its spiritual association, not to its architectural qualities.

New and enlarged lavatories and shower rooms were installed on each floor of the old building's north wing to remedy plumbing inadequacies. The walls were repainted, new flooring was laid, and new furniture was purchased. Within the next year the repair work included rewiring, installation of fireproof stairwells, erection of new showers and lockers in the basement, and other improvements. The total cost of renovating the old building was about $250,000. The new unit had cost approximately $2,000,000. This new unit was erected in the space between the present old and new buildings. The third unit of the new building, which is not expected to be built for another generation or more, will occupy the site of the old building. It will contain the college department's classrooms and living quarters presently located in the old building.

Construction of a boiler house, first unit of the expansion program of St. Gregory's Preparatory Seminary, began in November of 1955. Archbishop Alter turned the first spadeful of earth in a ceremony attended by the student and faculty members. With the archbishop was Monsignor Robert J. Sherry (rector), and Robert J. Beischel, contractor.[49]

It was completed in the winter of 1956-1957 at a cost of $240,000 and is located at the rear of the new building.[50]

On March 31, 1956, a fire completely gutted the south wing and a corridor connecting it with the central unit of the old seminary containing the chapel, refectory, college recreation rooms, and the living quarters of Monsignor Spence.

The fire, which consumed the sixty-two year old south wing of the old seminary building, began some time between 12:30 a.m. and 1:30 a.m. on Holy Saturday morning. Smoke was detected about 1:30 a.m. and a fire company was on the scene shortly thereafter. Water pressure was so weak that hose lines had to be laid two hundred years or more to outlets on Beechmont Avenue.

Seeing that they could not prevent complete loss of the south wing, the firemen concentrated their efforts on the fifty foot corridor connecting the south wing and the central building. The corridor was gutted but only part of the rear of the central building was burned.

Heat and smoke caused considerable damage to the corridor walls and professors' rooms in the central building. The pain on the walls was blistered and smoke-stained, and many paintings and photographs were damaged. Fire doors prevented damage to the north wing.

The fire was thought to have started in the basement next to the boiler room. Power lines were concentrated there, and lights and telephone service went dead soon after the fire started.

Estimates of the losses incurred from the fire ranged from $300,000 to $500,000. In addition to losing the structure itself, the seminary lost all of the chapel furnishings, costly vestments and sacred vessels, the organ, altars, rugs and other furnishings; equipment in the refectory and kitchens; furnishings of the students' recreation rooms on the second floor under the chapel; and a large number of trunks, suitcases, and other articles which the students had stored on the top floor of the south wing. Many years ago this floor (called "High Docks"), served as student dormitory, but in more recent years was used only for storage. Twelve students' rooms and a janitors' room on the connecting corridor were burned out completely.

Most serious personal losses were incurred by Monsignor Spence who occupied rooms on the second floor of the south wing. He lost practically all his personal effects, including a 10,000 volume library, which he had assembled over a period of forty years. Many of the books were rare copies of Latin and Greek classics. Lost also was a sizable collection of photograph records and data which Monsignor Spence had used in preparing the Ordo (liturgical calendar), for many dioceses throughout the country. A collection of Ordos and other ecclesiastical publications dating back many years were also consumed in the fire. Seminary expansion plans had called for the erection of the new refectory and chapel within the next few years, but the archbishop noted the part of the plan had been the continued use of the wing now destroyed by fire.[51]

The rector, Monsignor Sherry, in a statement acknowledging the help St. Gregory's received from many quarters during and after the fire, said it caused a serious loss but revealed that the institution had a multitude of friends. The statement follows:

Generosity to those in trouble and need is a virtue of most Americans. The recent tragic fire at St. Gregory's Seminary gave eloquent proof of this fact. People from far and wide as well as those nearby came to the assistance of the stricken seminary. Offers of food, clothing, shelter, and equipment poured for all sides.

McNicholas High School and Guardian Angels' Church opened their cafeteria to the personnel of the seminary. The Wittstein-Middleman Post, American Legion, offered its headquarters and commissary to the faculty and students. George Moehringer, commander of the Fourth District, American Legion, placed all nearby posts at the service of the seminary. [52]

Immediate construction of a new building to replace the south wing of St. Gregory's Seminary was announced by Archbishop Alter. The new building, expected to be completed as part of the seminary's long-range expansion program.

Work this more permanent structure was expected to begin as soon as possible. The one-story edifice was to form the foundation for the future chapel, and was to be faced with stone to match that of the seminary high school building completed in 1929.

The building which rose on the site of the destroyed south wing was constructed of cement block, and faced with brick to match the old seminary building. It was intended to serve as a temporary refectory and kitchen but was expected to provide many years of service as a reading room and stack-room library.

Since the lack of a chapel and refectory made it impossible to accommodate all three hundred students at the seminary, only the high school department students were to be kept there for the remainder of the year.

The 162 students in the college department were sent to three other seminaries for the next two months. Forty-two students in the second year of college were accommodated at Mount St. Mary's Seminary, Norwood; the seventy-five students in the first year of college entered the new Holy Cross Seminary in La Crosse, Wisconsin (at the invitation of Bishop John P. Treacy of La Crosse); and forty-five collegians in a group receiving special training in Latin and other subjects lived and studied at St. Francis' Seminary, Mount Healthy, the preparatory seminary of the Cincinnati Franciscan Fathers.

For the most part the students continued to be taught by members of St. Gregory's faculty. Some of the faculty members resided in La Crosse, and those now teaching at Mount St. Mary's and St. Francis' Seminaries continued to reside at St. Gregory.

When the high school department would open depended upon how soon the heat ducts damaged by the fire could be repaired. Although the boiler room at the rear of the old building was near the fire, it was not severely damaged, but the ducts leading from it to the high school building were damaged by excessive heat, water and falling debris. They were put back into operation within a few days. Heat had been restored to the old building by the opening date of April 9. The 138 high school students, now in need of a refectory, ate dinner each evening in the new cafeteria of McNicholas High School located nearby on Beechmont Avenue. Arrangements were made to serve the students breakfast and lunch at the seminary. The large study hall in the high school building was converted into a chapel.

...Here in the Archdiocese of Cincinnati our seminary program has been traditionally sustained by an enlightened interest, a generous measure of self-sacrifice, and sincere appreciation of its achievements. We gladly make public acknowledgment of the favorable position which we have heretofore enjoyed in this respect. Today, we address ourselves to this question of the seminaries with particular solicitude. The recent disastrous fire at St. Gregory's has impoverished our physical resources and made it necessary to make a special appeal to the devoted faithful of the archdiocese for their assistance.

It is true that our losses were partly covered by insurance; but it must be borne in mind that the buildings which were destroyed were more than sixty years old and that their replacement will cost many times the original investment...For many years plans to build a chapel and other permanent facilities at St. Gregory's have been held in abeyance. The college students are still housed in old buildings which are dangerous in event of fire. The delay has lasted now thirty years since the permanent high school building was completed. The chief reason for the delay in completing the original program was the urgent need of using our resources to meet the expanding needs of our growing parishes and institutions. Now we have reached a stalemate. Unless the number of our vocations increases we cannot staff the parish with the necessary personnel; and unless our seminary facilities are adequate we shall not be able to train the candidates who apply.[53]

Six contractors were invited to submit bids for construction of the basement section of the chapel wing which was to be erected adjacent to the existing "new" (built in 1929) stone building. The basement section was to include a permanent dining room and kitchen, as well as a mezzanine area with living quarters for maintenance workers. The contract was awarded to Allen and Beischel of Cincinnati whose bid of $493,687 was the lowest.

Announcement of the beginning of work on the chapel wing was made by the archbishop in a letter thanking benefactors who responded to the appeal for funds to restore the seminary buildings after the disastrous Holy Saturday fire.[54]

In September of 1956, just six months after the fire, ground was broken for the first section for the proposed new addition. The construction now started was actually the second step in the seminary construction program, although it marked the beginning of work on the expansion of the new main building. Total cost of the structure, which housed the seminary's permanent refectory and auxiliary rooms was estimated at $725,000.

In September of 1958 Archbishop Karl J. Alter expressed hope that it would be possible to begin work the following spring on the remainder of the building program at St. Gregory's Seminary.

"The next step in the building program," Archbishop Alter said, "will be the erection of the chapel and new wing to the north (in the direction of the older seminary building). Construction of the chapel and the new wing will be undertaken next spring if bids for this next phase of the building programs are not to high.[55]

He revealed that improvements made in the previous two years, at a cost of about $1,500,000, had been entirely paid for without touching the seminary's funds or burses. Improvements made at St. Gregory's in recent years have included the installation of modern plumbing facilities and stairwells in the college buildings; construction of a temporary refectory on the site of the south wing (destroyed by fire in 1956); the erection of a boiler house; and a new permanent refectory and kitchen.

When the new refectory was opened, the building which had temporarily housed it became the new seminary library. The former college library was converted into students' rooms.

The last phase of the full expansion program—the new chapel and north wing—was begun, as hoped for, in the spring of 1958. The wing contains administration offices, classrooms, utility and recreation rooms, and residential quarters for three faculty members and sixty students. The cornerstone of the new chapel was set on September 8, 1961 and the building was occupied in September 1962. The altar was consecrated and the new wing blessed by Archbishop Alter on May 25, 1963. The chapel dedicated on August 27, 1963, by his Eminence, Albert Cardinal Meyer. This marked an end of the extension building program which had been initiated almost a decade before.

SUMMARY

The years between 1950 and 1960 were important years in the history of the two seminaries of the Archdiocese of Cincinnati. During this decade, all units and affiliations of the Athenaeum were dropped with the exception of the two seminaries. At the end of the decade they alone comprised the Athenaeum of Ohio.

An extremely vital educational advance was made when the reorganized Athenaeum of Ohio became a member of the Ohio College Association, and obtained accreditation from the North Central Association of Colleges and secondary schools. This important step was initiated by Archbishop Alter and implemented by Monsignor Schneider.

This accreditation from the North Central Association had a most profound effect on seminary administrative policy. The seminaries were put under the unitary control of the archbishop of Cincinnati as chairman of the board of trustees. The rector of Mount St. Mary's Seminary served as president of the Athenaeum. Reports of inspections by committees and self-surveys conducted by seminary faculty members, made in the process of becoming part of the Ohio College Association, resulted in refinements of certain administrative procedures and significantly raised the level of operating efficiency of the two seminaries.

This chapter also dealt with the curriculum of the Athenaeum during this decade. In both the College of Liberal Arts and in the School of Theology, it can be seen that its offerings were impressive and equal to the curriculum offerings of the other similar colleges of liberal arts in the country.

In this chapter it has been seen that the building program which was started in 1929 by Archbishop McNicholas was brought to completion by Archbishop Alter. The lower division, the college of liberal arts of St. Gregory's Seminary, now was equipped with complete and adequate facilities for the first time in almost fifty years.

NOTES
[1] *Catholic Telegraph*, April 28, 1950, p. 1.
[2] *Ibid.*,, September 9, 1949, p. 1, June 21, 1957, p. 3.
[3] *Ibid.*,, November 11, 1949, p. 1.

[4] "Minutes of the Board of Trustees, May 28, 1951," Book #4. Office of the Registrar. Mount St. Mary's Seminary.

[5] "Minutes of the Board of Trustees, May 28, 1951," Book #4.

[6] "Minutes of the Board of Trustees, May 29, 1952," Book #4. "Minutes of the Board of Trustees, May 25, 1953," Book #4.

[7] "Minutes of the Board of Trustees, May 28, 1951," Book #4.

[8] Campion Robert Baer, "The development of Accreditation in American Catholic Seminaries, 1890-1961." An unpublished Doctor's Dissertation, University of Notre Dame, 1963, p. 367.

[9] "Minutes of the Board of Trustees, June 18, 1957," Book #5.

[10] *Ibid.*, June 18, 1957," Book #5.

[11] "Minutes of the Board of Trustees, May 25, 1953," Book #4.

[12] "Memorandum," p. 241. Book #4. Office of the Registrar. Mount St. Mary's Seminary.

[13] "Minutes of the Board of Trustees," Book #5.

[14] *Self Evaluation Report of the Athenaeum of Ohio.* 1955-1956, 1956-1957, June 1958.

[15] "Memorandum," p. 241. Book #4.

[16] *Ibid.*, p. 241. Book #4.

[17] "Minutes of the Board of Trustees," Book #5.

[18] "Student Activity Survey of the Athenaeum of Ohio," 1955.

[19] "Minutes of the Board of Trustees, May 28, 1956," Book #5.

[20] *Ibid.*

[21] *Ibid.*

[22] "Minutes of the Board of Trustees, May 28, 1956," Book #5, August 1, 1956, Book #5.

[23] *Catholic Telegraph*, December 26, 1958, p.1.

[24] "Minutes of the Board of Trustees, October 12, 1959," Book #5.
Harlan C. Koch, (ed.), "Retroactive Accreditations," The North Central Association Quarterly. October 1959, Volume XXIV, Number 2, p. 150. "At the annual meeting of 1959 the Commission on Colleges and Universities postponed decisions on the accredited status of a number of institutions, authorizing the Executive Board to secure additional date and to take the appropriate action. After securing additional information, the Executive Board, at its meeting on September 29, 19d59, voted to accredit the following institutions, as indicated, retroactive to April 24, 1959: Applying institution accredited as a Master's degree-granting institution, The Athenaeum of Ohio, Cincinnati, Ohio." The Athenaeum of Ohio was authorized on June 28, 1964 to expand its offerings on the graduate level and to confer the degree of Master of Arts in theology upon graduates of the Honors Course in Theology.

[25] *Announcements 1958-1959*, p. 5. The Athenaeum of Ohio.

[26] *Announcements 1960-1961*, p. 44. The Athenaeum of Ohio.

[27] *Ibid.*

[28] *Ibid.*

[29] *Ibid.*, 45.

[30] *Announcements 1960-1962*, p. 44. The Athenaeum of Ohio.

[31] *Announcements 1960-1961*, p. 45. The Athenaeum of Ohio.

[32] *Ibid.*, 45.

[33] *Ibid.*, 45.

[34] *Ibid.*, 46.

[35] *Ibid.*, 46.

[36] *Ibid.*, 69.

[37] *Ibid.*, 69.

[38] *Ibid.*, 69.

[39] *Announcements 1953-1954*, pp. 11—14. The Athenaeum of Ohio.

[40] *Ibid.*, 14-16.

[41] *Ibid.*, 16-17.

[42] .Chapter VIII

[43] *Announcements 1960-1961*, p. 4. The Athenaeum of Ohio.

[44] *Ibid.*, 5.

[45] *Ibid.*, 11-12.

[46] *Ibid.*, 13.

[47] *Ibid.*, 16-18.

[48] *Catholic Telegraph*, July 11, 1952 p.1.

[49] *Ibid.*, November 18, 1955, p. 1.

[50] *Ibid.*, November 4, 1955, p. 1.

[51] *Ibid.*, April 6, 1956, p. 1.

[52] *Ibid.*

[53] *Ibid.*, April 20, 1956, p. 2.

[54] *Ibid.*, August 3, 1956, p. 1.

[55] *Ibid.*, September 5, 1958, p. 1.

CHAPTER TEN

Summary and Conclusions

PROBLEMS AND PROCEDURES

Purpose of the Study—The Athenaeum of Ohio as it functions today is the educational institution which comprises the two seminaries of the Archdiocese of Cincinnati, Mount St. Mary's Seminary in Norwood and St. Gregory's Seminary in Mount Washington. The prime purpose of this dissertation has been to document the history and development of the Athenaeum from its founding in 1829 to the present day. Since there was no comprehensive and complete history of this institution and since the educational needs of the times make it imperative that much more be known about the development of the individual Catholic seminaries in this country, this dissertation has presented a detailed historical study of a particular and individual diocesan seminary institution in the United States. The one essential purpose, therefore, of this chronological record has been to be of help to those who, in the future, must proceed with the work of evaluating and assessing Roman Catholic seminary education in the United States.

Closely allied with this purpose were several others. Since the past is but a guide to the future, this history was written with the idea of presenting the ideas and plans of the past in such a way that they might be of benefit to those engaged in the present planning for the future needs of the Athenaeum. Another purpose of this dissertation was to give due recognition to the many excellent rectors and dedicated professors of the Athenaeum lest their names be forgotten and their work go unheralded. Lastly, in an age of transition, it is helpful to be aware of the traditions of the past. It is hoped that this dissertation will preserve the best of those traditions.

Investigational Procedures—The historical method of research is the major procedure used in the writing of this dissertation. The primary and secondary materials which could be found have been assembled, studied, analyzed and interpreted as far as possible in accordance with the principles of historical research.

Sources of Date—The primary sources which provided the basic data and information for this dissertation were, in very large measure, found in the archives and library of Mount St. Mary's Seminary in Norwood. The 131 volumes of the *Catholic Telegraph,* dating back to 1831, were the most useful source material. Extensive use also was made of the vast amount of letters, diaries, memorials, and ledgers contained in the archdiocesan archives. Very helpful were the actual minutes of the faculty meeting and the minutes of the Board of Trustees of the Athenaeum of Ohio. The important documents on early American Catholic church history were investigated in the archives of the University of Notre Dame: the archives of the Ursuline Sisters in Brown County also proved helpful. Father Lamott's

History of the Archdiocese of Cincinnati was the most important source of information outside the primary sources listed above. Interviews were conducted with many priests of the Archdiocese of Cincinnati on various points pertinent to the history of the Athenaeum.

Delimitation of the Study—The study was confined to the history and development of the institution known today as the Athenaeum of Ohio. It comprises the two seminaries of the Archdiocese of Cincinnati, and is composed of a school of theology and a college of liberal arts. In dealing with the historical account from the date of its founding in 1829 up to the year 1960, particular emphasis was placed upon (1) the growth and development of seminary administration and organization; (2) the depth and quality of the faculty; and (3) the changes occurring in the curriculum and in the teaching methods.

Review of Related Studies—Several histories of individual Roman Catholic seminaries were read and consulted for treatment of matter and similarity of trends. In addition, several works treating on historical trends in both administration and organization, and works on curriculum development were studied. It was found that the bibliography on Roman Catholic seminaries in the United States was not extensive.

On the subject of the history of various other institutions of this country, related doctoral and master's dissertations completed at the University of Cincinnati and the University of Notre Dame were reviewed and studied.

SUMMARY OF THE HISTORY OF THE ATHENAEUM OF OHIO

The first plans for the seminary and college in the early history of the Archdiocese of Cincinnati were conceived by Bishop Fenwick who had been made one unsuccessful attempt to start a college and seminary before seeing the actual beginnings of St. Francis Xavier Seminary (1829) and the Catholic College of the Athenaeum (1831). In Bishop Fenwick's time the seminary and college were considered to be two separate and distinct institutions joined together in a common educational purpose. This type of educational arrangement resulted in a corporate institution known as a seminary-college. In its very earliest days the college section of the Athenaeum was "mixed" that is, it was both preparatory seminary and a lay college. Mainly due to the uncertainties of obtaining qualified men for administration and teaching, Bishop Purcell (successor of Bishop Fenwick), turned the college over to the Jesuits in 1840; but the diocesan seminary of St. Francis Xavier continued its precarious existence despite great hardships. Eleven years later, in 1851, it received a permanent home and a new name, Mount St. Mary's Seminary of the West.

The history of the seminary of Mount St. Mary's of the West from 1851, the date when it was established on Price Hill, to 1879, the year it was closed because of the financial failure of the archdiocese, was truly remarkable. Purcell's plans for the financing and erection of a seminary on Price Hill date back to the late 1840's. The new seminary became a reality and was opened in 1851 with Hallinan as rector. In these days there was talk of establishing it as a regional seminary. In these days there was talk of establishing it as a regional seminary. During the meeting of the First Provincial Council of Cincinnati, pontifical status and the power to award degrees were sought. All came to naught. In 1855 the seminary itself was incorporated as an educational institution under the laws of the State of Ohio. During the tenure of Quinlan as rector of Mount St. Mary's Seminary, Mount St. Mary's College was opened (1856) with Rosecrans as president. In 1859 the brilliant Barry became rector of the seminary and was succeeded in 1863 by Pabisch. In 1863 the college section of the Price Hill institution was closed due to the war. The seminary was closed in 1879 because of the financial failure of the archdiocese. It had enjoyed a reputation second to none in the Midwest.

The seminary reopened in 1887. Thomas Byrne was appointed rector and the seminary started the long, difficult process of rebuilding. In 1894 John Murray became rector, and the institution was just on the verge of recapturing its former glory when the decision was made to change to a new location. In 1904 Mount St. Mary's of the West was moved to Mount Washington, then known as Cedar Point.

The year 1890 marked the founding of the preparatory, seminary had existed in one form or another in the diocese from the inception of St. Francis Xavier Seminary and Athenaeum on Sycamore Street. Purcell, who had always favored the idea of a "mixed" college, ultimately found it expedient to give way to a classical course for "preparatorians." The minor and major seminaries were still considered to be two separate units of one corporate institution. The founding of St. Gregory's Seminary at Cedar Point resulted in the minor seminary now becoming autonomous in administration and separate in locale from the major seminary. J. C. Albrink was the first rector, and he was succeeded in 1892 by Henry Brinkmeyer who remained rector until 1907. In 1904 the minor seminary was moved from Cedar Point to downtown Cincinnati where it existed for three years as a day school. The downtown location was closed in 1907, and the diocese was without a minor seminary until 1924.

The history of Mount St. Mary's Seminary during the years 1904 to 1923 was one of quiet transition. The years during which the major seminary was located in Mount Washington constituted an interim period, and was not a period of significant accomplishment. During these years Mackey, Shee, and Beckman served as rectors.

In 1923 the newly erected Mount St. Mary's Seminary located at Norwood, Ohio, was dedicated. Preliminary plans for building the major seminary in Norwood had begun in June 1906, long before it became an actuality. The years 1923 to 1949 were years of rapid progress and major accomplishments. Beckman, Nau, Vehr, Rehring, and O'Brien served as rectors of the major seminary during these years.

During this period an extensive program of post-graduate studies was inaugurated. This program was initiated to provide a broad base from which to select subsequent faculty members. When the Athenaeum of Ohio was founded in 1928, Mount St. Mary's became one of the original units of the educational corporation. Subsequent approval of the Athenaeum by the State of Ohio enabled Mount St. Mary's Seminary to again award academic degrees for the first time in over seventy-five years. This period, 1923 to 1949, witnessed changes in the curriculum necessitated by entrance into the area of secondary education.

St. Gregory's, the minor seminary which had previously been located in Mount Washington, Ohio (and then moved to downtown Cincinnati in 1904) was closed in 1907. Following the move of Mount St. Mary's major seminary from the Mount Washington location in Norwood in 1923, St. Gregory's minor seminary was reopened at its original location. Joseph Sieber was the new rector, followed by Vehr, Sherry, and Roddy. New buildings had been erected and the faculty, administration, and curriculum of the minor seminary were rapidly improved. For the first time in the history of the two seminaries, the philosophy classes were separated from the theological classes, only to be united again in 1949.

The Athenaeum was founded in 1928 by Archbishop McNicholas and was designed to unify and coordinate the educational institutions of the archdiocese. Mount St. Mary's Seminary and St. Gregory's Seminary were the first units of this organization; the old Teachers' College was the third. Later the Institutum Dive Thomae and various other affiliations were added. These were all governed by the decisions of a central board of trustees.

During the 1950's the Teachers' College, the Institutum Dive Thomae, and other affiliations were dropped from the organization. Now the Athenaeum consisted only of the two seminaries of the archdiocese, Mount St. Mary's Seminary and St. Gregory's Seminary. The Athenaeum, thus constituted, was admitted as a member of the Ohio College Association in 1957, and was accredited by the North Central Association in 1959. During this period there was a significant improvement in the administrative functions of the two seminaries.

CONCLUSIONS

The findings of this dissertation will be presented in this section in three categories: Organization and administration of the seminaries; the quality and competence of the faculty; and the development of the curriculum and methods of teaching. In the span of 135 years covered in the history of the Athenaeum of Ohio, an excellent opportunity is afforded to judge and consider the unfolding development of a Catholic Seminary in three aspects. being the second oldest seminary system in the Midwest, and the forth oldest in the United States, the Athenaeum provided a marvelous opportunity for an insight into the historic developmental patterns involved in Roman Catholic seminary education in the United States.

Organization and Administration—The organizational and administrative patterns of Roman Catholic seminary education are a vitally important subject of controversy in the current struggle of the seminaries to approach standards set in secular universities and colleges. Much of the criticism , both positive and negative, has been directed toward the way the seminaries of today are organized and the manner in which they are administered. The findings of this thesis, although derived only from the history of the Athenaeum of Ohio, are significant in that they show the development which has taken place in these important areas. When changes are called for or demanded, it is felt that the findings of this thesis can be of significant value in appraising the plans and proposals for future improvement.

(1) On the matter of financial support of the seminaries in Cincinnati, it can be said that they have fared well. In the early days of the Athenaeum the matter of financial support was a problem but with the moving of the seminary to Price Hill, Purcell gradually solved this difficulty. With the sole exception of its closing during the year of 1870 the seminary has always functioned with exceptionally good financial backing. This has been very evident in the building programs of the seminaries which have kept pace with the increased demands of succeeding generations.

(2) As to organization, the history of the Cincinnati seminaries shows that they have passed through three phases: the seminary-college combination (1829-1863); the major-minor seminary at one location (1863-1879); and the major-minor seminaries at separate locations (1887-1960). The seminary-college combination was the first form of organization used in the history of Cincinnati seminaries. This organizational pattern was retained in the Cincinnati seminaries for a period of thirty-two years, culminating in the successful Mount St. Mary's College on Price Hill. In 1863 this college section was eliminated. The major and minor seminaries remained at one and the same place and ultimately were brought under one administration. It was not until 1890 that the final separation was made. With the exception of the years when St. Gregory's was closed, separate minor and major seminaries had been the normal educational arrangement for the seminaries.

The first arrangement, the seminary-college combination, was a peculiarly American institution. It worked for the financial betterment of the seminary, and afforded the diocesan clergy a fertile field for recruitment. In this plan non-Catholics were admitted to the classical courses and freely mingled with the seminarians and professors. Both Bishop Fenwick and Archbishop Purcell favored this arrangement and, in many ways, it seems to have merited their confidence.

The second arrangement, operation of the minor seminary and the major seminary at one location, resulted purely from circumstances. Additional room was added for the seminarians and the college therefore had to be dropped. Except for minor disciplinary problems it seems to have worked out very well.

The system of operating the minor seminary separate from the major seminary is the result of several historic factors. This was certainly the arrangement desired by the Holy See in the late nineteenth century. In the case of the Cincinnati seminaries, it was demonstrated that the nationalistic factor, as a result of German immigration, played an important part in instigating the separation.

(3) During the entire history of the Athenaeum, the normal number of years allotted for the classics course has been six. It is truly significant that this six years allotment to the classical course was never altered until just a few years ago.

(4) The number of years allotted to philosophy and theology has not remained constant. From a maximum of two or three years in the early days of the seminary on Sycamore

Street, it has developed into a six-year course. The philosophy and theology courses have been expanded through the addition of one extra year every thirty-five years. It would seem, therefore, that as the demands on the ministry increase, the courses in both philosophy and theology in this country tend to become more extensive. Perhaps, if such be the case, added study could be obtained not by delaying the date or ordination beyond the present six-year course, but rather by post-ordination studies in the seminaries on the graduate level.

(5) The history of the Athenaeum of Ohio also indicates that the theology course has nearly always been given at the same place as the philosophy course. The only time philosophy was separated from theology was when the seminary moved to Norwood in 1923, which separation lasted for twenty-six years. There are arguments for and against this particular arrangement but this study does indicate that the classic six-six arrangement, six years of minor seminary and six years of major seminary, has been the patter adopted in the Cincinnati seminaries.

(6) A subject of interest in regard to seminary organization has bee the talk about establishment of "regional" seminaries. In this thesis it was found that Purcell tried to establish such a regional seminary more than one-hundred years ago. In the light of present day debates concerning the proliferation of seminary facilities, it is interesting to note that the idea of a central seminary which would draw students from a central area, and not just from an individual diocese, is an idea which as been germinating in the mind of Catholic America for a long time without having borne such fruit.

(7) The system of administration in the early days of the Athenaeum was exceedingly primitive. Over the years, however, the administrative functions of the seminary have increased and developed. Generally speaking, the seminaries have been very well administered. Membership in the Ohio College Association and accreditation by the North Central Association exerted a strong influence toward spurring the seminaries on to a very high level of achievement in administrative policies. At the time of writing this dissertation, it can be said that the administrative structure of the Athenaeum of Ohio is fully in lien with any existing qualified American College.

(8) As for accreditation, this thesis tends to confirm the recent findings on accreditation of Catholic seminaries, i.e., it is thought better to seek accreditation from an accrediting agency other than one formed by Catholic seminaries themselves. Furthermore, it was evident that there was not a great deal of interest shown in degrees or accreditation until the seminary began the added function of preparing teachers for the secondary school of the diocese. The attempt of the Athenaeum (as incorporated in 1928) to maintain educational standards did not prove successful.

(9) The seeking of accreditation immeasurably improved the administrative standards of the Athenaeum of Ohio. There can be no doubt that the inspection of the Athenaeum by

accrediting teams and the self-surveys conducted by the administration and faculty have improved seminary administrative standards to a remarkable degree.

The Quality and Competence of the Faculty—Since the quality and competence of the teachers of any educational institution are the heart and soul of that institution, a great deal has been written today concerning the faculties of this thesis in the area of faculty competence allow insight into the phase which might otherwise not be obtained.

(1) Over the years the two seminaries of the Archdiocese of Cincinnati have had very capable faculties. From the very earliest days of the Athenaeum, the academic training and devotion to seminary education of the men who have taught at Mount St. Mary's or at St. Gregory's have been in general of very high caliber.

(2) In the first fifty years of the seminary's history, laymen were quite frequently members of the faculty. At one time, in 1858, there were as many laymen on the faculty as there were clerics. Conservative tendencies prevailing in the early years of this century tended to almost exclude laymen. In recent years there has been some evidence to indicate a willingness once again to employ laymen on the faculty.

(3) Beginning in the time of Archbishop Purcell (1851), most of the members of the faculty were sent away to obtain post-graduate degrees in philosophy and theology. From that time on most of the faculty teaching in the seminaries have obtained doctoral and master's degrees.

(4) In the last quarter of the last century, and during the first quarter of this century, extensive use was made of foreign priests, especially those from Germany, to fill faculty vacancies. They were always well educated in the fields of theology and, in the majority of cases, had brilliant careers as teachers at the seminaries.

(5) Prior to the time of Archbishop McNicholas, the few priests who were sent away for further studies were almost certainly slated for a teaching post on the faculty of the seminary. Because so few were sent there was never an adequate reserve of priests available for seminary teaching. Archbishop McNicholas' policy was to send many of the diocesan clergy away for further studies, and the reserve of priests capable of teaching at the seminary was immeasurably increased. This undoubtedly favorably influenced the quality of seminary instruction.

(6) The faculties of the two seminaries have not published a substantial amount of material, however the books and articles which have been printed have been of generally high quality. The lack of any considerable amount of published material is due mainly to the time-consuming pastoral work carried on by the resident professors.

The Development of Curriculum and Methods of Teaching—In regard to the curriculum and the methods of teaching in the major and minor seminaries of the Archdiocese of Cincinnati, the history of the Athenaeum shows that there has been extensive development in one sense, and a great deal of atrophy in another sense. This thesis tends to show that the curriculum in the minor seminary has developed and progressed satisfactorily in relation to the needs of the day. The curriculum of the major seminary, which changed very rapidly in the first seventy-five years, has been fairly well standardized and unaltered since the turn of the century. Teaching methods have not varied a great deal from the lecture system of instruction.

(1) One of the most significant findings of this thesis was the modification of purpose with regard to seminary education which occurred in 1925. As a result of Archbishop McNicholas' program of extended secondary education, diocesan priests (for the first time in the history of the Archdiocese of Cincinnati), began to employed as teachers in secondary schools. For almost the first one-hundred years of the history of the Athenaeum of Ohio, the sole purpose of seminary education was to provide the professional training required for the pastoral and parochial ministry. Pedagogy was taught but only in connection with the pastoral function of catechetics. Through the program of Archbishop McNicholas, the curriculum was designed to make the students eligible for teaching certificates enabling them to teach in the secondary schools of the Archdiocese. This new function of the seminary sparked the drive for degrees and ultimately accreditation. It was also the basis for the summer school program for the seminarians which continues up to the present day.

(2) The curriculum of the minor seminary (the six-year classical course) has always been very adequate, thorough, and complete. This thesis confirms the fact that through all the years of its existence, the minor seminary has maintained a consistently high standard of excellence.

(3) Curriculum development in the minor seminary (the six-year classical course) has come about in a very interesting way. During the early years of the Athenaeum on Sycamore Street, and later at Brown County, great emphasis was placed on study of the Latin and Greek classics. In the days of Mount St. Mary's College, although Latin and Greek were still held in high esteem, English and English literature now received due recognition and emphasis. In the first period at St. Gregory's (1890-1907) the curriculum was expanded to include scientific subjects. When St. Gregory's returned to Mount Washington in 1923, balance among the three was maintained. All through the 30's and 40's Latin and Greek were still honored subjects, but English and science were given added stress. Later Latin and Greek continued to be emphasized, but English and science held respectable places in the curriculum. Today, Latin, English, and English literature are still emphasized; Greek is studied but is not stressed; and social studies have tended to be emphasized to the expense of science.

(4) The curriculum of the major seminary (the six-year course in philosophy and theology) has maintained a striking degree of stability over the years. The core subjects (dogma, moral, Sacred Scripture, canon law, and church history), have remained the same for practically the entire history of the Athenaeum.

(5) Since the latter part of the last century the curriculum of the major seminary has remained fundamentally unchanged with regard to the subjects taught and the amount of time allotted to each subject in class. Subsequent instructions and decrees of the Holy See have served only to reiterate and stress what already was being done.

(6) The use of Latin in the study of philosophy and theology resulted in two things: textbooks printed in Latin, and the periodic speaking of Latin by the professors when teaching, as well as its periodic use by the students in both oral and written work. The use of Latin textbooks for both philosophy and theology has a very long tradition of use. Most certainly Latin textbooks were used at Mount St. Mary's in the early days; most probably the were used from the very birth of the seminary.
Despite adverse criticism in educational circles, the practice of using textbooks printed in Latin for the study of philosophy and theology is a tradition which still survives.
Periodically attempts have been made, in the form of directives, to revive the practice of having the professors speak in Latin and the students recite and write in Latin. Athenaeum records indicate that every twenty-years or so this matter is brought up, but the attempt to implement Latin in this fashion has always failed.

(7) In the philosophical and theological courses, the lecture method of teaching has been the one most often employed. During the time the seminary was on Price Hill, outside reading was very strongly encouraged. At the turn of the century, most probably due in great measure to the difficulties experienced by the church with the inroads of modernism and Americanism, outside reading was severely curtailed and restricted. For the greater part of the first half of this century most students were required to know the content of their texts, little more. In the last decade (the 1950s) of the history of the Athenaeum, ever increasing emphasis has been placed upon outside reading.

PROBLEMS FOR FURTHER STUDY
Regarding the areas for further research, additional consideration can be given the areas dealing with the organization and administration of the seminary; the quality and competence of the faculty; and the curriculum and methods of study. Use of the following suggested avenues of further study would give valuable insight into many matters presented in the course of this thesis.

The organizational patterns of the seminar—the seminary college combination (1829-1863); the major-minor seminary together (1863-1879); and the major-minor seminary separated (1887-1960), merit a great deal more research and investigation in order to evaluate the comparative success of each one. Taking into account the number of priests ordained under each system in relation to the entire Catholic population, it would be interesting to see which system, if any particular one, met with more success than the others in recruiting students for the diocesan clergy; which system was better adapted for equipping the American clergy to play a more significant role in the intellectual life of the community; which system exerted more influence upon the laity, both within and without the church; and which system actually made the most efficient and economical use of its faculty without unnecessary duplication. Studies in these areas and the data accumulated there-from could indeed be vitally significant in advancing seminary education and the Catholic church in America.

The seminary from 1923 to 1948 was organized on the basis of four years of high school, four years of college, and four years of theology. Since 1948 the seminary, for practical reasons, has reverted to the traditional system of the six-six course—four years of high school and the first two years of college, plus the final two years of college and the final four years of theology. Since many of the alumni of these two systems are still living, a solid study could include all of these graduates and their preferences for one or the other system. There is a great deal of controversy concerning the merits of each system, and it would be interesting to see the results of such a study.

At the time of this writing (1964), no history of Mount St. Mary's Alumni Association and its contributions to the seminary has been compiled. Founded in 1901, it has had an illustrious past which should not go unrecorded.

Much more could be learned, thence known, concerning the lives and works of many of the more eminent members of the faculties of the two seminaries. In many instances they are not much more than names. More research into the individual correspondence of these men, as presently contained in the archives of the seminary, would undoubtedly cast much light upon certain policy changes and developments about which little is known. Of special importance would be more research into the correspondence of the various archbishops of the diocese concerning the affairs of the two seminaries should be completed. Examination of their writings would indeed supply much insight into the reasons for certain changes and developments.

Examining the names of all the men who taught at the seminaries of the diocese, it would be satisfying to see a study made of their educational backgrounds. At what schools did they do their post-graduate and graduate work? Has the European influence predominated? Has any particular European country and/or school exerted the greatest influence? It would seem that the American influence has been rather insignificant.

A study should be made in the area of curriculum during the history by an examination of the textbooks used in each coarse during the history of the two seminaries. The various texts used in the courses since 1851 are very well known. Comparing each text with the related course of the period, research could be done on the developmental sequence of curriculum down through the years.

The lecture method teaching in the seminary could be easily examined and compared with the other methods which are in the experimental stages in other seminaries. Could visual aids, educational television, field trips, and in-service training, in part, do a better job than the present system of lecturing? All of these methods have been tried in the seminary from time to time. It may be that limited studies could be made to compare the results.

Concerning methods of teaching, it has become very evident that the use of one professor to cover all the material of one course which embraces many disciplines in no longer adequate. For example, the course is fundamental dogma embraces pertinent material in Sacred Scripture, history, psychology, and anthropology, not to mention the discipline of dogma itself. More investigation could be made into the area of providing teams of professors to teach those courses which demand specialization in so many phases. Team teaching could prove to be very effective in many of the courses in philosophy and theology.

BIBLIOGRAPHY

BOOKS

Acta et Decreta Quatuor Conciliorum Provincialium Cincinnatensium, 1855–1882 (Cincinnati: Typis Benziger Fratrum, 1886), pp. vii, 319.

Allen, Yorke, Jr., *A Seminary Survey* (New York: Harper and Brothers, 1960), pp. vii, 640. Alzog, Johannes. *Handbuck der Patrologiae oder de Altern Christlicken Literurgschichte.* Feuburg in Bereisgau, 1876.

Alzog, Reverend Doctor John. *Manual of Universal Church History.* Translated by F. J. Pabisch and Reverend Thomas S. Byrne. Volume II (Cincinnati: Robert Clarke and Company, 1876), pp. xv, 1096.

Anniversary Addresses of Priests and People of the Diocese of Cincinnati on the Twenty-Fifth Anniversary of the Episcopate of Most Reverend John Baptist Purcell. (Cincinnati: John P. Walsh, Bookseller and Stationer, 1858), p. 99.

Baker, Henry Given. "Transylvania: A History of Pioneer University of the West, 1780–1865." Unpublished doctor's dissertation, University of Cincinnati, 1949, pp. x, 368.

Barry, Colman J. *The Catholic Church and German Americans* (Milwaukee: The Bruce Publishing Company, 1952), pp. xii, 348.

Boffa, Conrad Humbert. *Canonical Provisions for Catholic Schools* (Washington, D.C.: The Catholic University of America Press, 1939), pp. x, 211.

Braun, Right Reverend Henry A. *History of the American College of the Roman Catholic Church of the United States, Rome, Italy* (New York: Benziger Brothers, 1910), p. 570.

Brinkmeyer, Henry. *The Lover of Souls: Short Conferences on the Sacred Heart of Jesus* (New York: Benziger Brothers, 1906), p. 180.

Bruns, Reverend J. A. *The Catholic School System in the United States* (New York: Benziger Brothers, 1908), p. 415.

Butler Nicholas Murray. Editor. *Education in the United States* (New York American Book Company, 1910), pp. xxiii, 1068.

Callaghan, Emily A. *Memoirs and Writings of the Very Reverend James F. Callaghan, D. D* (Cincinnati: The Robert Clarke Company, 1903), pp. viii, 568.

Catholic Churches of Cincinnati and Hamilton County, Ohio, Edition (Cincinnati: United States Church Album Publishing Company, 1896), p. unrecorded.

Catholic Colleges and Schools in the United States (Washington: The National Catholic Welfare Conference, 1942), p. 164.

Character Glimpse of Most Reverend William Henry Elder, D. D (New York: Frederick Pustet and Company, 1911), p. 180.

Cist, Charles. *The Cincinnati Miscellany.* Volume I. (Cincinnati: Caleb Clark Printer, 1845), p. 272.

Clerus Cincinnatensis: Official Publication for the Clergy of the Archdiocese of Cincinnati. Volume I, Numbers 1–5 (Cincinnati: No publisher stated), May 1942.

Clerus Cincinnatensis: Official Publication for the Clergy of the Archdiocese of Cincinnati. Volume II, Number 2 (Cincinnati: No publisher stated), October 1946.

Clerus Cincinnatensis: Official Publication for the Clergy of the Archdiocese of Cincinnati. Volume V, Number 2 (Cincinnati: No publisher stated), September 27, 1960.

Connaughton, Edward A. *A History of Educational Legislation and Administration in the Archdiocese of Cincinnati* (Washington, D.C.: The Catholic University of America Press, 1943), pp. xxvii, 309.

Cosgrove, Reverend J. J. *Most Reverend John Lancaster Spalding* (Medota, Illinois: The Wayside Press, Incorporated, 1960), p. 160.

Coulton, G. G. *Romanism and Truth.* Part II. "The Struggle Against Common Sense" (London: The Faith Press, 1931), pp. vii, 388.

DeHerdt, P. J. B. *Pontificalis seu Ceremonialis Episcoporum.* Three Volumes (Louvanii: Vanlintheret Fratres, 1863).

DeLaney, John J. and Robin, James Edward. *Dictionary of Catholic Biography* (Garden City, New York: Doubleday and Company, Incorporated, 1961), pp. vii, 1245.

"Diamond Jubilee Number of Mount St. Mary's Convent of the Good Shepherd, Cincinnati, Ohio" (Cincinnati: No publisher stated, 1932).

Diocese of Columbus, the History of Fifty Years. 1918, pp. vii, 611.

Directory of Catholic Colleges and Schools. Compiled by James H. Ryan (Washington, D.C. National Catholic Welfare Conference, Bureau of Education, 1921), pp. i, 980.

Dixon, Joseph. *A General Introduction to the Sacred Scriptures* (Baltimore: John Murphy, 1853), pp. xv, 271.

Documents of American History. Edited by Commager, Henry Steele. Fourth Edition (New York: Appleton-Century-Crofts, Inc., 1948), pp. xxiii, 781.

Drane, Augusta Theodosia. *Christian Schools and Scholars.* Second Edition (London: Burns and Oates, 1881), p. 738.

Dunigan, David R. *A History of Boston College* (Milwaukee: The Bruce Publishing Company, 1947), pp. xv, 362.

Easterly, Reverend Frederick John. *The Life of Right Reverend Joseph Rosati. C.M* (Washington, D.C.: The Catholic University of America Press, 1942), pp. xi, 203.

Ellis, John Tracy. *American Catholicism* (Chicago: The University of Chicago Press, 1955. Pp xi, 203.

——. *American Catholics and The Intellectual Life* (Chicago: The Heritage Foundation, Incorporated, 1956), p. 63.

——. *Documents of American Catholic History* (Milwaukee: The Bruce Publishing Company, 1956), pp. vii, 677.

——. *John Lancaster Spalding* (Milwaukee: The Bruce Publishing Company, 1961), p. 106.

——. The Life of James Cardinal Gibbons. Volume I (Milwaukee: The Bruce Publishing Company, 1952), p. vii, 207.

Evans, Mary Ellen. *The Spirit Is Mercy* (Westminster, Maryland: The Newman Publishing Company, 1960), pp. xi, 346.

Farrell, Reverend Melvin. *First Steps to the Priesthood* (Milwaukee: The Bruce Publishing Company, 1960), pp. v, 232.

Feeney, Bernard. *The Catholic Sunday School.* (St. Louis: Herder, 1901), pp. 233.

——. *The Ideal Seminary* (New York: The MacMillan Company, 1923), pp. vi, 152.

——. *Manual of Sacred Rhetoric: On How to Prepare A Sermon* (St. Louis: Herder, 1901), p. 336.

Fifty Years In Brown County Convent (Cincinnati: McDonald and Company, 1895), pp. x, 294.

Foote, John P. *The Schools of Cincinnati and Its Vicinity* (Cincinnati: C.F. Bradley and Company's Power Press, 1855), pp. vi, 232.

Fox, Sister Columba. *The Life of the Right Reverend John Baptist Mary David* (New York: The United States Catholic Historical Society, 1905), p. 188.

Gabriels, Right Reverend Henry. *Historical Sketch of St. Joseph's Provincial Seminary* (New York: The United States Catholic Historical Society, 1905), p. 188.

Garraghan, Gilbert J. *The Jesuits of the Middle United States.* Volume III (New York: America

Press, 1938), pp. v, 666.

Godecker, Sister May Salesia. *Simon Brute De Remur* (St. Meinrad, Indiana: St. Meinrad Historical Essays, 1931), pp. ix, 441.

Good, Carter V. *Introduction to Educational Research* (New York: Appleton Century-Crofts Company, 1959), pp. xii, 424.

Good, H. G. *A History of American Education.* Second Edition (New York: The MacMillan Company, 1962), pp. vii, 610.

——. *A History of Western Education* (New York: MacMillan Company, 1962), pp. ix, 620.

Grace, Sister Mary. "History of the Educational Work of the Sisters of Mercy in the Archdiocese of Cincinnati." Unpublished Master's dissertation, Department of Education, University of Cincinnati, 1941), p. 147.

A Guide to Colleges and Universities and Professional Schools. Compiled by Carter V. Good (Washington, D.C.: American Council on Education, 1945), p. 681.

Guilday, Peter. *A History of the Council of Baltimore* (New York: The MacMillan Company, 1932), p. x, 291.

——. *The Life and Times of John England.* Volume I (New York: The America Press, 1927), p. vii, 596.

Gury, P. Joanne. *Compendium Theologiae Moralis.* (Ratisbonae: George Joseph Manz, 1868).

Gury P. Joannis, and Ballerini, Antonii. *Compendium Theologicae Moralis.* Third Edition (Rome: Polyglotta, 1874).

Hamel, Dana B. "A History of the Ohio Mechanics Institute." Unpublished Doctor's Dissertation, University of Cincinnati, 1962, pp. iv, 168.

Hanna, Thomas H. "The Development and Status of Villa Madonna College." Unpublished Doctor's dissertation, University of Cincinnati, 1962. Pp ix, 484.

Heck, Reverend Theodore H. *The Curriculum of the Major Seminary in Relation to Contemporary Conditions* (Washington, D.C.: The Catholic University of America Press, 1935), pp. xii, 160.

Hickerson, Frank R. "The History of the University of Toledo." Unpublished doctor's dissertation, University of Cincinnati, 1941, pp. viii, 558.

The History of Brown County, Ohio (Chicago: W. H. Beers and Company, 1883), pp. vii, 1011.

Houck, Reverend George F. *The Church in Northern Ohio and in the Diocese of Cleveland* (New York: Benziger Brothers, 1887), pp. iv, 266.

Howlett, Reverend William J. *Life of the Right Reverend Joseph P. Machbuef, D. D* (Pueblo,

Colorado: The Franklin Press Company, 1908), pp. 419.

Hughes, Reverend Thomas. *History of the Society of Jesus in North America. Volume I, Part II* (Cleveland: The Burrows Brothers Company, 1910), pp. xi, 601–1222.

Jones, A. E. *Early Days of Cincinnati* (Cohen and Company, 1888), p. 133.

The Jubilee at Mount Saint Mary's (New York: Edward Dunigan and Brother, 1859), p. 288.

Kelly, Michael J., and Kirwin, James J. *History of Mount St. Mary's Seminary of the West, Cincinnati, Ohio* (Cincinnati: Keating and Company, 1894), pp. xiv, 409.

Kelly, Robert L. *Theological Education in America* (New York: George H. Doran Company, 1924), pp. v, 456.

Lamott, Reverend John. *History of the Archdiocese of Cincinnati, 1821–1921* (New York and Cincinnati: Frederick Pustet Company, Inc., 1921), pp. x, 430.

Latin Lexicon (Romae: Societas Lebraria "Studium," n.d.) pp. xi, 707.

Leineweber, Sister Mary Vincent de Paul. "History of Catholic Secondary Education in Cincinnati." Unpublished master's dissertation, College of Education, Butler University, 1955.

Lewis, John Jr. "An Historical Study of the Origin and Development of the Cincinnati Conservatory of Music." Unpublished doctor's dissertation, University of Cincinnati, 1949), pp. xiv, 436.

Lind, Reverend Christopher. *Priestly Studies in Modern Papal Teachings* (Washington, D.C.: The Catholic University of American Press, 1958), pp. vii, 100.

Liguori, Alphonsus. *Theologicae Moralis.* Three Volumes. Fourteenth Edition (Bossari: Roudenera, 1537).

McAvoy, Thomas T. *The Great Crisis in American Catholic History 1895–1900* (Chicago: Henry Regnery Company, 1957), pp. xi, 402.

McCann, Sister Mary Agnes. *Archbishop Purcell and the Archdiocese of Cincinnati* (Washington, D.C.: The Catholic University of America Press, 1918), p. 107.

McCluskey, Neil G. *Catholic Viewpoint on Education* (Garden City, New York: Hanover House, 1959. Pp 192.

McDonald, Lloyd Paul. *The Seminary Movement in the United States: Projects, Foundations and Early Development: 1784–1833* (Washington, D. C. The Catholic University of America Press, 1927), pp. v, 68.

McGinnis, Frederick A. "A History of Wilberforce University." Unpublished Doctor's dissertation, University of Cincinnati, 1940), p. viii, 340.

McGuire C. E. *Catholic Builders of the Nation* (Boston: Continental Press, Inc., 1923), p. 488.
McKeough, Reverend Michael J. *The Curriculum of the Minor Seminary* (Washington, D.C.: The Catholic University of America Press, 1952), pp iv, 99.

McPhesters, Alphonso A. "The Origin and Development of Clark University and Gammon Theological Seminary, 1889–1944." Unpublished Doctor's dissertation, University of Cincinnati, 1944, pp. v, 317.

Maynard, Theodore. *The Reed and the Rock* (New York: Longmans, Green and Company, 1942), p. vii, 273.

Meline, Mary M., and McSweeny, Reverend Edward F. X. *The Story of Mountain.* Volume II (Emmitsburg, Maryland: The Weekly Chronicle, 1911), pp. xiii, 555.

——. *The Story of the Mountain.* Volume I. (Emmitsburg, Maryland: The Weekly Chronicle, 1911), pp. vii, 477.

A Member of Brown County Convent. *Fifty Years in Brown County Convent* (Cincinnati. McDonald and Company, 1895), pp. xvi, 294.

Memorial Volume of the Centenary of St. Mary's Seminary of St. Sulpice (Baltimore: John Murphy and Company, 1891), pp. 163.

Miller, Edward Alanson. *The History of Educational Legislation in Ohio from 1803 to 1850* (Chicago: The University of Chicago, 1920), pp. xi, 248.

Missionarii Congregationis Immaculati Cordis Mariae. Directorium Seminariorum. 1949, pp. xxxix, 290.

Monica, Sister. *The Cross in the Wilderness* (New York: Longmans, Green and Company, 1930), pp. xii, 290.

Morris, William Stephen. *The Seminary Movement in the United States: Projects Foundations, and Early Development* (Washington, D.C.: The Catholic University of America Press, 1932), pp. viii, 118.

Mount St. Mary Seminary of the West—A Gateway to the Priesthood (Cincinnati: No publisher Stated, 1929), p. 76.

Myers, Rawley. *This Is the Seminary.* (Milwaukee: The Bruce Publishing Company, 1952), pp. 9, 123.

Nau, Louis J. *Manual of the Code of Canon Law* (New York, Pustet, 1933).

——. *Mary, Mediatrix of All Graces for All Men* (Cincinnati: Pustet, 1928), p. 73.

Niebuhr, H. Richard. *The Purpose of the Church and its Ministry* (New York: Harper and Brothers, 1956), pp. vii, 134.

O'Brien, John A. Editor. *Catholics and Scholarship* (Huntington, Indiana: Our Sunday Visitor Press), pp. 256.

O'Brien Kevin J. *The Proximate Aim of Education* (Milwaukee: The Bruce Publishing Company, 1958), pp. x, 267.

O'Connor, Paul L. *Vidit Mirabilia Magna.* An Address read at the Newcomen Meeting at the New York World's Fair on August 5, 1939, p. 28.

O'Daniel, Very Reverend Victor Francis. *The Dominican Province of Saint Joseph* (Somerset; Ohio: The Rosary Press, 1942), pp. xii, 517.

——. *The Father of the Church in Tennessee.* (Press of Saint Mary's Industrial School, 1926), pp. vii, 607.

——. *The Right Reverend Edward Dominic Fenwick, O.P* (Lancaster, Pennsylvania: Press of the New Era Printing Company, 1920), pp. xiv, 473.

O'Dea, Thomas F. American Catholic Dilemma: An Inquiry into the Intellectual Life (New York: Sheed and Ward, 1958), pp. xv, 173.

O'Donohoe, James A. *Tridentine Seminary Legislation: Its Sources and Its Formation* (Louvain: Publications Universitaires de Louvain, 1957), pp. vi, 187.

O'Donnell, Reverend George E. Editor. *St. Charles Seminary Overbrook: 1943–1953,* Volume II (Philadelphia: The American Catholic Society, 1953), pp. xi, 358.

O'Reilly, Bernard. *Life of Leo XIII* (New York: Charles L. Webster and Company, 1887), pp. 603.

Orlando, Vincent A. "A Historical Study of the Origin and Development of the College of Music of Cincinnati." Unpublished doctor's dissertation, University of Cincinnati, 1946. Pp xiv, 280.

Papal Teachings: Education. Translated by Rev. Aldo Rebeschini (Boston: Daughters of St. Paul), p. 668.

Parsons, Wilfred. *Early Catholic Americana: 1729–1830* (New York: The MacMillan Company, 1939), pp. xxv, 282.

Perrone, Joannes. *Praelectiones Theologicae.* Four Volumes (Paris: A. Jouby, Bibl and Roger, 1870).

Power, Edward J. *A History of Catholic Higher Education in the United States* (Milwaukee: The Bruce Publishing Company, 1939), pp. xiii, 383.

Purcell, Most Rev. John Baptist. *Pastoral Letter on the Decrees of the First Provincial Council of Cincinnati* (Cincinnati: John P. Walsh, Printer and Bookseller, 1858), p. 22.

Putz, Louis J., ed. *The Catholic Church, U.S.A* (Chicago: Fides Publishers Association, 1956), p. xxiii, 415.

Rahner, Karl. *Theological Investigations*, Vol. I. Translated and Introduction by Cornelius Ernst. (London: Darton, Longman, & Todd, 1961), pp. xxii, 382.

Rashdall, Hastings. *The Universities of Europe in the Middle Ages*. New Edition, F. M. Powicke and A. B. Emden eds., vol. II (London: Oxford University Press, 1936), pp. vi, 342.

——. *The Universities of Europe in the Middle Ages*. New Edition. F. M. Powicke and A. B. Emden, eds., vol. II (London: Oxford University Press, 1936), pp. vi, 342.

——. *The Universities of Europe in the Middle Ages*. New edition, F. M. Powicke and A. B. Emden, eds., vol. II (London: Oxford University Press, 1936), pp. vi, 558.

Reardon, Rev. Maurice E. *Mosaic of a Bishop* (Paterson, N. J.: St. Anthony Guild Press), pp. xiii, 365.

Rothenflue, Rev. Francis. *Institution Philosophiae Theoreticae*. Fifth edition. Revised (London: Perisse Fratres, Bibliopolas-Editores, 1854), pp. 429.

Ruppert, Arthur G. *The City of Norwood, Ohio: 1809–1957* (Norwood, Ohio: The Norwood Chamber of Commerce, 1957), pp. 151.

Ryan, Rev. Paul E. *History of the Diocese of Covington, Kentucky* (No publisher stated) 1953. P. 1051.

Sabetti, Aloysius. *Compendium Theologicae Moralis*. (Rabisbonae: Pustat, 1898), pp. 896.

Sacra Congregation de Seminariis et Studiorum Universitatibus. *Elenchus Seminariorum* (Roma: Typis Polyglottis Vaticanis, 1938).

Sauter, John D. *The American College of Louvain* (Louvain: Publications Universitaires de Louvain, 1959), pp. xii, 289.

Scanlan, Arthur J. *St. Joseph's Seminary. Dunwoodie, New York, 1896–1921* (New York: The United States Catholic Historical Society, 1922), pp. vii, 237.

Scanlan, Rev. Arthur J. and Duffy, Rev. Francis P. *St. Joseph's Seminary. Dunwoodie, New Jersey: 1896–1921* (New York: The United States Catholic Historical Society, 1922), pp. xv, 237.

Schnapp, Sister Mary Mildred. "The History of Diocesan Teachers Colleges in Ohio, with Particular Reference to the Athenaeum of Ohio." Unpublished masters dissertation, University of Cincinnati, 1942, pp. 85.

Schroll, Sister Agnes Claire. *The Social Thought of John Lancaster Spalding, D. D.* (Washington, D. C.: The Catholic University of America Press, 1944), pp. xxii, 299.

Sexton, John E. and Riley, Arthur J. *History of Saint John's Seminary Brighton* (Boston: Roman Catholic Archbishop of Boston, 1945), pp. 320.

Shea, John Gilmary. *History of the Catholic Church in the United States.* Vol. III (New York: D. H. McBride & Co., 1890), pp. xvi, 784.

——. *History of the Catholic Church in the United States.* Vol. IV (New York: C. H. McBride & Co., 1892), pp. xxix, 727.

Sisters of Divine Providence. *Character Sketches of the Rt. Rev. G. P. Maes. D. D* (Baltimore: John Murphy Company, 1917), pp. 187.

Smith, Rev. John Talbot. *Our Seminaries an Essay on Clerical Training* (New York: William H. Young & Company, 1896), pp. iv, 327.

Snyder, James M. "Analysis of the Objectives and Evaluation of Achievements of Sinclair College of the Y. M. C. A., Dayton, Ohio." Unpublished doctor's dissertation, University of Cincinnati, 1957, pp. xv, 418.

Soklich, Rev. Alexander F. *Canonical Provisions for Universities and Colleges* (Washington, D.C.: The Catholic University of America Press, 1956), pp. x, 178.

Spalding, J. L. *The Life of the Most Rev. M. J. Spalding, D. D* (New York: Christian Press Association Publishing Co., n.d.).

Spalding, M. J. *Sketches of the Life, Times and Character of the Rt. Rev. Benedict Joseph Flaget* (Louisville, Kentucky. Webb & Levering, 1852).

Stoll, Raymond F. *The Gospel According to St. Luke* (New York and Cincinnati: Frederick Pustet, 1931), pp. xii, 422.

Synodus Diocesana Cincinnatensis Tertia (No publisher stated, 1898), pp. 161.

Thonnard, F. J. A Short History of Philosophy. Translated from the revised and corrected edition by Maziarz, Edward A. (Tournai: Desclee & Cie, 1955), pp. x, 1074.
Tongiorgi, Salvatoris. *Institutiones Philosophicae* Three Volumes. (Bruxellis: H. Goemaere, 1864).

Verwyst, P. Chrysostomus. *Life and Labors of Rt. Rev. Frederick Baraga* (Milwaukee: M. H. Wiltzius & Co., 1900), pp. vii, 476.

Wagoner, Walter D. Bachelor of Divinity (New York: Association Press, 1963), pp. 159.

Warner, Louis H. *Archbishop Lamy: An Epoch Maker.* (Sante Fe, New Mexico: Sante Fe New Mexican Publishing Corporation, 1936), pp. 7, 316.

Wittke, Carl, ed. *The History of the States of Ohio* (Columbus, Ohio: Ohio State Archaeological and Historical Society, 1941), pp. v, 524.

Woywood, Rev. Stanislaus. *A Practical Commentary on the Code of Canon Law*, revised by Rev. Callistus Smith, Vol. I (New York: Joseph F. Wagner, Inc. 1948), pp. xii, 833.

——. A *Practical Commentary on the Code of Canon Law*. Revised by Rev. Callistus Smith, Vol. II (New York: Joseph F. Wagner, Inc., 1948), pp. xi, 905.

Zwierlein, Frederick J. *The Life and Letters of Bishop McQuaid* (Rome: Desclee & Company, 1926), pp. xii, 487.

——. *The Life and Letters of Bishop McQuaid* (Rome: Desclee & Company, 1927), pp. xii, 513.

MAGAZINES AND PERIODICALS

Brann, Henry A. "Reverend Charles Constantine Pise." *United States Catholic Historical Records,* (II, October, 1900), 354–357.

"The Catholic Church in Ohio," *The United States Catholic Magazine*, 6 (1847), 93–100.

Furey, Francis, J. "Il Pontificio Seminario Romano Maggiore," *American Catholic Historical Records,* 55 (December, 1944) 332–347.

Guilday, Peter. "Very Reverend V. F. O'Daniel, O.P.," *American Catholic Historical Society,* 53 (March, 1942), 88–85.

Herbermann, Charles G. "The Sulpicians in the United States," *Catholic Historical Records and Studies,* 8 (June, 1915), 7–82.

Meng, John J. "Growing Pains in the American Catholic Church, 1880–1908," *Historical Records and Studies,* 35 (1947), 17–37.

"Mount St. Mary's Seminary of the West," *American Ecclesiastical Review,* 18, (June, 1898), 561–578.

Stritch, Alfred G. "Political Nativism in Cincinnati, 1830–1860," *American Catholic Historical Society,* 48, (September, 1947), 227–278.

Tschan, Francis J. "The Catholic Church in the United States, 1852–1862: A Survey," *The American Catholic Historical Records,* 58, (March 1947), 123–132.

MANUSCRIPTS

Archives of Mount St. Mary's Seminary

Archives of St. Gregory's Seminary

Archives of the University of Notre Dame

Archives of the Sisters of Brown County

Minutes of the Board of Trustees, Athenaeum of Ohio. Book No. I. March 24, 1928 to October 7, 1836.

Minutes of the Board of Trustees, Athenaeum of Ohio. Book No. 2. May 25, 1937–May 23, 1942.

Minutes of the Board of Trustee, Athenaeum of Ohio. Book No. 3. May 26, 1943 to May 22, 1947.

Minutes of the Board of Trustees, Athenaeum of Ohio. Book No. 4. May 25, 1948 to May 20, 1954.

Minutes of the Board of Trustees, Athenaeum of Ohio. Book No. 5. June 13, 1955 to October 12, 1959.

PRINTED MATERIALS

Catalogue-Teachers' College, Athenaeum of Ohio. Volume I, 1928–1935.
Catalogue-Teachers' College, Athenaeum of Ohio. Volume I, 1936–1940.
Catalogue-Teachers' College, Athenaeum of Ohio. Volume III, 1941–1945.
Catalogue-Teachers' College, Athenaeum of Ohio. Volume IV, 1946–1948.
Catalogue-Teachers' College, Athenaeum of Ohio. Volume V, 1949–1952.

Catalogue of Mount St. Mary's Seminary, 1905–1906.

A Statement of Receipts and Expenditures of Mount St. Mary's Seminary, 1869–1870.

Catalogue of St. Gregory's Seminary, 1904–1905.

Prospectus of St. Gregory's Seminary, 1904–1905.

Annual Announcements, Mount St. Mary's of the West, 1924–1931.
Annual Announcements, Mount St. Mary's of the West, 1931–1941.
Annual Announcements, Mount St. Mary's of the West, 1941–1953.
Annual Announcements, Mount St. Mary's of the West, 1953–1960.

Athenaeum of Ohio—Announcements, 1953–1960.

Annual Report of Subscriptions of the Theological Seminary, 1900–1901.
Annual Report of Subscriptions of the Theological Seminary, 1906–1907.
Annual Report of Subscriptions of the Theological Seminary, 1909–1910.
Annual Report of Subscriptions of the Theological Seminary, 1913–1914.
Annual Report of Subscriptions of the Theological Seminary, 1916–1917.
Annual Report of Subscriptions of the Theological Seminary, 1917–1918.

NEWSPAPER ARTICLES

The *Catholic Telegraph,* the official newspaper of the Archdiocese of Cincinnati began in the year 1831. From October of 1831 until August 2, 1849, it was known as the *Catholic Telegraph.* Volumes 1-18 take in the period below these respective dates.

On August 2, 1849, this newspaper became the *Catholic Telegraph and Advocate.* Under this title are included Volumes 19-32.

On January 1, 1862, the newspaper once more was known as the *Catholic Telegraph.* Under this title are included the Volumes 33-107.

On September 19, 1937, the same paper became the *Catholic Telegraph-Register.* Under this name are included volumes 108-132.

On January 5, 1962, the paper once more reverted to the original title of the *Catholic Telegraph* and included volumes 133–135.

CHRONICLES

Hussey, Edmund. *Mt. St. Mary's Seminary Chronicle for the Scholastic Year 1955–1956.*

Hussey, Edmund. *Mt. St. Mary's Seminary Chronicle for the Scholastic Year 1956–1957.*

Rudemiller, Edward L. *Mt. St. Mary's Seminary Chronicle for the Scholastic Year 1957–1958.*

Fisko, James. *St. Mary's Seminary Chronicle for the Scholastic Year 1958–1959.*

Reinhart, Robert. *Mt. St. Mary's Seminary Chronicle for the Scholastic Year 1959–1960.*

Mantel, Robert. *Mt. St. Mary's Seminary Chronicle for the Scholastic Year 1960–1961.*

Bank, Donald. *Mt. St. Mary's Seminary Chronicle for the Scholastic Year 1961–1962.*

INDEX